Name

Address

New .95

Used 6.00

USED BOOKS
Cost Less And
Serve as New
E-3-76

Follett's

MIAMI CO-OP STORE

110 E. High St.   Oxford, Ohio

COMPLETE DISCOUNT
523-2900   RECORD DEPARTMENT   523-4900

★ $ $ We Pay Cash For Used Books $ $ ★

Design for the Stage

First Steps

Darwin Reid Payne

With 117 drawings by the author
and 16 photographs

SOUTHERN ILLINOIS UNIVERSITY PRESS
Carbondale and Edwardsville

Feffer & Simons, Inc.
London and Amsterdam

Library of Congress Cataloging in Publication Data

Payne, Darwin Reid.
  Design for the stage; first steps.

  Includes bibliographies.
  1. Theaters—Stage-setting and scenery.   I. Title.
PN2091.S8P35   792'.025   74-3090
ISBN 0-8093-0654-9
ISBN 0-8093-0669-7 (pbk.)

To Mordecai Gorelik

Contents

Part 3: FROM TEXT TO DESIGNS

List of Figures

Acknowledgments

No book is ever the sole accomplishment of a single person. Certainly many people have aided in preparing this one. And yet, out of that number, two have been particularly thoughtful in their advice. In the manuscript stage, Dr. Archibald McLeod made many valuable suggestions which have been incorporated into the final text. A special thanks must be paid to Mordecai Gorelik for his many years of helpful counsel as well as the useful example of his own work; his philosophy of what constitutes that very special art of scene design certainly informs much of what is presented in the following pages. Lastly, I would like to express my great appreciation for the photographic work of Bob Jones whose great skill I have often relied upon both in the preparation of this book as well as in past projects.

Special acknowledgment is made to the following publishers and copyright holders to quote from their works:

A number of statements by Arthur Miller from *The Ideal Theater: Eight Concepts* have been reprinted with the permission of The American Federation of Arts which has the copyright.

Portion of a letter reprinted from "To Directors and Actors: Letters,1948–1959," by Michel de Ghelderode, translated by Bettina Knapp. First published in the *Tulane Drama Review,* Summer 1965. Reprinted by permission of Bettina Knapp.

The entire article, "The Building or the Theater," by Sean Kenny, from *Theatre Crafts* 2, no. 1 (January–February 1968). Reprinted by permission of *Theatre Crafts.*

"Practical Dreams," by Jo Mielziner, in Ralph Pendleton, *The Theater of Robert Edmond Jones* (Middleton, Conn.: Wesleyan University Press, 1958). Reprinted by permission of Wesleyan University Press.

Art and the Stage in the Twentieth Century, by Henning Rischbieter. Reprinted by permission of the New York Graphic Society, Greenwich, Conn.

"On Being Upstaged by Scenery," by Robert Hatch. © Copyright 1962 by American Heritage Publishing Co., Inc. Reprinted by permission from *Horizon,* September 1962.

"How I See the Woman without a Shadow," by Robert O'Hearn. Reprinted from *Opera News,* September 17, 1966, by permission of the publishers, The Metropolitan Opera Guild, Inc."

"Theory of Design," by Norman Bel Geddes in *Encyclopaedia Britannica.* Reprinted by permission of *Encyclopaedia Britannica.*

A review by Robert Lewis Shayon of *Death of a Salesman,* in *Saturday Review,* May 28, 1966. Reprinted by permission of Robert Lewis Shayon.

"A Director Views the Stage," by Tyrone Guthrie, in *Design Quarterly,* no. 58 (1963). Reprinted by permission of *Design Quarterly,* copyright Walker Art Center.

"The First Dialogue," by E. Gordon Craig. Reprinted from *On the Art of the Theatre,* by E. Gordon Craig, copyright 1956 by Theatre Arts Books, with the permission of the publishers, Theatre Arts Books, New York; and also by permission of Heinemann Educational Books, Ltd., the British publishers.

From *The Empty Space* by Peter Brook, published by Atheneum. Copyright © 1968 by Peter Brook. Reprinted by permission of Atheneum Publishers, New York; and also by permission of MacGibbon & Kee, the British publishers.

From *Designing for the Theatre* by Jo Mielziner. Copyright © 1965 by Jo Mielziner. Reprinted by permission of Antheneum Publishers.

From *Shakespeare, Our Contemporary* by Jan Kott. Copyright © 1964 by Państwowe Wydawnictwo Naukowe. Introduction and Text Copyright © 1964, 1965, 1966 by Doubleday and Company, Inc.

From *Problems of the Theatre* by Friedrich Dürrenmatt, translated by Gerhard Nellhaus. Copyright © 1958 by Gerhard Nellhaus, and Copyright 1955 by Peter Schifferli. Reprinted by permission of Grove Press, Inc.; and also by permission of Verlags AG "Die Arche," Zürich.

From *Brecht on Theatre* by Bertolt Brecht, translated by John Willett, copyright © 1957, 1963, and 1964 by Suhrkamp Verlag, Frankfurt am Main. This translation and notes © 1964 by John Willett. Reprinted with the permission of Farrar, Straus & Giroux, Inc.; and also by permission of Methuen & Co., Ltd., the British publishers.

From *Towards a Poor Theatre* by Jerzy Grotowski. Published by Simon & Schuster. Copyright © 1968 by Jerzy Grotowski and Odin Teatret. Reprinted by permission of Odin Teatret.

From *Theatre and Its Double* by Antonin Artaud. Translated from the French by Mary Caroline Richards. Copyright © 1958 by Grove Press, Inc. Reprinted by permission of Grove Press, Inc.; and also by permission of Calder & Boyars, the British publishers.

Introduction

There is nothing even mildly extraordinary about me except that I think I am durable and inquisitive in a comprehensive pattern. I have learned much; but I don't *know* very much; but what I have learned, I have learned by trial and error. And I have great confidence in the meager store of wisdom that I have secured.

R. Buckminster Fuller

The fundamental reason for the existence of this book is to present to beginning students a particular way of approaching scene design; in it design for the stage will be treated as an art, not just a craft. Too often these two aspects of design are separated; the student of scene design becomes so intrigued with the making of working drawings, models, and sketches of interesting possibilities for the stage that he forgets his contribution is not an end in itself but part of a larger effort involving the work and esthetic judgments of many others, not his alone. And yet it is possible for the designer, despite this seemingly severe restriction on his personal expression, to make his contribution to the production at the same level as those of the director and performer. Meeting the stated demands of the script or satisfying the specific requests of the director is certainly part of the designer's job; but it is also possible for him, with his special vision that spans all the arts, to make suggestions that may extend and amplify the underlying meanings of the production in ways that neither the playwright, director, or actor had envisioned. Of course he cannot accomplish this without being an able craftsman; it is imperative that he be a master of the mechanical skills of his profession in order to implement his special visions. But it is entirely possible to be an expert draftsman, carpenter, electrician, and scene painter and still not be an artist of scene design; too often this is the case. While this book is no more than an introduction to that area which lies beyond the basic craft of design, it does attempt to expose some of the elemental yet important questions most students have in their initial confrontation with this second aspect of scene design. Although these questions can never be answered completely, certain directions and possibilities they suggest are indicated and discussed. And, of course, it is in the lifelong pursuit of these answers that the craftsman can become an artist.

For a number of years I have taught scene design in university theaters. My first impulse, and the course of action which I followed for some time, was to teach design solely as a craft, with only passing affirmation that it could be more than that. The considered reason for pursuing that approach was a belief that since one could not be expected to teach a student to be an accomplished artist during some arbitrarily prescribed period of time, perhaps the subject need not be considered at all. While there has not been in my teaching a complete reversal of the early approach, it has been modified greatly; the mechanical skills of design still must be taught, but the emphasis in the classroom now rests more in showing how these serve the highest aims of the theater and drama. It now seems to make more sense to demonstrate from the outset of the designer's education that craft and art are not separate activities with different aims, but that each should assist the other to something greater than either one; ideally, each should grow out of the other.

All too often the beginning designer does not consider very deeply the theoretical basis of his profession. He is impatient with the scholarly approach to his art (in many instances quite rightly so) and eager to get to the "real" business of the designer which is almost exclusively, he believes, to draw sketches and make plans. And for many years, in my own classes there was little question of any conceptual approach other than that which was casually and more or less arbitrarily imposed. Nor did there ever seem to be time for any study more exhaustive than the unavoidably shallow research into architectural styles or the accurate copying of period design elements. For instance, when a student selected *The Beggar's Opera* as his project, the eighteenth-century ballad-opera by John Gay, he would usually be more interested in the style and dimensions of a Newgate Prison window and only slightly concerned (if at all) with the action which transpired in the room where it was to be placed. Asked what might be taking place in the London street just outside the prison, and whether that action might have any bearing on the dramatic situation inside the prison or if those actions would have any bearing on his particular design, the student might reply, "Just what difference does it make?" The fact that what the designer creates does have a very real influence on both the actor and director, and ultimately on the way the play itself is perceived, made me realize that mechanical skill was not enough, that there was a great deal more we should be considering in the classroom but were not. Further, I began to realize that it is not uncommon for a designer (and not just the student), with the very best intentions, to thwart the larger aims of a production, not to mention the work of the other members of the artistic team with which he is working, by striving too hard to make a strongly individual impression on an audience. These issues, it became more and more evident, should be broached and discussed in the formative stages of the designer's education. A designer must not only know *how*, important as technique is, he must also be fully aware of *why;* he must be, moreover, a conscientious man of the theater as well as an expert specialist.

Finally, it should be stated that a basic core of knowledge assimilated by one means or another from a number of areas spanning all human activity is essential to the student desiring to make the best use of this book. His progress in the art of scenic design will, in fact, be largely dependent upon his becoming knowledgeable in all these areas, first as a student and second, as an expert in their use in the practice of his profession.

Briefly, this basic core of knowledge would consist of the following:

1. A general familiarity with and an understanding of theater history and the development of the drama.

2. A basic knowledge of art history and an understanding of periods and styles of architecture, painting, sculpture, furnishings, and costume.

3. A familiarity with principles, techniques, and materials in pictorial and three-dimensional design.

(And the following which will not fall within the scope of this book:)

4. A basic knowledge of stagecraft and theatrical production techniques and materials, including the mechanics of the stage and an understanding of the fundamental principles of stage lighting.

5. Skill in fundamental drafting procedures and in executing mechanical drawings.

This may sound like an unusual amount and variety of information and skills for the beginning student to possess. It is. And most designers do not have them when they first begin the study of scene design. Many continue to try to do without them, but most finally acquire the necessary education and skills often independently of a formal academic process. Still, acquire it they must for there is no way for the aspiring designer to progress in his art without this solid grounding in all the skills and techniques listed above. Indeed, he must have a firm understanding of all the arts, including literature, music, and the dance as well as those more nearly allied to his own field. The successful designer should be, in the best sense, an educated man. And, make no mistake, our best designers are and have been just such men and women. Three of the most influential designers of the last hundred years—Gordon Craig, Adolphe Appia, and Robert Edmond Jones— have been keenly interested and vastly knowledgeable in all the arts, not just those of theater.

A Note on Outside Reading Materials and Allied Texts

Reading is not only essential to the designer seeking to build his store of practical information related to the art he practices, it is also a necessary and positive step toward the creation of a philosophical framework without which his craft will lack direction, his art purpose. Knowledge of the literature of his own and of related arts is important since scene design is an art whose scope is nothing less than the whole world outside the theater: one man simply cannot by himself discover all he needs to know about the design of scenery unless he avails himself of these outside sources.

Most creative artists, especially in their student days, do not read enough, not only generally, but even in their field of major interest. The average student designer is usually grossly ignorant of the litera- ture of his chosen profession, ignorant of both its extent and nature. He would probably read more if he knew what to read and where to find it; the fact that texts and articles on scene design are often hard to find (after all, it is not a greatly overcrowded profession and far fewer are writing about it than are practicing it) or not widely available. At the same time, much of the available material is not very informative; in content a great deal is inadequate, misleading, or too general to be of any real use to the beginning student. In the formal classroom situa- tion, moreover, the student is confronted with a dilemma; assigned to read a certain book or article by a certain time, information the instruc- tor feels is useful or necessary to his understanding and development at that time, more often than not he finds the book out of the library or the article missing. For these reasons, the outside readings in this book are presented in the following manner:

1. As is usual in most textbooks, direct quotations of short length will be used to make specific points concerning the material under im- mediate discussion.

2. At certain points, complete sections from larger works (such as a complete chapter from a book or an entire article from a magazine or journal) will be inserted into the main body of the text. These sections will allow the student to read a more comprehensive statement (rather than a limited quotation) in its entirety without having to check out

from the library the complete book or to track down the article. Having read a portion of a book will, hopefully, encourage a further reading in it at a later time.

3. At the end of Parts one and three in the book, there will be a highly selective list of books (some of which will already have been read in part under the provisions of the above heading) and most of which would form the basic core of the designer's personal library. There is no formal bibliography at the end of the book.

These readings, then, along with others the individual instructor will doubtlessly include in his own presentation, should give the student designer a good basic groundwork on which to build his understanding of the literature in the fields of scene design and the related arts.

A Note to the Instructor

No book can teach a course; only the individual instructor can do that. How helpful any text is to the student is largely dependent on how and to what extent the instructor uses that text within the structure of a course. For these reasons, the basic—and perhaps obvious— assumption of the author is that the greater responsibility of teaching any student the fundamentals of stage design is still where it always has been, with the individual instructor.

For approximately twelve years this book, in various forms and stages, has been the basic outline for an introductory course in theater art. Undoubtedly it will be more useful as a source book and point of departure than as a rigid all-inclusive guideline. It will become quickly apparent that the book has been written in a strongly personal tone; but the reason for this approach has less to do with ego gratification on the part of the author than it is a tacit admission that no text could ever be written which would set down once and for all the principles of this art completely and impersonally. If nothing else, some of what is discussed here may give the student something to react against; and in so reacting define more concretely his own growing artistic awareness. While this may seem to be a negative point, all artists realize that it is the right and duty of those who come after them to question the accomplishments and approaches of their predecessors, certainly not blindly follow them. So while examples are given within the book which demonstrate solutions to specific design problems (indeed, the whole second half of the book is primarily devoted to just such examples), they are not presented as the definitive solutions to those problems. Nor would examination of these examples alone further the student's education to any appreciable degree. For this reason it is the responsibility of each instructor to create and evaluate different problems and projects for his own students rather than to rely on a predetermined set of exercises devised by the author of a text. Materials of this nature, therefore, are missing from this book altogether. After all, the whole point of any creative course is—or should be—to allow (to force, in fact) the student to think for himself, not "play back" information or facts to which he has been recently exposed. And what is more important, each instructor must interpret this book (or take exception to) in the light of his own experience and to a greater extent than he might were he to use a more practically oriented manual on stagecraft or sceneography.

Darwin Reid Payne

Southern Illinois University
September 1973

PART 1   The Scene Designer

§ 1
The Designer: A Brief Examination of His Function

Before any philosophy of practice can be formulated or explored, it must first be accepted that there is a uniqueness to that practice that makes it worthy of study. The essential point to remember about the twentieth century's conception of scene design as an art is that prior to this century scene design was, almost always, only an adjunct to a production, not necessarily an integral part of it. In fact, there was little coordination between any of the various departments responsible for the mounting of a production. The designer, while he may have received some general directions from the owner of a company producing plays or the general manager of an opera house, relied pretty much on his own judgment; any discussion of the appropriateness; of a setting usually took place after the fact. If the settings were grand enough or sufficiently ornate no one particularly cared about the possibility they did not really fit the tone of the play or opera or the other elements of the production. If the settings were appreciated, the designer received more commissions, if not, others were given an opportunity to demonstrate their skills; in that respect, the same competitive situation still exists today. But the great difference between then and now lies in the fact that the designer of the past spent very little time working with others—directors, costumers, playwrights—in preproduction planning. Ostensibly the designer's task was to provide pictorial backgrounds for performers to be seen in front of, although his relationship to these performers was virtually nonexistent.

And yet it would not be entirely accurate to maintain that the designer of the eighteenth and nineteenth centuries was only the servant of actor-managers and playwrights. Often they were highly respected artists in the theater and there is ample reason to believe many were guilty of considering the actors, singers, and dancers mere additions to their work. Nor is there any real proof that the designer paid much attention to the playwright as a reliable source for determining the way a setting should look onstage; it is doubtful if many playwrights were consulted or given a chance to exercise any real control on how their plays were mounted. It is certainly doubtful if many designers ever gave much thought to the playwright's purposes that lay beneath the surface of the text and explicit directions written there. And if one inspects the pictorial records of the various forms of theater during the eighteenth and nineteenth centuries, it appears as if few designers saw much difference between any form of theatrical production; play, opera, masque, and ballet all received pretty much the same sort of treatment. The designer's only real concern was to what extent these different forms gave him opportunity to demonstrate his skill in creating fanciful stage pictures and spectacular effects (fig. 1). But, in fairness to the designers of these periods, it should be pointed out that this approach to stage design was exactly what was expected of them.

Perhaps we should not be too hard on the accepted conventions of

1. *Design for an opera by Joseph Galli Bibiena,* 1740

another age without understanding some of the reasons why certain practices were maintained. For instance, we are now fairly certain that, although providing a background for the performer was part of the early designer's function, the most important purpose for which scenery was invented lay in a somewhat different direction than mere service to the actor; in *Changeable Scenery,* Richard Southern draws our attention to a point that sheds light on the attitude of the early designers.

There is one remarkable fact to be found in a study of scenes and scene-changing which outshines even the intriguing details of the machinery by which the scene-changes were worked. This fact is both surprising and important; it controls the whole structure of scenery and supplies the prime reason for stage machinery; it clears up many puzzles in the staging of plays of the past, and its recognition is an essential to any understanding of the development of scenery today. This fact is that the changing of scenes was intended to be visible; it was part of the show; it came into existence to be watched.

For the most part, scenery is no longer created for its own sake and, as that mode of thought has radically altered, so has the designer's function and purpose in the theater. We have progressed to the point, at least, where scene design is now primarily a serviceable and integral part of the total production, not merely a decorative overlay.

But not only has the function of the designer changed over the years, the basic skills of his profession have also undergone a change. From the middle of the sixteenth century until late in the nineteenth, the designer almost without exception was a painter and quite often an architect (especially during the late Renaissance and baroque periods). But even as an architect, often only his skills as draftsman were utilized, not his knowledge or ability to manipulate actual three-dimensional form and space; his designs were almost always transferred to the stage in flat pictorial terms although there was a distinct attempt to produce an illusion of depth of space and solidity of form. Many of the designers creating settings for the baroque and romantic theater knew that what they had designed could only be realized on the stage as oversized pictures, never as real structures. Quite possibly many took a certain pleasure in being able to allow their imaginations full play without having to consider the limitations of actual structural practice and cost, weight, and unmanageability of gross building materials. Even today many designers begin their careers in areas and disciplines that deal primarily with two-dimensional design, painting for instance, and slowly become, as they begin to comprehend that the theater is not just a picture come to life, something else than a painter, something more than an architectural draftsman.

Although by the end of the nineteenth century there was a general dissatisfaction with painted scenery since it did not fit the trend toward realism that theater was taking (Strindberg was only one during this time to inveigh against the antiquated system of scenic art: "stage doors are made of canvas and swing back and forth at the lightest touch . . . nothing is more difficult than to get a room that looks something like a room although the painter can easily enough produce waterfalls and flaming volcanoes"), even as early as 1808 a few discerning critical voices were beginning to call attention to the essential stupidity of contemporary scene design practices. Wilhelm Schlegel, a German theater critic of the time, makes us realize that there were some even that long ago who did not blindly accept the current stage conventions as a proper and artistic mode of production.

> Our system of stage decoration has several unavoidable defects . . . the breaking of the lines on the sides of a scene from every point of view except one; the disproportion of the player when he appears in the background and against objects diminished in perspective; the unfavorable lighting from below and behind; the contrast between painted lights and shades; the impossibility of narrowing the stage at pleasure, so that the inside of a palace and a hut have the same length and breadth. The errors to be avoided are want of simplicity and of great and reposeful masses; the overloading of the scene with superfluous and distracting objects, either because the painter is desirous of showing off his strength in perspective or because he does not know how otherwise to fill up the space; an architecture full of mannerism, often altogether, nay, even at variance with possibility, colored in a motley manner which resembles no species of stone in the world. [Wilhelm Schlegel, quoted by Lee Simonson, *The Art of Scenic Design*]

Although Schlegel's remarks anticipate the revolution in scene design that would take place at the end of the century, at the time his feelings were not widely shared. Nowhere is the attitude of his period better displayed than in an event which took place in the Weimar Theater during the last portion of Goethe's reign there as the managing director. In 1816 a special evening was arranged at this theater. The occasion was not to present a new play or opera, but only to view a new stock of settings especially painted by a scenic artist named Friedrich Christian Beuther, whose work had greatly impressed Goethe. Not a single actor performed nor were any scenes given within these new settings; they were simply there to be looked at. After all the various settings had been displayed and applauded, the audience was allowed to come to the stage for a closer look at Beuther's artistry. Even though it is doubtful that a general audience of today would be even remotely interested in such a "performance," some designers even as late as the fifth decade of this century (Eugene Berman for one) strongly upheld the contention that stage design should be first and foremost decorative and visually exciting by itself. Leon Bakst, Diaghilev's greatest designer for his Ballets Russes, makes a special plea for this point of view.

> In the modern theater there are . . . tendencies which, in one way or another, affect the character of décors. The . . . tendency, which I call "Protestant," takes as its point of departure renunciation of beautiful, sumptuous, and dominant decor, claiming that such settings impede full apprehension of the word. [Leon Bakst, "Painting and Stage Design," *Art and the Stage in the 20th Century*]

There are few designers now who would be completely sympathetic with this point of view (although probably there are more than would admit it). Still, by and large, he does not speak to or for most designers today who are much more self-effacing than Bakst (or the designer he envisions) would ever allow himself to be. For if there has been one major change in the designer's role from the first uses of scenery until now, it is that he has become less and less a creator of scenic effects and more an artist who is deeply involved with the problems of the performers who must live in the special world the playwright defines in words and he, the designer, creates on the stage out of those words.

But why did this change come about? Actually the major reforms in theater production did not come until near the very end of the nineteenth century and were in great part due to the work and theories of men who were born near or soon after the peak of the romantic movement which began around 1815. These men were to have strong influences in the theater of their day and those influences still inform production practice today. Richard Wagner, Gordon Craig, and Adolphe Appia, to name the most important although not the only influential visionaries of the past hundred years, are directly responsible for freeing the stage of an increasingly stultifying realism in stage settings. In their writing and practice originated the concept—the most basic one in the whole philosophy of scene design—that scene design is not a peripheral theatrical activity (either physically or conceptually) but an art which is a vital element in dramatic production. And not too many years after these pioneers, the American theater gained one of its greatest artists, the undisputed father of American stage design, Robert Edmond Jones. Jones, whose design for *The Man Who Married a Dumb Wife* in 1915 not only heralded a new designer for the New York stage but also a whole new era in the American theater, was our first, and in many ways our most important, link with the new attitude toward scene design that was already well established in the theaters of Europe. Since that production it is quite possible that American scene design has been more influenced by this man, through his writings and many disciples, than any other.

Jones was a stern critic of what theater in general had become; in Europe he had seen numerous instances of a new approach toward theater design. This movement was called "the new stagecraft." In production after production there he saw how all the elements of design, direction, and acting were merged into a unified whole. Here in America, he felt, the prevailing practices of those working in theater had become shoddy and purposeless, that theater had become primarily "show business," the main purpose of which was to give an audience an evening of entertainment, often superficially exciting or spectacular but rarely meaningful or deeply moving. While he believed entertainment was an important part of the theater, it could and should offer more than that. Nor was he alone in his vision of a revitalized theater which would in its visual beauty and dramatic power appeal to the higher instincts of an audience. Norman Bel Geddes, another of the American theater's most important designers during the first thirty years of this century and a contemporary of Jones, also felt that theater could be more than it had been in the last decades of the nineteenth century and the first two of the twentieth. In the fourteenth edition of the *Encyclopaedia Britannica* he wrote the following:

> To the Greeks, the theatre was their most vital creative expression, and they succeeded in achieving results that for "pure theatre" have never been surpassed. They built them to look like theatres and to dignify what transpired within them. . . .
> We live in an industrial age. We should have theatres that belong to our time, drama that voices this time. Instead our theatre is a secondary expression. . . .

. . . The theatre is in a state of sham. The plays, the actors, the scenery, all try to make audiences forget they are in a theatre. The buildings themselves are made to look like office buildings, taverns, museums, Renaissance palaces, Spanish missions or casinos. . . .

To any student of the subject, the development of the theatre since the Greeks shows gradual deterioration. The single item that has most influenced these changes is the proscenium arch. . . . Its two dimensional aspect imposes an effect which is deadening, as compared with the exhilaration of an audience surrounding the actors, such as we get in the circus. There is no more reason or logic in asking an audience to look at a play through a proscenium arch than there would be in asking them to watch a prize fight through one. . . . In an art gallery, looking at a piece of sculpture, you instinctively walk slowly around the object to view it from different directions, rather than merely standing and looking at it as you would a painting. The exaggerated importance of the picture-frame stage of the past generation is undoubtedly due to lack of imagination of the minds working in the theatre. . . .

The end we seem to be going toward has a more plastic three dimensional stage structure, formal, dignified and neutral, as a basis, its various acting platforms inviting a variety of movement, and provided with adequate space for lighting instead of the cramped condition of the present. Such a structure is designed for the playing of a sequence of scenes of diverse mood, locale and character, not imitative in geographical terms, but creative in dramatic terms, with emphasis on the intensity of dramatic action and its projection to an audience.

The style of scenery both Jones and Bel Geddes were reacting against is shown in figure 2.

While there have been many influences which have changed the look of stage design during the last eighty years, the most revolutionary aspects of these influences did not really begin to manifest themselves until the 1950s. A few of these changes could be listed (many of them interrelated) as follows:

1. A tendency to prefer radical stage-audience relationships (many of these open stage or variations of open stage forms, but some like the experimental audience placements of Jerzy Grotowski in Poland which will be discussed at a later point in this book) rather than the standard proscenium arch relationship to the audience.

2. An emphasis toward sculptural building rather than employing

2. *Design for* The Seagull, *Moscow Art Theatre,* 1896

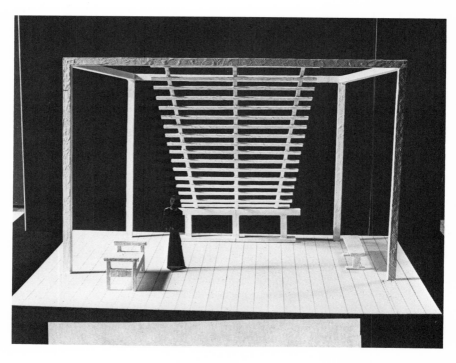

3. *Design for* The Crucible

flat units painted to represent three-dimensional form and, another facet of this same trend, a definite predisposition toward the use of open skeletal structural forms rather than cutting off the backstage area from the playing area by a single closed-off unit such as a box set (fig. 3).

3. The use of actual three-dimensional textures rather than painted simulation of textures and, at the same time, making use of twentieth-century materials (lightweight synthetics such as foam plastics, rubber castings, etc.) and technology instead of traditional building materials and stagecraft techniques.

4. A much greater use of metaphorical and symbolic imagery as a basis for the design concept rather than direct observation of nature (and then attempting to reproduce those observations on the stage) or the accurate copying of historical detail (fig. 4).

5. A general desire to simplify the settings into forms and materials that directly reflect and relate to the abstract qualities of the script.

6. An increased use of multimedia so that there is usually more

4. *Design for* As You Like It

than one focus (if any focus at all) of attention on the stage at one time; the effect and aim of the production to be more an accidental and accumulative experience rather than a linear progression of calculated images and rehearsed actions.

7. There has also been a noticeable difference in the manner in which the twentieth-century designer regards the setting on the actual physical stage; in addition to thrusting out of the proscenium arch or returning to open stage forms, there has also been a distinct movement from designs that are horizontal in orientation (fig. 5); to designs that employ a much deeper acting area and that have scenic elements which rise great heights from the stage floor plane (fig. 6).

All these tendencies are evident to some degree in the design for *Oedipus* shown in figure 7. Perhaps the greatest single preoccupation of the present-day designer lies in the manipulation of stage space. But just what is stage space; how does it differ from space outside the theater? These questions are not easy to answer, even by the designer who has been confronted with them for years and, oddly enough, whose success depends greatly on solving these questions time after time.

Let us first look at the problem of space on the stage in a historical perspective. Until approximately eighty years ago, the unstated but observable attitude toward scenery was that it should be, as we have pointed out before, *decorative* rather than *functional*. This attitude toward the role of scenery could be presented diagrammatically something like that in figure 8. Here we see that scenery stands on three sides of the actor but does not necessarily influence him; the only real way in which he relates to it is by being seen against it. The setting for him is something he does not take an active part in. Strangely enough, the actor of the seventeenth and eighteenth centuries—and well into the nineteenth—had little conception of how he related to his scenic

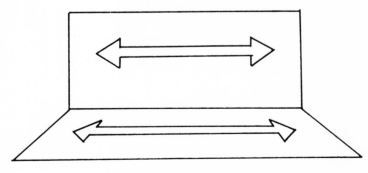

5. *Diagram showing design emphasis*

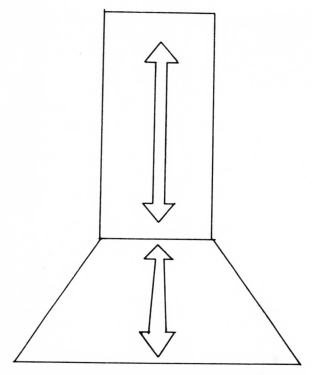

6. *Diagram showing design emphasis*

environment and, in most instances, simply ignored it even though he happened to be closest to it.

During the twentieth century, however, the director and the designer, and to some extent the playwright, have literally forced the actor to become more integrated with his environment by creating scenery that he cannot avoid using, scenery he must move in, around and through (fig. 9).

The designer, the moment he begins to assume responsibility for expanding the actor's possibilities of movement (nor can one design any setting without entailing this responsibility), must also begin to consider how he is able to affect the actor's movement; he can, for instance, restrict the actor by putting obstacles in his path (fig. 10); or cause him to conform to an accepted convention (physically he *could* walk through the "walls" [fig. 11]); or make him move in certain predetermined paths (fig. 12).

7. *Design for* Oedipus

The designer working in today's theater seems to be much less inhibited than his immediate predecessors about creating playing areas that do not correspond to the oblong shape of the traditional proscenium arch theater, even when he is working on such a stage. Perhaps

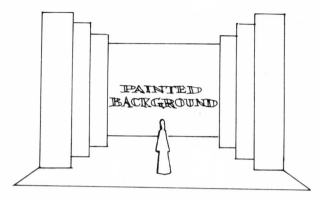

8. *Diagram of scenery style*

9. *Diagram of scenery style*

the most predominant trend during the past decade—from 1960 to 1970—so far as the proscenium arch theater is concerned, has been extending the playing area out beyond the curtain line (consequently making the curtain unusable) and into the auditorium as shown in figure 13.

When the designer conceives such a set, however, there must be a

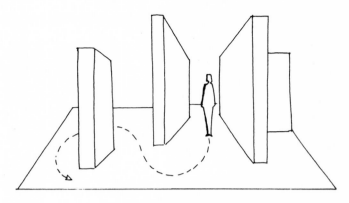

10. *Actor's possible movements*

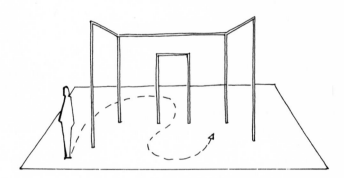

11. *Actor's possible movements*

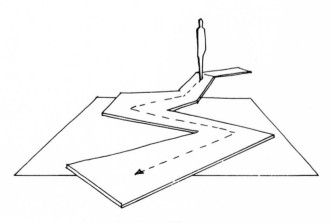

12. *Actor's possible movements*

14

13. *Design for* Hughie

much more careful working out of space relationships to accommodate and control the movement of the actors. In a later section we will examine how the designer arrives at the point where he knows what paths these movements should follow and how to determine the shape of the playing area from this information. There is always the temptation to create an interesting shape as a floor plan and then try to make the movement patterns of the play fit it. This is not, nor should not be, the manner in which these floor shapes are evolved. Working in this way also means, in most cases, that the designer does not use all of the space (the total amount of square footage actually on the stage) available to him; what he does use, therefore, must be meticulously considered. It is in this restrictive role that the designer has the more dangerous assignment since it is possible for him to limit the actor's movement and effectiveness purposelessly or hinder it merely to facilitate the design—that is, hamper the progress of the actor in order to preserve the pictorial effect of the setting.

The scene designer's most significant function, then, is that of a manipulator of stage space in its relationship to the human actor; the successful artist-designer is a master of this particular form of space manipulation. But what does that statement really mean? How, for instance, does the scene designer's job differ from that of the interior decorator? Or does it?

First of all, let us determine just what is meant by the term *space* as it relates to the human being—what its features and possibilities (but not necessarily in stage terms). Space, as utilized by the human being, can be categorized roughly into two major parts—private space and public space. For now we will consider the area of private space only.

Private space can be either inside a building structure or outside it, but in both instances there is some attempt to cut off that space—either by one person or small group—to make it clearly personal or somehow unique. The room is probably the most elemental unit of private space; no matter if the room is owned by the inhabitant(s) or just being used for a temporary period, it always, directly or indirectly, shows the effects of private use and ownership. But in what ways is the personal quality of a room brought about? Roughly this happens in three ways:

1. By seeking help of someone (an interior decorator most often) who can delineate and coordinate the functions of the room and at the same time produce a particular "look" and "feel" which reflects the owner's personal taste and sensibilities.

2. By the individual who owns the room assuming the responsibility for the planning and ordering of the room into workable units and an esthetically pleasing whole. Many individuals feel that space they inhabit cannot be arranged or made pleasing by anyone other than themselves. And many people approach the decoration of a room with the "I don't know, perhaps, what is good, but I know what I like" philosophy. Rooms that are consciously planned often tell what the person who occupies it would like to be accepted as rather than what he actually may be. In this way rooms are often like costumes or clothes.

3. By not consciously considering the planning of a room as a problem at all. (The natural demands of day-to-day living would require from the room only its functional and utilitarian properties.) Most characters in plays operate in this third category. The person who lives in a particular place for a period of time creates, although it is almost entirely unconscious, a highly distinctive and personal environment. This sort of room is slow in evolution however, and the overall effect is primarily accumulative in nature, not, as stated before, consciously planned. This is the most difficult type of room for the designer to plan and execute since the only way in which he can be suc-

cessful in his aim is to fully understand the person or persons who created it.

Quite often the young scene designer gets the function of the interior decorator and his own confused. (It is a well-known fact among professional scene designers that some of their colleagues are nothing more than interior decorators.) But, ultimately, it is not a matter of class distinction or hierarchy that separates the scene designer and the interior decorator; it is, rather, a distinct difference in purposes and goals.

The interior decorator has and uses in his work certain skills that allow him to analyze a room in a manner that the scene designer must also use. It is true that the interior decorator usually attempts to make the room he designs reflect the personality of his client; but, at the same time, it is almost impossible for him to keep his own out of the picture. Actually, he was probably chosen because of a distinctly personal approach to the decoration of a room; his client, in all probability, chose him precisely because of the style with which he has come to be associated. The point to be observed here is that the interior decorator, while he is greatly interested in making a room esthetically pleasing and stylish, is primarily concerned with the predictable functions of that room as outlined by his client's stated wishes and is responsible for the successful resolution of all those functions. He may be, for instance, called upon to provide a conversation area greater for client A than for client B since client B does not have nearly so many parties as client A. His task is to combine all demands (no matter how diverse the individual elements) into some unified and workable whole. Once he has done this his job is complete; he is paid and he need not concern himself with that particular room again. His task is finished when the people move in; what they do after that moment is their business, it is no concern of his.

We might ask, then, doesn't the scene designer perform many of the same functions as the interior decorator, operate in much the same manner? Is not his work complete when he has provided the characters in the play with a room that satisfies their physical needs, and (like the clients of the interior decorator) is his job not finished when the actors move into the setting? Actually this is not one question but several; yes, some of his functions are similar, but, no, he cannot consider his task done when the actors take up "tenancy" of the room he has created. What he must concern himself with, in fact, is what they do *after* they move into the setting. This is the main distinction and greatest difference between the work of the scene designer and the interior decorator. Let us be a little more specific as to what this difference implies.

Although the interior decorator has influenced certain aspects of behavior of the people who live in this room, he cannot be responsible if, say three weeks after he has completed his work, a murder is committed in that room. But what of the scene designer? He may have created a room that uses all the skills of a decorator, be identical in almost every way with one primary difference; he knows *everything* that will transpire in that room for the whole time that that room exists. If there is to be a murder in it he is quite aware that it will happen; he is literally forced to plan for it in some ways. The designer cannot relate to the characters of the play in the way that the decorator relates to his client; the designer's task is more complex since he must constantly work on more than one level at a time. Not only do the events of the play need understanding and coordination, the characters of the drama, unlike the decorator's client, never speak directly to the designer and very rarely reveal or discuss what they feel about the place where they live or find themselves. In almost every script, however, it is possible to glean from character study the necessary information that is directly useful in the construction of space relationships.

But what about stage space? How does it differ from the kind of space we have just been discussing? It is not uncommon for the playwright sometimes to call upon the designer to organize the stage into separate areas that will represent different locales although actually only a nominal distance from one another. While these locations are supposedly miles apart, they are in reality no more than a few feet, sometimes inches, apart. The same requirement is made in relation to time as well; Willy Loman in *Death of a Salesman* must literally walk in the space of a few feet from his backyard to another city, and, at the same time, into the past. This use of space on a stage in such a free and unrestricted manner is not a modern innovation however; Shakespeare, to mention but one playwright from the past, made similar demands on the theater's ability to mold time and space to its needs. The very nature of stage space is amorphous and subject to change; no set of rules, no firm principles can be formulated that will once and forever set the limits of how this space may be used. The problems the playwright presents the designer must be solved over and over with each new production. In most cases the problems are fairly simple; nevertheless, the designer must always be prepared, should it be necessary, to redefine the total space under his control into a workable framework that will aid and forward the progress of the production. Space on the stage, therefore, can never be simply equated with space outside the theater even though they can both be measured in feet and inches. The manipulation of stage space is, perhaps, one of the most

difficult areas for the designer to master; it is certainly of more importance to his fellow collaborators—the director and the actor—than the
creation of pictorial backgrounds. It is also the one significant aspect of
theater practice that separates scene design from all other arts.

It is now time, perhaps, to begin a closer and more detailed study
of the designer as he performs his multipurposed profession. In the
following pages we must examine him not only in relation to the
various physical demands and limitations he will encounter in his job,
but also, and probably more importantly, as he relates to the other creative personalities with whom he must collaborate. One thing the student of design must never forget: no matter how significant his contribution to a production, he is always a "community artist," an artist
whose success depends almost entirely on the service he gives to the
other members of his community—the actor, the playwright, and the
director.

§2
The Designer's Role in the Production Plan

The scene designer is an artist unlike almost every other creative
artist. While he is an individual, he is also a member of a team; his
work, no matter how unique, is not complete without the work of the
other members of that team. It is something of a paradox that the
greater the cooperation between these individual contributors to the
production is, the more singular becomes the artistic rewards for each.
Conversely, when there is a disparity in the various elements of the
production, when it is obvious that those who are responsible for the
final product have not meshed their skills and efforts into a unified
whole, no one emerges with successful results.

But just how does the designer work with other members of the
production staff? Just what is the organizational plan for the putting
together of a stage production? These questions cannot be answered
completely or finally for every production or for every producing organization; there are, however, certain common features in the planning
of most productions and these can be listed and discussed.

First of all, let us examine a diagram which shows the progress of a
production from the beginning of a project until performance. (This
diagram [fig. 14] assumes that the designer is responsible for the entire
production design and that his work cannot really be separated from
that of the director working with him.)

George Abbott once said of plays being produced for the first time

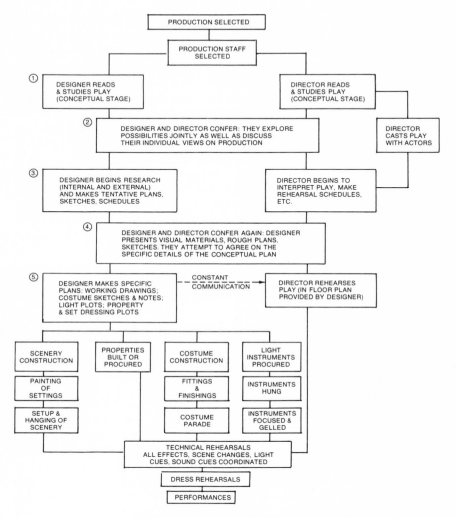

14. *Chart of functions of designer in production*

that they were not so much written as they were rewritten; something of the same philosophy applies to the manner in which the designer must go about his job. Perhaps the most obvious fact that emerges from study of the foregoing diagram is that the designer's task is a complex one, that it cannot be done all in one place (as a painter or sculptor can in his private studio) or all at one time or that he, the designer, is the only one who influences what the final result will be. It should also be apparent that the designer's ideas are constantly being shaped and altered not only by the progress of his own thoughts but those of other artists as well, most notably the director. And while the painter or sculptor can begin a project and pursue it, if he wishes, in an unbroken line of work taking as much or as little time as he decides, the designer finds that his job must be accomplished in bits and pieces in many places (scenic shops, libraries, paint studios, theaters).

Still, practically all production schedules follow, sometimes only roughly, a similar pattern of development as the one we have just seen. But the designer should always keep in mind that his work is conditioned by a number of factors that have little to do with the artistic merit of a design, important as that factor is. No designer, then, can plan a production without taking the following elements into consideration:

1. Budget available to him for building and finishing the setting and properties (and sometimes the costumes).

2. Time available for construction, painting, rigging, and lighting the setting. (In the professional theater time very definitely is money.)

3. The skill of his technical staff: carpenters, metal workers, painters, properties personnel, lighting technicians, and stage crew. (In the nonprofessional theater this is an area to consider carefully. There are very few designers indeed who do not realize that they are only as good as the people who work with them and for them.)

4. The limitations of the plant where the production is prepared and those of the theater where the production will be presented.

It is very much part of the designer's job to be fully aware of all these factors during every step of the construction, painting, setup, and lighting of his setting; he cannot simply deliver the sketches and working drawings to the various shops and then forget about the production until dress rehearsals. Nor should he feel he is at the mercy of the above limitations; ingenuity in overcoming these limitations actively builds the skill and prowess of the designer. But to blindly ignore them can only lead to frustration at every stage in the preparation of a production.

It would be well to consider at this time the place where the designer does spend a great deal of his time when preparing a production: his own studio. Doubtless no two designers could be expected to have identical work patterns; the individual manner in which each designer works, therefore, probably accounts more for the great variation one encounters from studio to studio than architectural differences. Nevertheless most studios of scene designers could be expected to have certain features in common.

Practically all artists find that the place they work has a definite effect on the kind of work they do; partly in the amount they are able to produce and also in the quality of that work. And the deeper they become involved in their profession, the more particular they are about not only the tools and materials of their craft but where they employ them. To the working designer, organization of his work area is not a restrictive activity, it is one that allows him to advance most freely. But what are some of the work needs of the designer? How are they expressed in work areas? Some of these needs one would almost certainly encounter in most studios would be:

1. A place to think, make rough sketches, confer with others concerned with the production.
2. A place to make finished sketches: watercolor, pastel, pen and ink, etc. (with a water supply near this area if possible).
3. A place to create and experiment with models and to be able to work with three-dimensional materials.
4. A place to make large-sheet working drawings (a drafting table).
5. Storage areas for: reference books (shelving); file clippings, catalogues, etc. (file cabinets); working drawings (flat files); sketches and set drawings (flat files or racks); drawing materials, drafting supplies, model materials (shelving, chests); finished models (shelving); slides and projections (slide files).
6. Display areas for current ideas, notes, schedules, etc., near working areas (bulletin boards).
7. A projection screen on which to show slides and a permanent setup for projector.
8. An all-purpose work table on which to lay out work in progress, draw up full scale details, etc.
(All these areas should have general lighting [from the studio's overall illumination] but should also have specifically directed light sources in each individual area.)
9. And, although not an absolute necessity, provision for refreshment—an area for coffee-making, etc.—and marginal entertainment: phonograph, radio. A designer spends a great deal of time in his studio; although it is a working place, it should be as comfortable as he can make it.

After only a few years, most designers find they need additional storage space for past projects (or for materials they might not need to use very often). The working designer, therefore, should examine his studio from time to time and store in some other place all the things he does not absolutely need. Nothing is quite as exasperating as trying to

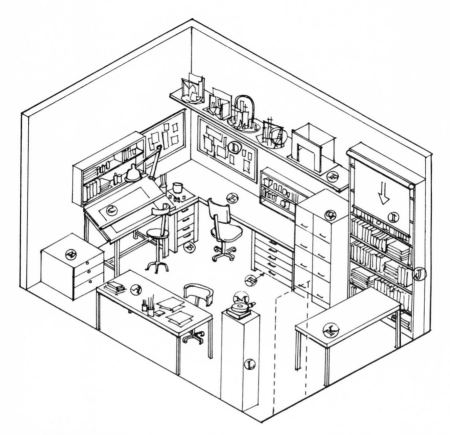

15. *Designer's studio:* A, *study and conference area;* B, *storage for drafting mate-rials and art supplies;* C, *drafting table—immediate reference materials and sup-plies kept in shelving above;* D, *bulletin board;* E, *sketching and model building area;* F, *storage shelving for models;* G, *file cabinets;* H, *flat file cabinets;* I, *projection screen—pulls down when used;* J, *book shelving;* K, *all-purpose work table;* L, *slide storage;* M, *slide projector*

put together a complicated production and having its component parts constantly being lost in a welter of past projects or unimportant mate-rials. Few professional designers can afford the luxury of being un-organized.

Figure 15 is a drawing that incorporates these work necessities into a workable studio layout.

§3
The Designer and the Playwright

When the English playwright David Storey was being interviewed by a reporter of the *New York Times* concerning his new play *Home,* his answer to a familiar question that many playwrights are asked was this:

REPORTER (*to Storey*): What do you say to people who ask what your play is really all about?
STOREY: No idea.

While this may seem a flippant reply to such a question, even a paradoxical one, more than one playwright has answered just such questions in much this way. Do they really not know what they are doing or what they have done, or is there something else, a deeper more profound meaning that touches on the nature of playwriting itself behind the words of this reply? What does such an answer mean, moreover, to the designer attempting to understand the purpose and scheme underlying the playwright's creation? Should he, for instance, always take the playwright's written directions at face value or should he be free to interpret them?

Friederich Dürrenmatt, in discussing his function as a playwright, has written down some of his thoughts concerning what he means to do and what he actually, in the end, does accomplish when he writes a play. Here is a brief extract from an essay called "Problems of the Theatre" (translated by Gerhard Nellhaus) in which he comments on his work and what that work "means":

For me, the stage is not a battlefield for theories, philosophies and manifestoes, but rather an instrument whose possibilities I seek to know by playing with it. Of course, in my plays there are people and they hold to some belief or philosophy—a lot of blockheads would make for a dull piece—but my plays are not for what people have to say: what is said is there because my plays deal with people, and thinking and believing and philosophizing are all, to some extent at least, a part of human nature. The problems I face as a playwright are practical, working problems, problems I face not before, but during the writing. To be quite accurate about it, these problems usually come up after the writing is done, arising out of a certain curiosity to know how I did it.

What I am concerned with are empirical rules, the possibilities of the theatre . . . the artist indeed has no need for scholarship. Scholarship derives laws from what exists already: otherwise it would not be scholarship. But the laws thus established have no value for the artist, even when they are true. The artist cannot accept a law he has not discovered for himself.

. . . Scholarship sees only the result; the process, which led to this result, is what the playwright cannot forget. What he says has to be taken with a grain of salt. What he thinks about his art changes as he creates his art; his thoughts are always subject to his mood and the moment. What alone really counts for him is what he is doing at a given moment; for its own sake he can betray what he did just a little while ago.

Here we have the playwright stating clearly and explicitly the idea that he, along with all those who read his play, find meaning in this work only *after* it is done; meaning is not necessarily a conscious goal the writer pursues at the time of creation or works out according to a preconceived plan. But, he also points out, with the completion of the writing his work is done; he is under no obligation to explain it further.

What, then, do those who take the playwright's work and produce it on the stage owe him; in particular, how closely should the designer follow the playwright's wishes, assuming he can discern them in the first place; and just what is the designer's role in relation to the written text of the play?

There are no easy answers to these questions nor is it possible to ever answer them finally; the nature and scope of the designer's task changes with each individual script. And it must be pointed out that though the designer and playwright are both creative artists, their raw materials, their purposes—even though they are attempting to produce a unified work—cannot be compared to any great extent. The biggest difference between the two, however, lies in the fact that the designer, though not a "scholar" in the sense Dürrenmatt uses that word, is always engaged in a form of research that in many ways resembles scholarship; he is not, usually, creating something completely new and original on his own. He is, in fact, an interpretive artist whose product depends largely on how successful he is in digging out meanings and information the playwright has hidden in his work and may even be unaware that he did so. It is a paradox that a production staff (of which the designer has become an increasingly important member) must sometimes consciously come to know more of the playwright's subconscious purposes than he himself might have been aware of were he directly confronted with the information.

Of course, no single rule can be formulated as to the obligation of the designer to the playwright which will satisfy all situations, all plays; the obligations imposed on the designer in the name of interpretation vary too greatly from script to script and from designer to designer. And while there are designers who have designed productions without actually having read the script, the more common fault is not not having read it, but not reading it with any degree of perception. It probably would not be a gross exaggeration to point out that there are far too many designers working today who think their job done when they have satisfied the most basic physical demands of the play's written directions: providing a door when a door is called for, a window because the script "says so."

But even though Dürrenmatt seemed to imply that how his plays were to be produced or interpreted was not necessarily his business, he has had at least one occasion to reprimand a number of designers who apparently, in their zeal to make a distinct contribution to the "interpretation" of the play, did not conceive of the design as he would have it. (This is a common fault in many playwrights who have occasion to be around a production of their play; more than one designer has noted that the author is perfectly willing to accept any solution in production just so long as it happens to coincide with what he wanted in the first place.) In an afternote to *The Marriage of Mr. Mississippi*, the author feels impelled to issue this warning to the designer of any future productions of the play:

> Many productions, no doubt misled by the text, have made the mistake of using scenery that was too abstract. Since, among other things, this comedy is "the story of a room," the room in which everything takes place must at the beginning be as real as possible. Only so will it be able to disintegrate. The unreal and fantastic may safely be left to the text, to the author.

In all fairness to Dürrenmatt, though, in this case he has touched on a valid point. As a matter of fact, this note might very well have been written by Ionesco for his play *The Bald Soprano* which has often received much the same treatment. Although the play is an example of what has come to be known as theater of the absurd since it takes a nonsensical approach to dialogue and situation—a characteristic feature of this form of theater—the author asks for (even though most designers have not taken him seriously) a typical English room in a middle-class home. And what most designers do not realize is that that is exactly what he meant, that the force of the play (its effect at least) greatly depends upon the contrast of unreal dialogue against a very real physical background. The designer, in both cases, should, as Dürrenmatt points out, resist doing the playwright's work for him.

In the foregoing note, Dürrenmatt sounds a little upset with the designer. But what of the other side to this situation: How does the designer feel about his obligations to the playwright? Few have either the skill or inclination to make their views on the subject known in print; the playwright's "way" with words does give him a certain advantage in this respect. However, not many designers seriously question the right of the playwright to expect to be interpreted correctly; most would agree that that is what they try to do. Still, most designers resent the prevalent unspoken assumption that he is nothing more than a highly skilled servant to the playwright; he feels he has a right to expect certain concessions from this playwright (even though he may have been dead hundreds of years) as well as being obliged to him. Sometimes, however, designers do express in print their "gripes" with playwrights; Peter Larkin in *The Ideal Theatre: Eight Concepts,* for instance, raises some serious questions concerning the present-day writer who has become too dependent on the cinema technique of writing. Here is what he said:

> The writer starts theater.
> The author also is a victim of the movies. As he writes his play, he cuts and pans with a vengeance, where before he strove mightily to stick with the classic unities of time and space. . . . I attended not long ago a meeting at the Ford Foundation in which our finest playwright bawled all the designers out for our prehistoric, creaking old theater. Why were there no new techniques available to him? It is true our professional theater hasn't got answers for that. He placed the responsibility on the architect-designer's head. . . . You cannot develop what you believe to be an undiscovered wonder drug and then go looking for a new disease. Designers must not design stage sets but stages, architects not theater buildings but theater; and playwrights must stop writing movies and write in a new way for theater.

While Larkin's remarks concerning this particular point may be less warranted today than they were even ten years ago, we now have playwrights who, in their search for the new and original, are creating works that rely greatly on multimedia production. It is possible that many of them are creating works that might be better realized in some other medium, the cinema for instance. These playwrights, in their infatuation with the exciting possibilities of projections, slides, closed-circuit TV systems, and filmstrips, often rely on the scene designer to "make it all work." These techniques and mechanical contrivances, although legitimate in themselves and often interesting to an audience, in many instances become mere gimmickry which sometimes masks a lack of genuine creativity and originality on the part of the playwright who makes heavy use of them in his work; often what is presented is nothing more than a cover for inferior creative talent rather than a manifestation of it. All too often it is the designer who ends in making the pertinent and definitive statement rather than the playwright he ostensibly serves; this is simply because the playwright has done nothing much more with his script than write out a blank check for those in charge of the physical production to fill in to whatever amount they choose. Few designers really desire this situation no matter how satisfying personally such opportunities can be.

And yet playwrights vary greatly one from the other in their concern with how their works will be scenically realized on the stage. But it has only been during the last hundred years, approximately, that any have bothered themselves with the problem at all. During this century, however, we have had a rather extensive spectrum of writers who range all the way from writing complete directions into the scripts (as George Bernard Shaw did when he felt that internal guides and clues were not explicit enough to secure the proper interpretation of the script) to the author who apparently couldn't care less how his play is produced in the theater. A great deal of the difference lies, quite probably, in the individual writer's personal view of his function in relation to a producing situation. While some feel the "trappings" have little permanent influence on the worth of their play, others have done all within their power to have the final word as to how it will be viewed by an audience in the theater.

Perhaps a truer, more realistic attitude of the playwright toward the producing theater (and one that most designers and directors implicitly act on) has been voiced by Michel de Ghelderode in a letter to a prospective director of his play *Escurial.* Here is part of that letter.

> You don't have to take into account the wishes and advice of its author, who has been living, for a long time, a solitary life far removed from the theatre. There are several ways *Escurial*

can be played. Yours will be the right way; the style you give it, the incantory state you project upon it, will suit your temperament. These things escape me—they no longer belong to me: the play is yours and it is your obligation to bring it to live either from the inside or the outside depending upon the intensity of the reality or dream. That is your marvelous domain. I am not part of it. The stage is where you, in turn, become the creator. Everything I would tell you is suggested in the text: the cruel and hallucinatory aspect of this action is contained in the description of the decor and characters. The only thing that could be useful to you is this: *think of painting;* this play is painting become theatre. I shall explain. I was inspired to write *Escurial* after I saw two canvases of the Spanish School at the Louvre. An El Greco and a Velasquez on the same wall and not far from each other (this was in 1925–1926). El Greco inspired an anxious, haggard, visibly degenerate, pulmonary "King John"—in brief, a beautiful, clinical specimen. El Greco's brush brought forth a terrible, disquieting, unforgettable character—and I dreamt of him! Velasquez inspired a magnificent dwarf, swollen with blood and instinct. To bring these two monsters together was all that was needed. The play was the outcome—and its plasticity captivated you as did its peculiarly intense and spasmodic tone, its sudden modulation—the voices once again became human. Yes, everything is painting: gestures, attitudes, miming, parades, I can't think of anything else to tell you. [Bettina Knapp, trans., "To Directors and Actors: Letters, 1948–1959," *Tulane Drama Review,* Summer 1965]

But while some playwrights have, as de Ghelderode did in this instance, completely abdicated to the designer and director the responsibility for the realization of their play on the stage, others have been very specific in their desires concerning the production of their work. Eugene O'Neill, at least on one occasion, even went so far as to visit a power plant in order to make a sketch of its interior and equipment to give the designer Lee Simonson so that he would more nearly obtain the effect O'Neill wanted for his play *Dynamo* (fig. 16).

Few playwrights ever go quite this far; at best the practice has limited application. Most designers would not take kindly to a script that came with exact pictures of the playwright's wishes. Most playwrights actually count on the designer's collaboration as an artist with ideas of his own; while there have been many occasions where authors have

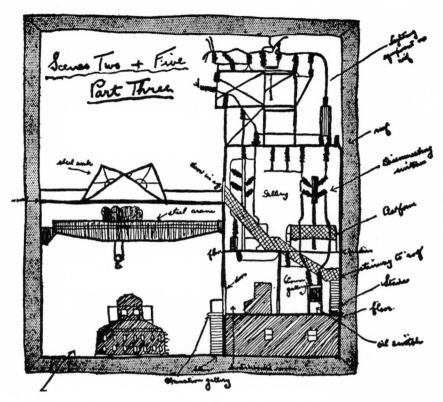

16. Dynamo *sketch by Eugene O'Neill. Used by courtesy of Yale University*

been dissatisfied with the productions of their plays, few would want the responsibility for it themselves.

The playwright is often more helpful to the designer when he stays within his own province; O'Neill is much more useful when he is less specific visually and makes his wishes known in terms that, while they guide the designer in certain paths, inspire him to make a contribution on his own. Read, for example, his description of the play's locale for *Desire Under the Elms:*

> The action of the entire play takes place in, and immediately outside of, the Cabot farmhouse in New England, in the year 1850. The south end of the house faces front to a stone wall with a wooden gate at center opening on a country road. The house is in good condition but in need of paint. Its walls

are a sickly grayish, the green of the shutters faded. Two enormous elms are on each side of the house. They bend their trailing branches down over the roof. They appear to protect and at the same time subdue. There is a sinister maternity in their aspect, a crushing, jealous absorption. They have developed from their intimate contact with the life of man in the house an appalling humaneness. They brood oppressively over the house. They are like exhausted women resting their sagging breasts and hands and hair on its roof, and when it rains their tears trickle down monotonously and rot on the shingles.

This leaves something for the designer to do; the playwright is saying, "Here is the way I *feel* about this place. These are things I think are important for you to consider when you begin to design an actual structure where the characters of my play must live. And I don't feel I am encroaching on your art if I tell you about it. But, it is up to you to find a way of putting these thoughts and suggestions on the stage; at the same time it allows room for you to exercise your own art too."

§4
The Designer and the Director

In *Creativity in the Theater,* Philip Weissman writes,

no performance of a written work of art can be more than a single interpretation. The greatness of a director depends on his capacities to identify with the creator and to create in performance an optimal and original communication which enhances the author's creation without distorting it.

A director identifies with the contents of the created work and interests himself in communicating its contents. He is more identified with the dramatist or composer than with the audience. He re-creates the originator's creative expression.

In an article by Harold Clurman called "In a Different Language," a director says this of his profession:

That action speaks louder than words is the first principle of the stage; the director, I repeat, is the "author" of the stage action. Gestures and movement, which are the visible manifestations of action, have a different language from that which the playwright uses, although the playwright hopes that his words will suggest the kind of action that ought to be employed. The director must be a master of theatrical action, as the dramatist is master of the written concept of his play. . . .

It is rarely the director's intention to alter the playwright's meaning. (Of course this has often been done—consciously as well as unconsciously—and occasionally with very happy results.) But it is a mistake amounting to ignorance to believe that the playwright's meaning is necessarily conveyed by merely mouthing the playwright's dialogue and following his stated instructions. In a sense the playwright's text disappears the moment it reaches the stage, because on the stage it becomes part of an action, every element of which is as pertinent to its meaning as the text itself. [*Theater Arts* 34 (January 1950)]

The thoughts and criterion of interpretation inherent in these statements apply to the designer as well as to the director. They also, in part, help to clarify the similarity of purpose and the artistic bond between them; although their materials and techniques are different, as well as their points of attack, the aims of both are often similar. In a successful collaboration, both personalities might very well be evident, but, just as some aspects of observation are directed by thought and some by purely visual response, so it is with the director's and designer's contributions. The designer's role is to act as an eye to the director-mind; but these activities bear the same relationship in the total creative effort as do the activities of the different parts of the single human body; they are not separate and unrelated but, rather, all part of the same single function: interpretation of the playwright's script. In a successful production, it is impossible to separate these two influencing forces into individual contributions. That all too often the work done by the director and designer exist side by side with little relationship one to the other, is testimony to the fact that this desired collaboration does not come about automatically or effortlessly. In fact, the odds always seem to be heavily weighed against it.

Some directors are able to think in terms similar to the designer's (some, in fact, are or were designers before becoming full-time directors) and are able to speak his language, to make their ideas clear to the designer with whom they are working. These directors, strangely enough, are often less dictatorial than those to whom the designer's function and art is a foreign language. Very few designers have not had the experience of working with a director who simply could not visualize in one scale—the working plans, models, sketches—what would eventually be rendered in another. And how often has a designer heard the complaint, "I didn't know that *that* was what it would really look like," or the defense, "I don't know what I want until I see it on the stage."

There are directors, though, that are able to express their directorial concepts in images the designer can understand and make use of in his own search for a design concept; most designers do not feel this is an intrusion into their private area of creativity. As a matter of fact, it is not uncommon for a designer to become so involved in the problems of the director that he actually begins to direct himself. Take for instance the example of Franco Zeffirelli; a successful designer who has become an even more successful director. While this might be considered a special case since he often designs and directs at the same time, it in no way negates the relationship between the designer and director when they are separate artists; if anything, it supports it and perhaps points the way to what this relationship should be. Here are some random thoughts by Zeffirelli from *Directors on Directing*, edited by Toby Cole and Helen Chinoy, on the problems of directing. It is interesting to note that he is unable to keep his "designer's eye" from determining much of the action.

> You don't need many ideas [in directing a play], you need one. On that you work and the idea carries you if it's right. . . . Each of his interpretations he reports is based on a controlling image, a core. In *Cavalleria* [*Rusticana*] I have always seen the core as a wide white street going uphill in a Sicilian village, that and the sky. At night the wind blows, and a tiny figure with a black shawl comes down running, closing under her shawl her pain and sorrow. It is the destiny of some Sicilian women. I built the set that way. The stage hands at Covent Garden can tell how fussy I was about the platform. The curtain goes up on the prelude. After that it's easy. You are on your path and you follow the consequence. What happens at dawn in Sicily? All the old women come to church. And so on. . . . For *Lucia* [*Di Lammermoor*], mine was the image of a woman shouting in a tremendous room, a castle hall, with her wedding veil covered with blood, crying and chasing her cries. How would a woman arrive at that point? How? I couldn't bear a kind of mechanical bird performance in the mad scene. It's a great tragic scene.

Although Zeffirelli is by no means only a pictorial director (those who have seen his work in both the theater and on the screen realize that although he has a strong interest in scenery and costume, environment and people are his major concern), we do have a director reinforcing the concept that the correct scenic image is all-important to the successful resolution of the director's function and objectives. Zeffirelli has, in fact, used designers other than himself in most of his cinema productions. And while his way of thinking was clearly evident in the designs for costume and setting, at the same time his designers were not simply copying his style or instructions slavishly; their own personalities were evident as well as his. Much of Zeffirelli's motion-picture work clearly shows that both the director and the designer can, as separate creators, interest themselves in the other's function, as in the case of Zeffirelli's *Taming of the Shrew* and *Romeo and Juliet,* often with stunningly successful results.

Sometimes, however, although the designer and director may work in close harmony and understanding, the resulting collaboration is something less than artistically successful. Why should this be; how does this situation come about? It is easy to understand failure when they do not cooperate with one another. What possible explanation could there be for failure when these two do work together? Peter Brook, in his book, *The Empty Space,* touches on this matter and offers some thoughts from the director's point of view.

> In performance, the relationship is actor/subject/audience. In rehearsal it is actor/subject/director. The earliest relationship is director/subject/designer. Scenery and costumes can sometimes evolve in rehearsal at the same time as the rest of the performance, but often practical considerations of building and dressmaking force the designer to have his work cut and dried before the first rehearsal. I have often done my own designs. This can be a distinct advantage, but for a very special reason. When the director is working this way, his theoretical understanding of the play and its extension in terms of shapes and colours both evolve at the same tempo. A scene may escape the director for several weeks, one shape in the set may seem incomplete—then as he works on the set he may suddenly find the place of the scene that eludes him; as he works on the structure of the difficult scene he may suddenly glimpse its meaning in terms of stage action or a succession of colours. In work with a designer, a sympathy of tempo is what matters most. I have worked with joy with many marvellous

designers—but have at times been caught in strange traps, as when the designer reaches a compelling solution too fast—so that I found myself having to accept or refuse shapes before I had sensed what shapes seemed to be immanent in the text. When I accepted the wrong shape, because I could find no logical reason for opposing the designer's conviction, I locked myself into a trap out of which the production could never evolve, and produced very bad work as a result. I have often found that the set is the geometry of the eventual play, so that a wrong set makes many scenes impossible to play, and even destroys many possibilities for the actors. The best designer evolves step by step with the director, going back, changing, scrapping, as a conception of the whole gradually takes form. A director who does his own designs naturally never believes that the completion of the designs can be an end in itself. He knows that he is just at the beginning of a long cycle of growth, because his own work lies before him. Many designers, however, tend to feel that with the delivery of the sets and costume sketches a major portion of their own creative work is genuinely complete. For them, a completed design is complete. Art lovers can never understand why all stage designing isn't done by "great" painters and sculptors. What is necessary, however, is an incomplete design; a design that has clarity without rigidity; one that could be called "open" as against "shut." This is the essence of theatrical thinking: a true theatre designer will think of his designs as being all the time in motion, in action, in relation to what the actor brings to a scene as it unfolds. In other words, unlike the easel painter, in two dimensions, or the sculptor in three, the designer thinks in terms of the fourth dimension, the passage of time—not the stage picture, but the stage moving picture. A film editor shapes his material after the event: the stage designer is often like the editor of an Alice-Through-the-Looking-Glass film, cutting dynamic material in shapes, before this material has yet come into being. The later he makes his decisions, the better.

Of course it would be impossible to set down an ideal work plan which the designer and director could always follow to insure a successful collaboration; too many factors exist and these factors change from production to production. Certain principles, however, can be evolved (as Peter Brook implies in the above statement) which might help the designer to open channels of communication. During the rest of this book this need should always be kept at the back of the mind; the designer cannot perform his job successfully unless he finds ways to cooperate with the directors with whom he works and still preserve his own artistic personality. It is often difficult but it can be done.

§5
The Designer and the Physical Stage

It is not possible to design for any theater without first examining the various physical forms the stage within it can assume. It is, perhaps, the designer's first, and in some ways his most important, duty to reconsider the possibilities that lie open to him when he is given a production to design in even the most formalized and rigid of theater structures. He does not often have the opportunity (or need) to completely remake the stage and auditorium for one particular production, as did Norman Bel Geddes for Max Reinhart's production of *The Miracle,* but designers are more and more not content to accept as inviolate the flat floor and picture frame which characterize most theaters in this country. They are beginning to feel less inhibited about extending their settings into the audience's area in ever new and different relationships.

It would be well to examine briefly just what basic relationships between the acting area and the audience are possible in the two types of theaters the designer of today is apt to encounter: the open stage and the proscenium stage.

The Open Stage

What concerns us in this book is not so much the historical aspects of the open stage (although the designer should be aware of this form's development) as with the role the designer plays when working for it. And to fully understand that role we must also be aware of how the actor moves on that stage and how the director guides that movement.

Basically, this movement tends to be circular in nature; directors find, because of the audience-actor relationship, that they must cause the actor (A, fig. 17) to move in such a way that (1) he does not spend any appreciable time with his back to any one section of the surrounding audience, and (2) so that when he is speaking, he is generally in a position that allows him to face both his partner (B, fig. 17) and the greatest number of the audience possible at the same time.

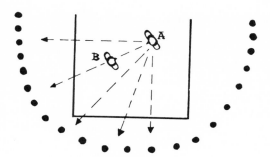

17. *Actor-actor relationship*

The basic action that puts the actors in a favorable position both to be seen and heard (although actors in this form of theater must often deliver lines with their back to a large portion of the audience) is known as an "exchange." This movement (again basically circular) allows the actor on whom the focus has been placed because he has lines to speak or actions to perform to give over his position when the focus changes from him to another. Directors for the open stage find that they must also continually keep the actors moving in order to keep the audience's attention properly focused; the amount of physical action, it would be possible to say, in the average open stage production would be at least two-thirds as much again as in the average proscenium production (fig. 18).

At the same time, space on the open stage is almost always more restricted; that is, there just isn't as much of it as would be on the average proscenium stage. The director and designer, therefore, must

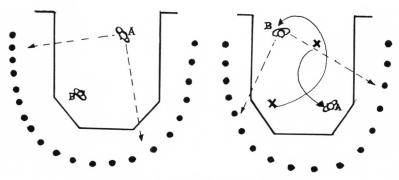

18. *Two-part actor-actor-audience relationships*

be expert in the use of this limited space. A director, for example, will often require the designer to provide sitting arrangements around the periphery of the acting area so that the speaking actor (or the one with the focus on him) can gain dominance through (1) height—he is standing, the one to whom he speaks is sitting, and (2) through position on the platform—he faces the larger number of the audience, the one to whom he speaks faces up to him (fig. 19). We have already noted that the designer can and does affect the actor by restricting and channeling his movement; on the open stage it is imperative that the director and designer work closely together so that the available space is used most effectively.

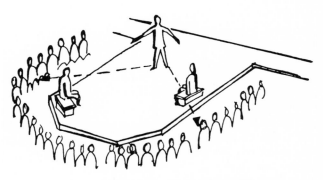

19. *Actor-actor-audience relationship*

Actors like the open stage generally for several reasons. Being closer to the audience and being among them, not separated and isolated to one side as they are in the proscenium theater, actors need not work as hard to secure the proper effect, either vocal or physical; their characterizations, therefore, can be more natural, more subtle in interpretation. At the same time, they are able to establish better relationships and more deeply motivated involvements with their acting partners since they do not have to "cheat" toward the audience while trying to maintain the illusion they are relating to other actors on the stage. One of Stanislavsky's most desired reforms was to bring the attention of the actor more to the stage, to the objects on it as well as to other actors, and less to the audience. (It was a hallmark of nineteenth-century theater that the actor, no matter how realistic the intent of the play he was performing, almost always was more aware of the audience he was playing for than of the other performers on the stage. Stanislavsky did not want the actor to ignore the audience, as he has often been accused; he merely felt that an audience would be more deeply engrossed in the drama if the actors themselves were.)

Even though the pendulum has swung from a naturalistic theater (the direction it was taking at the end of the nineteenth century) to a more theatrical one, much of the open stage technique of acting and directing has now found its way onto the proscenium stage; more and more settings, for this reason, are "violating" conventions of the proscenium arch, that is, being built across the curtain line and into the auditorium so that the performance of the actor can be more immediate than if it were contained wholly on the stage behind the arch line.

During the past three decades there has been a renewed interest in the open stage form. The most successful new theaters built in this hemisphere have been, perhaps, those that exhibit the basic features of such a theater even though there has been no attempt to reproduce exactly any historical open stage in detail. The Stratford Theatre in Ontario, Canada (fig. 20), and the Tyrone Guthrie Theatre in Minneapolis, Minnesota, are only two of the outstanding examples of new theaters built primarily to present works from the various ages of the theater and yet have been highly successful in accommodating modern plays as well. Some of the Guthrie's most popular presentations have been works by Chekhov who wrote exclusively for a theater whose form and style is all but diametrically opposed to that of the open theaters of the past. Nevertheless, his plays have not only withstood the transfer from one form to the other, in many cases they have greatly benefited from the advantages the open stage has to offer.

If one man were to be singled out as having popularized this type of theater in our own time, it would probably have to be Tyrone Guthrie; for a number of years he has been one of the most successful directors working on the open stage. Here is an article, "A Director Views the Stage," written by him in which he attempts to explain why the Minneapolis theater—the one named in his honor—was designed as it was.

In designing an auditorium, the prime consideration should be the relation of performer to audience. Since the middle of the seventeenth century when Italian opera took Europe by storm, theatres have been designed almost exclusively in the manner best suited to operatic performances. Such designs have a raised platform in front of which is a horseshoe-shaped auditorium, usually in several tiers of seating. Between stage and auditorium a great gulf is fixed, literally a pit, in which the orchestra plays. The stage of the opera

20. *The Festival Stage, Stratford, Ontario. Designed by Tanya Moiseiwitsch,* 1957

house is further removed from the audience by a partition with a large hole through which the spectators view the performance. This proscenium opening is often decorated as a picture frame to enhance the illusion that the performance is a picture in which the figures magically move, dance, or sing.

When the performance demands that the picture be changed, a curtain falls and appropriate pulling and hauling prepares the stage for further surprises to delight the audience. When all is ready, the stagehands are replaced by painted mummers in fine raiment, and the curtain is raised. For many years I have worked in such theatres, and it never crossed my mind that a theatre could or should be otherwise. When I was in my early thirties, I was hired to direct the Old Vic Shakespeare Company. Gradually it became clear to me that trying to put Shakespeare's plays into the conventional framework for opera was wrong. The plays had been written by a master craftsman for a theatre of altogether different design. It was certainly possible to adapt them to the requirements of conventionally planned theatres. It seemed more desirable, however, to adapt some commonplace building than to adjust a masterpiece. As is often the case, the obviously sensible building plan was too expensive to execute. Yet, I realized that a more logical and easy way to stage these plays existed. It led to an examination of the whole premise of illusion which is the basis for the proscenium stage.

It has always seemed to me that people do not submit to illusion in the theatre much after the age of ten or eleven. They are perfectly aware that the middle-aged lady uncomfortably suspended on a wire is not Peter Pan but an actress pretending to be Peter Pan. For a performance to attempt to create an illusion is as gallant but futile as Mrs. Partington's attempt to sweep the Atlantic Ocean out her parlor. In planning the Tyrone Guthrie Theatre, it was necessary to decide whether the stage should be the conventional platform separated from the audience by a proscenium arch or whether it should be an open stage such as the Elizabethan theatre and the ancient Greek and Roman theatres. A third alternative was available. We might have asked our architect to create a flexible design which could adjust to both types. We rejected this, however, on the ground, that an all-purpose hall is a no-purpose hall—that insofar as a purpose is flexible, it is not wholehearted; that it was better to be firmly and uncompromisingly of one kind than to attempt a compromise between opposites which we considered to be theatrically and architecturally, theoretically and practically irreconcilable. We argued for the open stage for the following reasons: first, our intended program is of a classical nature, and we believe that the classics are better suited to an open stage than to a proscenium one. Second, the aim of our performances is not to create an illusion, but to present a ritual of sufficient interest to hold the attention of, even to delight, an adult audience. Third, an auditorium grouped *around* a stage rather than placed in front of a stage enables a larger number of people to be closer to the actors. Fourth, in an age when movies and TV are offering dramatic entertainment from breakfast to supper, from cradle to grave, it seemed important to stress the *difference* between their offering and ours. Theirs is two-dimensional and is viewed upon a rectangular screen. The proscenium is analogous to such a screen by forcing a two-dimensional choreography upon the director. But the open stage is essentially three-dimensional with no resemblance to the rectangular postcard shape which has become the symbol of canned drama.

No claim is made that the open stage is better than the proscenium stage for every type of play. But, in our opinion, the open stage is more desirable for the kind of plays we propose to perform and the kind of project we propose to execute. [*Design Quarterly,* no. 58 (1963)]

Figure 21 is a design for the Harold Pinter play, *The Caretaker,* a work that is particularly suitable for the open stage. Notice that the furniture is not arranged, as it would be in the proscenium theater, so as to favor any one direction. And yet there is in this arrangement, casual though it may seem, a certain amount of planned orientation imposed on the actors working in this setting; when one sits on the bed (A), or in the chair (B), or at the table (C), he naturally would be forced to face toward anyone in the general area of the center of the stage, the area where most movement is possible. Actor-to-actor relationships are thus strengthened (almost forced upon the actors) by the placement of the furniture and the layout of the playing area (fig. 22).

As it has been pointed out, there is probably a great deal more movement occasioned by open stage productions than on the proscenium stage; the better the director, however, and the more skilled the actor, the less likely the audience will be able to perceive or be aware of the fact that the life they are seeing on this type of stage is much more active than that outside the theater or in the proscenium theater. For this and other reasons, then, the designer's task is often more difficult—if not more extensive—than when working in other stage forms.

21. *Design for* The Caretaker

The Proscenium Theater

In proscenium theaters, the audience is isolated on one side from the action on the stage. The performance is therefore viewed two-dimensionally; that is, primarily as a picture. This kind of relationship cannot help but force the designer to compose his setting more pictorially than spatially. But what is even more detrimental is that this relationship cannot avoid separating an audience and the performers into two distinct groups. Lines of communications are, for the most part, in one direction: from the stage to the audience. In this form of theater, the members of the audience feel less called upon to participate as actively as they might in the arena situation or while attending the open stage form of theater; there seems to be a willingness on the part of the audience to extend its attention to the open stage or arena more than to the proscenium arch stage. In any case, the proscenium arch does act as a barrier and the integration of audience and performer is at a minimum. And if there is one trend apparent in the

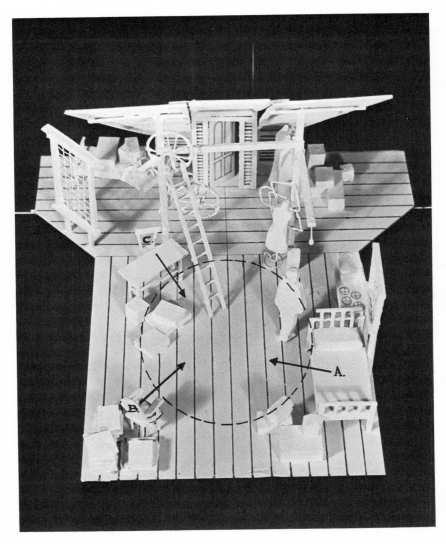

22. *Actor-to-actor relationships in* Caretaker *design*

present day theater it lies in the abolition of barriers rather than in
their construction. For some time, moreover, there has been a growing
dissatisfaction with the proscenium theater. Much of this feeling stems
from and is in reaction to the playwrights and producers who made a

conscious attempt, starting in the late nineteenth century, to keep the stage and audience apart in separate units. And that desire in turn was a reaction by the more progressive playwrights and producers of the period (Strindberg being one of the most outspoken members of the "new wave") against what they felt was too much audience-performer fraternization which, they also felt, would defeat the purpose of the newer trends in the theater, the principle one being naturalism. This point of view, as we know, eventually won out over the more theatrical approaches to producing plays with the result that the bulk of the dramas written since Ibsen has sought to present on the stage an illusion of life as it appears outside the theater.

In the realistic play the viewer must be kept at a safe distance from the actor and the scenery; at least this was felt to be the best way to maintain the illusion of reality. In such a position, what the audience would see could be strictly controlled; what it was not meant to see could be in the same manner carefully regulated. The proscenium theater is more compatible than any other form with the creation of an illusion that what is seen on the stage is "real" or at least realistic enough to complement a style of acting that was also at this same time being formulated to simulate life as it occurred outside the theater.

The influence of this movement to an illusory theater as opposed to a nonillusory theatrical one is still very strong, especially in the area of acting; in production this is less true. And, during the past two decades, both here and abroad, there has been a steady assault on the proscenium theater, as well as the drama it engendered, as the dominant philosophy of theater. As a result, more varied forms of stages exist concurrently now than the total number of forms in all theater history.

In 1959, the Ford Foundation Program for Theater Design initiated a program to study theater structures; what they were and what they should be. In 1962, the American Federation of Arts issued a catalogue showing the results of stage designers working in close relationship with architects to formulate new ideas in theater design. This book, called *The Ideal Theater: Eight Concepts*, represents the thoughts of a number of the best designers and architects working in America today. The book has probably had, during its short existence, a strong effect on contemporary theater building; possession and study of this work is a must for all designers, especially for young designers training now.

One of the more interesting portions of this book is a number of statements by Arthur Miller concerning the proscenium theater.

I have no doubt that plays are not being written just because of the limitations of New York's theaters. . . . You just can't write for these "shoe boxes" with the same ideas, with the same emotional scope, as you would for a (more adaptable) theater. . . . The New York theater is a limitation to the playwright at least to the degree that it is no inspiration to him—he is dragging it around on his back half the time.

. . . You can't hope to make one theater which is absolutely perfect for all kinds of plays. It's just a contradiction of terms. I think the first thing any theoretician has to face is that there is no universal solution to this; I think it's a false chase.

In some kinds of plays, the actors have to come and say, well here I am; but the proscenium says, here I am not. In fact, here you aren't.

The proscenium is a limitation for a hell of a lot of plays. . . . You see, the drama has become more and more a first person thing. Even such a really traditional writer as O'Neill started talking biographically as he grew older. There's a subconscious analogy, I think, between the proscenium theater and the third person, here, the play is pretending to take place without any author; these people are supposed to be really talking to each other, and we are overhearing them. . . . You see, it's all a question of how much you're pretending that this isn't a play, or that this is a play—whether the emphasis is on the author or the actor—presentational or representational. The proscenium favors the latter. . . .

. . . What we are trying to do now is make a theater of essences. That is, where an Ibsen would create the surrounding documentation of social existence (a new discovery—people weren't aware of themselves in society to the degree that they are now)—well, we take for granted that kind of documentation. So, when Ibsen would get to the essences at about the last third of each act—the first two-thirds being the setup for the social situation—we share an awareness of our situation to the degree that numerous plays can simply deal in essences. . . .

. . . You know, every flight from one form is always the attempt to fly into the most direct confrontation with the essence. You break up a form because its appurtenances keep you further and further away from the center. But then when you get into the center, it gradually begins to move out into the periphery again—and somehow you've got to get back into the center again. Time after time, scientists believe that they have reached the ultimate understanding of some process—then it turns out that there is a smaller world inside of the one discovered, a new path into a more recessed center always requires new kinds of documentation if the vision of it is to be proved to others.

The proscenium arch theater has been primarily devoted to the use of scenery and often is a highly complicated mechanism. American theaters are traditionally less well equipped with permanent stage machinery than European stages, particularly German theaters. Broadway, the center of the American professional theater, has stages that often are nothing more than empty shells, their only permanent features being equipment for flying hanging scenery in and out. Most of them do not have permanent lighting control boards, which must be rented along with lighting equipment from production to production. On the other hand, the new Metropolitan Opera House at Lincoln Center is one of the best-equipped theaters in the world.

Regardless of the complexity of the stage mechanisms, the relationships of audience to stage in the proscenium theater is approximately what we see in figure 23. Partly through necessity, but mostly from habit and practice, performers generally orient themselves directly toward the audience; this is also true for the placement of furni-

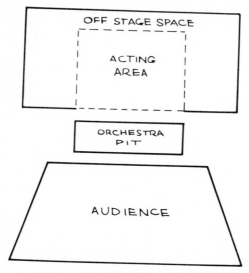

23. *Proscenium theater stage-audience relationship*

ture, important entrances, and scenic effects (fig. 24). Although there is a general tendency to disguise the practice, more today than in the past, patterns of movement tend to be horizontal (A, fig. 25). This horizontal relationship to the audience causes a certain strain on the performers since they must orient both to the audience (to be seen and heard) and to each other (to maintain the necessary involvement with

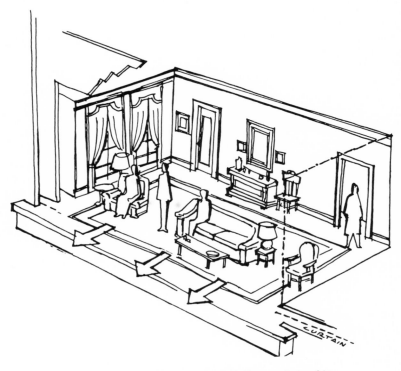

24. *Proscenium theater actor-audience relationship*

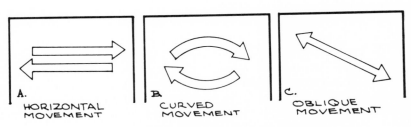

25. *Movement possibilities on the proscenium stage*

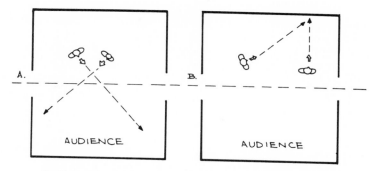

26. Two-part actor-audience relationships on proscenium stage

one another) at the same time; the three-quarter down position seems to be about the best compromise possible (A, fig. 26). In the recent past, directors and actors have become more bold and have begun using the three-quarter up and full back positions as well (B, fig. 26).

When, in 1893, Strindberg wrote *Miss Julie,* he included with it a preface stating his views on how the new theater of that time should be presented to the public. In many ways, the theater has not changed all very much in the past eighty years.

> Of course, I have no illusions about getting the actors to play *for* the public and not *at* it, although such a change would be highly desirable. I dare not even dream of beholding an actor's back throughout an important scene, but I wish with all my heart that crucial scenes might not be played in the centre of the proscenium, like duets meant to bring forth applause. Instead, I should like to have them laid in the place indicated by the situation. Thus I ask for no revolutions, but only for a few minor modifications. To make a real room of the stage, with the fourth wall missing, and a part of the furniture placed back toward the audience, would probably produce a disturbing effect at present.

Until recently the designer rarely (if ever) bothered himself with the problems and incongruities the box setting presented. He merely lined up the furniture so that the audience could see the actors sitting on it and to make it easier for the actors to speak to them as directly as possible. Although few in the audience even thought to question this arrangement, the characters in most plays apparently spend most of their lives facing one wall, which, fortunately for the audience, happens to be facing them and, even more fortunate, isn't there.

The theater has made some progress in this regard since Strindberg. We do see furniture with its back to the audience, or at least not lined up as it was in the old arrangement. Both the director and designer are trying to make the actor's environment appear more natural even if they often "cheat" these furniture relationships toward the arch opening. In fact, there has been, on the part of directors and actors, a general reorientation of the problems of movement on the proscenium stage. (To cite only one example in this regard: when Charles Laughton directed a revival of *Major Barbara* in 1956, during some of the longer "set" speeches in the first act, he seated two of his actors on a low bench directly downstage center with their backs to the audience. In the arsenal scene, at least five actors did most of the scene facing up toward the rear of the stage.)

Elements of the Proscenium Arch Stage As Shown in Figure 27

1. Proscenium arch
2. Stage floor—(A) Trap in stage floor. (Opened here, closed when not in use.)
3. Apron
4. Offstage space (Wings)
5. Orchestra pit (In some theaters, slightly recessed under stage.)
6. Back wall of theater (Usually contains loading door.)
7. Grand drape (Often decorative and used to cut down arch opening.)
8. Main curtain (In many theaters this curtain can be either lowered from above or can be opened laterally from a draw line at the side of the arch.)
9. Second portal (This arch, usually black velvet or some light absorbing fabric, comes after the main curtain; its purpose to help mask off backstage and side lighting arrangements.)
10. Gridiron (A number of supports suspended from the ceiling of the stage house which allows scenery to be flown up and out of sight.)
11. Fly gallery (Usually suspended some distance from the stage floor and where the lines attached to the flown scenery are manipulated after it has been counterweighted.)
12. A Cloth drop suspended from the gridiron (These drops have a rigid batten at top and bottom, sometimes wooden, often pipe.)
13. A cut drop suspended from the gridiron (These drops have a wooden batten at top but are free at bottom.)

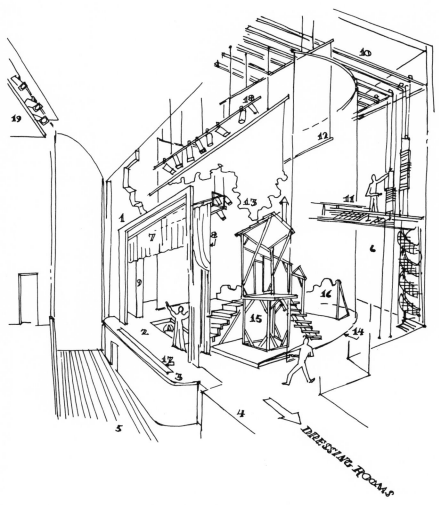

27. Proscenium theater mechanics

14. Cyclorama (Horizont—surrounds most of the stage area, unlike a sky drop which is flat.)

15. Scenic unit (Composed of flats, platforms, steps, all built on a movable wagon.)

16. Groundrow (Cut and painted to simulate a distant view: hills, houses, etc. Sometimes these groundrows are built as are cycloramas, semicircular rather than flat.)

17. Footlights (Not built in many recent theaters but a feature of most theaters built in the last two hundred years. When they are included in modern day theaters, they are usually recessed and are able to be covered over when not in use.)
18. Light batten suspended from gridiron (These battens most often have attached to them permanent lighting connections which feed into known circuits and are not used for anything else but lighting equipment.)
19. Front of house lighting portals (Usually built into the theater ceiling although older theaters do not have them. They are in most cases self-masking and have wire mesh over the front openings to insure the safety of the audience seated below. Generally there is more than one portal.)

New Stage Forms

During the last fifty years a number of theories concerning the nature of theater art have challenged the old ideas as to what the theater art is and where it should be performed. There has been an increasing desire on the part of some directors, actors, and playwrights to abolish the standard forms of the stage along with the accepted audience-actor relationships that exist in order to render the stage a more flexible instrument capable of acting on the spectator in a much more direct manner and with a greater impact than heretofore. These newer forms would allow the actor to involve the audience to a degree and in a manner not possible in theater forms of the past (fig. 28). Until recently the leading exponent of such a new theater—a place that is more environment for the spectator than it is platform for the actor—was Antonin Artaud. At least he has been the major prophet of this movement. Although not able to create this theater in his lifetime, in his book *The Theater and Its Double* he describes how this theater should be realized. Here are some of the basic requirements he proposes:

> The Stage—The Auditorium: We abolish the stage and the auditorium and replace them by a single site, without partition or barrier of any kind, which will become the theater of the action. A direct communication will be re-established between the spectator and the spectacle, between the actor and the spectator, from the fact that the spectator, placed in the middle of the action, is engulfed and physically affected by it. This envelopment results, in part from the very configuration of the room itself. . . .

28. *Scenic arrangement for* Kordian

Thus, abandoning the architecture of present-day theaters, we shall take some hangar or barn, which we shall have
reconstructed according to processes which have culminated
in the architecture of certain churches and holy places, and of
certain temples in Tibet. . . .

In the interior of this construction special proportions of
height and depth will prevail. The hall will be enclosed by four
walls, without any kind of ornament, and the public will be
seated in the middle of the room, on the ground floor, on
mobile chairs which will allow them to follow the spectacle
which will take place all around them. . . . The scenes will be
played in front of whitewashed wall-backgrounds designed to
absorb light. In addition, galleries overhead will run around
the periphery of the hall as in certain primitive paintings.
These galleries will permit the actors, whenever the action
makes it necessary, to be pursued from one point in the room
to another, and the action to be deployed on all levels and in
all perspective of height and depth. . . .

. . . However, a central position will be reserved which,
without serving, properly speaking, as a stage, will permit the
bulk of the action to be concentrated and brought to a climax
whenever necessary.

Artaud's theories have been widely accepted and put into practice in numerous instances especially during the past decade. Probably the most famous group to make use of these concepts has been the Laboratory Theater of Jerzy Grotowski in Poland, who, in 1959, after becoming increasingly dissatisfied with the conventional theater—its purposes and form—decided to create a theater of his own partially based on the writings and philosophy of Artaud. Since that time he has become increasingly influential both in Europe and in America, primarily because he was one of the very first directors to successfully realize many of the ideas that Artaud had only dreamed of. In many of Grotowski's productions, the audience is fragmented into small unequal groups and placed in various spatial combinations in a larger space that has also been broken into smaller acting areas of unequal size. He has, in fact, completely disavowed all stage forms and relationships as they exist today. Here is what he has to say concerning his philosophy of what the theater should be:

> By gradually eliminating whatever proved superfluous, we found that theatre can exist without make-up, without autonomic costume and scenography, without a separate performance area (stage), without lighting and sound effects, etc. It cannot exist without the actor-spectator relationship of perceptual, direct, "live" communion. This is an ancient theoretical truth, of course, but when rigorously tested in practice it undermines most of our usual ideas about theatre. It challenges the notion of theatre as a synthesis of disparate creative disciplines—literature, sculpture, painting, architecture, lighting, acting (under the direction of a *metteur-en-scene*). This "synthetic theatre" is the contemporary theatre, which we readily call the "Rich Theatre"—rich in flaws. . . .
>
> The Rich Theatre depends on artistic kleptomania, drawing from other disciplines, constructing hybrid-spectacles, conglomerates without backbone or integrity, yet presented as an organic art-work. By multiplying assimilated elements, the Rich Theatre tries to escape the impasse presented by movies and television. Since film and TV excel in the area of mechanical functions (montage, instantaneous change of place, etc.), the Rich Theatre countered with a blatantly compensatory call for "total theatre." The integration of borrowed mechanisms (movie screens onstage, for example) means a sophisticated technical plant, permitting great mobility and dynamism. And

if the stage and/or auditorium were mobile, constantly changing perspective would be possible. This is all nonsense. . . .

No matter how much theatre expands and exploits its
mechanical resources, it will remain technologically inferior to
film and television. Consequently, I propose poverty in theatre. We have resigned from the stage-and-auditorium plant:
for each production, a new space is designed for the actors
and spectators. Thus, infinite variation of performer-audience
relationships is possible.

Actually, Grotowski has not created a new theater so much as he
has returned to that very first relationship which began the theater, jet-
tisoning everything between then and now. His theories (which, if we
accept his words at face value, are more rediscoveries than original inventions), and his experiments will undoubtedly have an effect on the
theater of the future. Few who have seen and studied his work would
doubt its depth of accomplishment or Grotowski's sincerity of purpose.
Directors such as Peter Brook, influential critics such as Jan Kott and
companies such as the Living Theatre have been greatly affected by
him and they, in turn, are influencing others. Still, it is probable that
the inherent limitations both in the methods he uses to produce this
form of theater plus the smallness (and specific type) of audience he
appeals to will keep it from being quickly or ever totally assimilated into
the mainstream of acting or production. There are many, in fact, who
do accept the idea of a synthetic theater as a defensible esthetic of theater which, of course, Grotowski does not. This book is tacitly based on
the supposition that synthetic theater is a defensible and viable attitude
which will be with us for some time to come.

If one salient point can be derived from the investigation of theater forms and actor relationships it would probably be that no single
point can be made. Quite possibly there is, for every single person who
works in the theater, a single theater form that he feels most comfortable working in. Nevertheless we must always recognize that "best" for
A may be acceptable (not first) for B and totally unacceptable for C.
And who has the ultimate right to make a final priority which will
decide this question of theater form once and for all? It is more than
likely the designer will find himself confronted with the problems and
virtues of many stage forms during his career; learning what those
problems and virtues are is part of his development, a very important
part. Nor should we really entertain the idea that one stage form is
inherently superior to another. Perhaps the only real point we should

make here is that no single stage and auditorium could ever be expected to satisfy all the philosophies that exist concerning the physical
theater. There is more truth than we might care to admit in Tyrone
Guthrie's statement that, "an all-purpose theater is a no purpose theater."

§6
The Designer's Areas of Influence

The Stage Floor

There is a great deal of soundness in the proverbial basic requirement for theater—three boards and a passion. There is no better way
in which the designer can serve the actor than to provide an appropriate place for him to perform, since there is nothing more or quite as
important to him as what he stands on.

Once the stage floor was nothing more than just a floor; something
to be walked upon, but not to be considered to any great extent by itself. It was merely a neutral area with no definite shape or boundaries
except those of the back and side walls of the theater. As the designer
became more involved with the performer's actions on this floor, his interest in its scenic possibilities also increased. Now, for many designers,
this area has become the single most important element in the total
design. The emphasis of scene design, once almost totally confined to
the periphery of the stage area, has now all but given way to the treatment of the stage floor; once only a simple horizontal plane (slightly
tipped in older theaters to facilitate the sight lines of an audience seated
on a flat floor), this area is now being fractured, extended, raised,
lowered, and angled in literally every possible combination. To resolve
the stage floor into appropriate acting areas is the first major step in
designing a production (fig. 29).

It is surprising that only in the last century has the proper attention been given to this most important of considerations. Yet, it has
been only relatively recently that the scene designer has considered the
stage floor as scenery at all.

The General Background

This general background includes walls, backdrops, overhead
units, etc. While actors do not necessarily involve themselves with the
background, they will always be seen in relation to it. Nothing can be

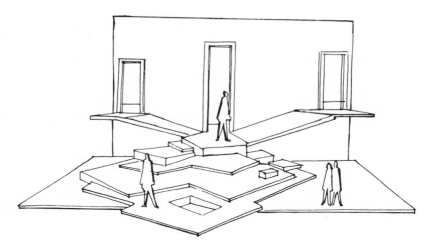

29. *Stage floor and levels*

seen without relationship to some sort of background and therefore, no matter how little it is actively used in the design or by the performers, it must be carefully considered even when it is the desire of the designer to have it totally ignored. Settings for the ballet (and, until recently, opera) consist mainly of backdrops and wings, the floor space being left open and unencumbered. Keeping scenery out of the dancer's way is one of the problems of designing for the ballet (although modern dance, and especially such companies as that of Martha Graham have made active use of their scenic environment, sometimes, in fact, taking this involvement to the point of making the dancer part of it). Painters who have made their reputations elsewhere than the theater are often used for creating ballet settings. Nor are they asked to think or create works in a manner contrary to their already established styles. This means that they do not really attempt to work as the theater designer does; he, more often than not, strives to integrate his work into the production as a whole. The famous painter, on the other hand, is simply expected to present himself as forcefully as possible and is accepted more for the success with which he does that than for his ability to become part of the total production. Picasso is expected to remain (and proclaim clearly that he is no other than) Picasso. As Richard Buckle has pointed out concerning the work of another famous artist, Salvador Dali, "It must be quite clear to anyone looking at . . . Dali's curtain and decor . . . that the celebrated Catalan illusionist does not design ballets—he allows dancers to take part in his painting."

This background can be, therefore, at one and the same time, the least important part of the design to the performer and the most potent visual element in terms of what the audience sees. Actors simply cannot compete with a background that is too bright or distracting. This is potentially the most dangerous area in which the designer works; it is also the area in which the greatest amount of adjustment takes place both in color, intensity of light, and placement of forms (fig. 30).

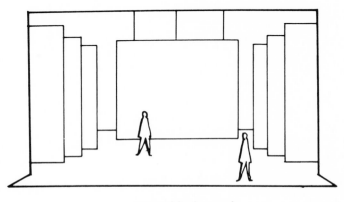

30. *General background*

Specific Units of Scenery

These units may be part of the general background, but what separates them into a different category is that they may, in fact often are, used directly by the actors and therefore become much more important to them. Doors, windows, platforms, steps, rocks, trees, etc., can be used by themselves, that is, separated from their surrounding background, to create the sense of a particular place without the connecting material—such as a wall—that would be found if the scene were completely realistic in conception. For instance, a room like the one shown in figure 31 can be defined simply by the placement of its architectural features and retaining the placement of its furnishings in a manner as if the actual walls were still there (fig. 32).

Actors have an instinctive desire to relate to units of scenery and playwrights have an equally instinctive urge to provide them for the actor to use; windows and doors especially have always had a special symbolic fascination for both the playwright and the actor. They pro-

31. *Drawing of setting*

vide, in fact, an invaluable means by which the actor can show what he thinks, how he relates to the larger world outside the window, and beyond the door of his immediate locale.

Although she was speaking of the window specifically in relation to its use in painting, Katharine Kuh, the eminent art critic and historian, has offered some provocative observations that apply to its use in the theater.

A window is to look through, both into and out of. Though often the symbol of an eye, it is not an eye, but a vehicle for light and for that volatile mirage we call atmosphere. A window is selective; it can frame nature in sweeping panoramas or in magnified close-ups. It provides access to inner visions more vivid than real ones. It can be nothing more than a blank, a vacant opening, or it can reproduce the unedited reflection of one's own image. Because windows imply secret revelations, because they are outlets to both the inside and outside world but, unlike doors, are rarely tangible passageways, they take on a variety of guises. Frequently ex-

32. Specific units of scenery

ploited in art as compositional devices, they have come into their own only recently since Freudian discoveries infused them with new meaning.

In the last moments of the last act of Chekhov's *The Cherry Orchard,* Madame Ranevsky is leaving the home she has known and loved all her life. The room where she is has been stripped of most of its possessions; outside the windows of this room her beloved orchard is being cut down, a sacrifice to progress and a signal that the old life she has lived heretofore is past, all its outward manifestations—the cherry orchard being the symbol of these things—vanishing. In a few moments she must walk out the door of this room never to enter again. What does she *feel* about the empty room where so many happy times were spent? More important, just what does she *see* as she looks out the window? Most important of all, how can the designer aid the actress playing Madame Ranevsky to reinforce the underlying emotions of these moments? How must he design them to show an audience, when no words are given the character except a few insignificant ones, why and to what extent she loves this room as well as what lies beyond it? Of course, most of this must be left to the skill and art of the actor; nevertheless, the designer cannot merely provide a Russian nineteenth-century country-house room and think his job completed. He must put himself in the place of the characters, seeing through their eyes. Moreover, not only must he see what they see at the moment, but with the eyes of their memory as well; in the first act of the play Madame Ranevsky's windows looked out on a happy contented life while now they present a bleak and dying world. How does the designer make these things clear? Or can he? Can a window be designed that somehow helps both the actor and audience to understand *something* about that which is happening outside it? It is the asking of such questions (not necessarily the quick solution to them) that separates the artist-designer from the man who is not.

Let us take another instance in which a door becomes greatly important to the progress of the play and to the actor who must use it. Consider the center doorway (always the palace in Greek theater) in *Oedipus*. What size should these doors be, how big and how heavy? Of what materials should they be made? What physical effort should it cause the actor to open these doors? How, for that matter, does the door open; with what speed or what sound, if any? Do they open in or out? Which way would be most effective? (Perhaps they might open the last time by themselves, as if moved by the gods.) These are but a few of the many questions that, although at first glance may seem unimportant, must be answered. Careful research will provide much of the information needed to satisfy the historical aspects of these questions; but that is only half of the designer's task. After this material is assembled and assessed, he must then consider questions that are beyond mere accuracy of period and style. He must create a door that contains in its design and structure elements of the tragedy of which it is a part. (Symbolically, this is the final door to the mystery he is attempting to solve and, of course, it is behind this door—his own house—that he finds the answers he seeks.) But how do these considerations affect the function of the door or its appearance?

We can, for instance, make some artistic judgments in relation to the width and height of the arch that contains these doors; not only does it determine how big these doors will be, it will also have an effect on the spectator watching Oedipus when he is seen in juxtaposition to it. We might ask, in this regard, how large or high or thick this arch *should* be to be most effective, and what the relationship of the width to the height should be. (fig. 33).

But, once these decisions are made, we still have another problem

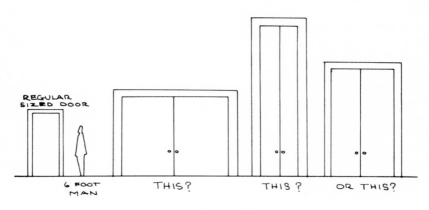

33. *Door heights*

to resolve—the *quality* of the doors themselves, what they are able to say to the audience (or help the actor to make clear).

A number of years ago a director was discussing this very problem with the designer who had been selected to design *Oedipus*. At that time all he could tell the designer was that it started out as "being the entrance to an 'unclean place', that it is majestic, that it holds power, but that dark and unclean things are hidden behind it, hidden from the sight of men." He also spoke of the doors moving like "heavy oil in a dirty machine—slow and sluggishly—not lubricating it but clogging it." This is what he wanted the doors to show: unclean, majestic, slow moving like heavy oil. . . . But, at the end of the play, he said, "this quality must be mitigated, in some way refined, made clear—the doors still majestic but now cleansed and bright."

Since the doors couldn't be changed (it wouldn't be desirable even if possible), they must contain the potential of both these images—dark and corrupt, light and clean. And the designer's job was to make both possible in the same door at different times.

In the first part of the play these doors are seen in a dark world full of shadows; as the light becomes progressively brighter, the shadows are dispelled. After all, the Greek plays actually did start, as far as we know, during the first light of dawn and progressed into the light of day. Is there a similar progress in the structure of the play itself: a progress from darkness into light? Things appear different in different light. Perhaps, thought the designer, this is a clue to how this problem could be solved, that the director have his images to support his thesis. In any case, the physical actualities of the doors and the director's images, had to be amalgamated into a single dynamic (changing) dramatic image.

After much discussion, thought, research, experimentation, and more discussion, a set of doors was designed that could, relying heavily on the properties of light (its ability to change radically color, direction, and intensity), satisfy the various demands made of them. The ornamentation of these doors consisted of massively carved entwined serpents in simulated antiqued bronze. At the beginning of the play these doors were lighted to capitalize on the three-dimensional qualities of the high relief, (the side which the light predominantly struck was also

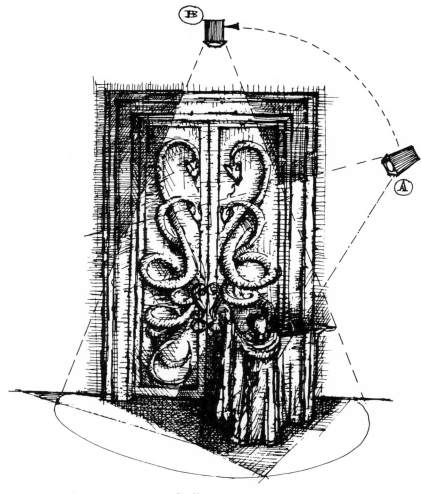

34. Oedipus *doors*

more heavily "corroded"—finished to resemble the green oxide colors and textures of old weathered bronze. The other side (A, fig. 34), which showed up during the later part of the play, was finished with brighter metallic colors. By changing the direction, color, and intensity of the light, it was possible to change both the color of the door and also its dramatic quality as well (B, fig. 34).

The undulating movements inherent in the carving of the coiling snake forms, as the source and intensity of the light changed, were forced back and flattened into the general background design of the doors. As they became flatter they lost much of their dramatic power; as they changed color, they lost much of the feeling of corruption (unclean things) and decay.

The doors matched, therefore, the progress of the play:

1. First part of the play—dark and heavily shadowed stage (Oedipus, literally and figuratively "in the dark").

2. Middle part of the play—with the coming of light (both physical and intellectual) the mysteries begin to resolve, the heavy snake forms lose their hard definition, their power lessens.

3. Last part of play—the light becomes brightest, all things become exposed to the light of day; the palace, formerly an unclean place has been purged and, by Oedipus' own action, cleansed of the defiler.

When the final moment comes for Oedipus to emerge from the palace to announce the catastrophe within and to disclose the action he has taken upon himself (his blinding of himself and his expulsion), what should we, who are outside the door, feel? What emotions should we experience as the doors open? The question has been, can the designer in his work create palace doors that not only have the necessary functional qualities but that can actually intensify the drama itself? The answer is very much so. But, as Robert Edmond Jones has said better than anyone else, it can only happen when the designer *thinks as a poet* and uses his poetic imagination in his designs.

Furniture and Set Properties

These elements are one step nearer the actor, both in physical proximity and usefulness to him as an artist. Although there are only a few major categories of furniture that man has devised, there are innumerable variations and permutations on these basic forms; he needs something to sit or lie on (chairs, benches, stools, beds), something to hold objects and material for his immediate use (tables in various forms), and storage units, sometimes open, often with lids or doors, in which to keep his needs and possessions (chests, boxes, shelves). All of man's furnishings fall within these categories; the manner in which he fashions and decorates them, however, tell much about him in relation to the age in which he lives and about how he views his position in relation to the world as a whole, past as well as present.

In his book *An Illustrated History of Furnishings,* Mario Praz gives some indication of the close relationship between man and those objects he makes, selects, or uses.

> Dickens and Gogol have written about the capacity that objects have for expressing their owner. Podsnap's silver (in *Our Mutual Friend*) was characterized by a "hideous solidity." "Everything was made to look as heavy as it could, and to take up as much room as possible." Twenty years before, in *Dead Souls,* Gogol described Sobakevitch's house: "Tchitchikov looked around the room again and everything in it, everything was solid and clumsy to the last degree and had a strange resemblance to the master of the house. In a corner of the room stood a paunchy walnut bureau on four very absurd legs looking exactly like a bear. The table, the armchairs, the chairs were all of the heaviest and most uncomfortable shape; in short, every chair, every object seemed to be saying 'I am a Sobakevitch too!' or 'I too am very much like Sobakevitch!' ". . . .
>
> This is the house in its deepest essence: a projection of the ego. And furnishing is nothing but an indirect form of ego-worship.

And later he writes: "For this reason, perhaps even more than painting or sculpture, perhaps even more than architecture itself, furniture reveals the spirit of an age."

The scene designer, therefore, might be well advised to follow this simple principle in his research into period interiors: whenever seeking information concerning furniture or set properties, don't just try to find isolated pieces and objects; find, if at all possible, these items as they are being used.

A source picture such as the one shown in figure 35 is much more helpful to the designer than examination of each of the objects in the picture individually; as with a work of art, a good research picture is more than the sum of its parts.

The items that comprise this present category are far more necessary to the actor than either the general background (which he cannot use directly) or specific units of scenic architecture. But, as with this lat-

35. *Room interior showing furniture use.* Women Embroidering, *engraving by Phillip Galle from a painting by Jan Van der Straet*

ter category, it is also possible to create a sense of place and period—its characteristic form and atmosphere—by careful selection and placement of furniture and set properties. In the arena theater and on the open stage, creating this sense becomes critically important to the designer since furniture and set properties literally become the scenery.

It was said of Molière that he could place chairs on the stage so effectively that "they could almost speak." The designer, in the selection or design of furniture and set properties, is faced with the problem of making sure each piece is correctly made and finished; the creative designer must also, however, spend as much time or more considering the proper relationship of each piece of furniture to the function it will serve—the actor's use of it and its relation to the design as a whole—as well as overseeing its manufacture and its finish. Jean Cocteau, although a man of letters, was keenly aware of the importance of this principle; "A chair," he once wrote, "badly placed on the stage is almost as dangerous as a trapeze insecurely suspended from the roof." It is in this area, the selection and placement of furniture and set properties, that the designer and director should expend their greatest effort to communicate with each other. No part of the physical production should take precedence over this most important consideration. The decisions they make cannot be underestimated in importance to the performer who, in most instances, has an instinctive desire to relate to his immediate environment in a highly personal manner. While it has often been observed that young actors tend to hold on to a piece of furniture, even hide behind it, the mature actor also uses these objects—chairs, tables, set properties—but does so in order to expose his internal thoughts by direct physical contact with them in a meaningful way. The veteran actor realizes that these objects can be used to show what he is feeling or what he is reacting against.

Figure 36 shows a setting for *The Tiger,* a one-act play by Murray Schisgal, as it was presented in an arena theater. The locale of the play, a basement apartment of a not-too-tidy eccentric New York mailman obtained its atmosphere not only from the selection of appropriate furniture, but from the arrangement of it, from the clutter of newspapers, books (the protagonist is an avid reader but cares little about the book

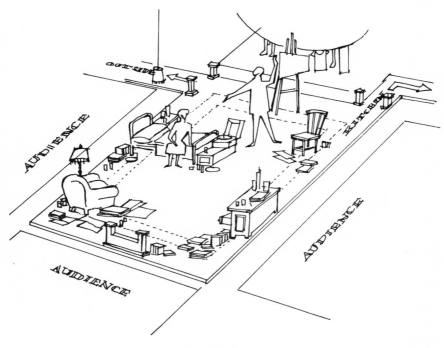

36. *Setting for* The Tiger

once read), and especially from the manner in which these items were composed and used. It was decided early in the discussions between director and designer that the person who lived in this room had intuitively carried over an arrangement he had been subjected to in his army days (a barracks type cot with foot locker at the end used as table and catch-all now) but had superimposed his own casual personality onto this living area by merely dropping what he is finished with as soon as it is no longer useful (newspapers, socks, books, etc.). This room says, quite plainly, the person who lives here is not concerned to any great extent with his immediate surroundings; his mind is somewhere else.

It is also possible for the designer, by careless selection or design of furniture to affect the actor's performance adversely. He can, for instance, cause the actor to sit in markedly different attitudes simply by varying the height of a chair a small amount in either direction from its normal seating height; a little too high, the actor may seem helpless and childish since his feet may have trouble reaching the floor; a little too low, he may appear oversized or awkward. Of course, there are many times when such alteration is done on purpose to produce just such effects, but there is a vast difference between the purposeful intention and the accidental result. It is not uncommon for actors to have strong opinions concerning the furniture they must use directly; it is doubtful if there is one working designer who has not had many confrontations with performers on this particular issue. Although some might just be hard to please—perhaps because they have been subjected to years of having to cope with uncooperative pieces of furniture that the designer selected or designed for visual effect rather than usefulness to the actor—most realize that it can affect their performance to such a degree and so directly that they feel it their prerogative to insure the designer does not thoughtlessly hamper them.

Hand and Personal Properties

It would be hard to overemphasize the importance of the role that properties play in the average production, or the care with which they should be selected or constructed. In many instances, as with a piece of furniture or a set property, a prop is the external focus for the actor's attention; in other words, he uses it to expose what he is thinking when he has been given no words to express these thoughts. Often the most important moments of a play take place in those silences between units of written dialogue, and many times an object—a prop—is used to make clear what no amount of words could. Here is an account of just how important such a prop can be. This particular example occurred in the 1966 CBS Television production of *Death of a Salesman*:

> Television rarely sees exciting bits of acting, but there was one recently that could make a viewer start with a sharp intake of breath. It happened on the CBS television network during Act Two of the two-hour color production of Arthur Miller's *Death of a Salesman*. . . .
>
> Willy Loman has been fired by his young boss. The aging salesman comes pounding hysterically into the office of Charley, his friend. Lee J. Cobb, playing Willy, finds Bernard, Charley's son, in the office. This is the school-grind, the anemic worm that Willy and his popular, athletic sons once scorned. Now Bernard is a successful lawyer on his way to Washington, carrying a tennis racquet to play on the private court of affluent friends. . . .
>
> Willy desperately tries to maintain the old razzle-dazzle about his own son Biff's "big deal." Bernard offers him a cigarette from a large, gold cigarette case. Willy stops talking, stares at the case, takes it, holds it, closes it and passes it back— in a silent passage of torment, despair, and envy. . . .
>
> The cigarette case is a symbol of everything Bernard has won in life—success, status, wealth—and a mocking sign of all that Willy and his two boys have failed to win. The pain on Mr. Cobb's face as his emotions overwhelmed him, the wordless eloquence of his baffled regard for that shining piece of rail that crushed his ego and pierced his boasting—were utterly communicated and shared. I think it was the production's finest moment. . . .
>
> Yet afterward, scanning a reading edition of the play, I found no mention of the cigarette case and this bit of stage business. Seventeen years ago I saw *Death of a Salesman* during its original run on Broadway at the Morosco Theater. Perhaps the bit was done on the stage but I don't recall it. . . .
>
> . . . Whoever suggested the bit gave the actor a rich opportunity and the viewers a rare experience. [Robert Lewis Shayon, *Saturday Review,* May 28, 1966]

As a matter of fact, this particular bit of business was created by Elia Kazan, the director of the original production, and appears in his *Notebook Made in Preparation for Directing "Death of a Salesman."* These notes appear in *A Theatre in Your Head* by Kenneth Thorpe Rowe. The original note reads like this: ("Bernard offers him a cigarette case. Willy takes it, examines it with awe, hands it back. Bernard opens it, offers cigarette, he shakes his head.")

Properties are classified, roughly, in two categories: set properties and hand properties. Set properties are almost always the responsibility of the scene designer while hand props are sometimes selected by him only in part. Many times, as indicated in the above passage, these props may not exist in the original script; often a director will call for them. Sometimes the designer may himself suggest an item and in so doing make a distinct contribution to the actor's characterization.

In the amateur theater, properties are not often given the attention they deserve. Too often the making or procurement of them is relegated to a person who, rather than considering each item needed as a separate and integral objective, tends to think of them only as a list of things to be gotten as quickly and effortlessly as possible. In theaters such as the Stratford, Ontario, Festival Company, the properties are not only carefully designed but are beautifully executed by a number of highly trained artisans under the guidance of the designers. The conscientious property man finds out not only what is needed, but how it is to be used and how it has been used in the past.

The great American designer Robert Edmond Jones had a keen appreciation of the importance of properties. Jo Mielziner, another distinguished designer, recalls an incident that illustrates the care with which Jones approached the selection of objects to be used on the stage. In an article he wrote for the book of Jones's designs and drawings *The Theatre of Robert Edmond Jones,* Mielziner relates the following story:

> I recall that Arthur Hopkins' business manager very hesitantly and politely inquired of Bobby one day, "Is it necessary to have those eighteenth-century quills and sand shakers on the desk up-stage in the corner of the set? You must realize, Mr. Jones, that even the first row of the orchestra can't appreciate an object so small at that distance." Bobby turned and glared. "Do you think," he said, "that only people on the other side of the footlights need exaltation? What about the actor? Surely he should *feel* the *sense of period* when working in this set?"

Unfortunately, all too few designers think as Robert Edmond Jones and far too many as the business manager. Not only is this attention to detail a quality most of the great designers do share, it is also a mode of thought that certainly should be cultivated rather than denied, as it often is even in the professional theater.

It is interesting to note that many playwrights have taken particular care to specify exactly what the actor needs in the way of properties to make his motives clear, not necessarily in a formal stage direction but embedded in the text itself. Shakespeare, time after time, weaves into the fabric of a speech an object which would externalize a character's inner and deepest thoughts: the mirror Richard II dashes to the ground after reflecting on the image in it is far more dramatic than anything he might say at that point; Yorick's skull in which Hamlet finally sees the ultimate observation that can be made on life, not the philosophical speculation of ceasing to exist expressed in words, but in an actual piece of a human being he once knew and loved. Even Hamlet, who has a sentiment or word on practically every possible situation or event, is reduced to near speechlessness when confronted with this object that shows what death really means; all he can say is, "This?"

Costume

Although the practice of using another designer to create the costumes for a production independently of the scene designer is now common, the most desirable situation is for one designer to control all visual elements of a production. Costumes, like properties, are all-important to the actor; they concern him more directly than any property or item of setting. Every designer should be able to design costumes and know the fundamental practices of costume construction (fig. 37).

In his book *The Dramatic Imagination,* Robert Edmond Jones makes several excellent points concerning the design of costumes. Here are just a few of his remarks:

> In learning how a costume for the stage is designed and made, we have to go through a certain amount of routine training. We must learn about patterns, and about periods. We have to know what farthingales are, and wimples, and patches and caleches and parures and godets and appliques and passementerie. We have to know the instant we see and touch a fabric what it will look like on the stage both in movement and in repose. We have to develop the brains that are in our fingers. We have to experiment endlessly until our work is as nearly perfect as we can make it, until we are, so to speak, released from it. . . .
>
> A stage costume is a creation of the theatre. Its quality is

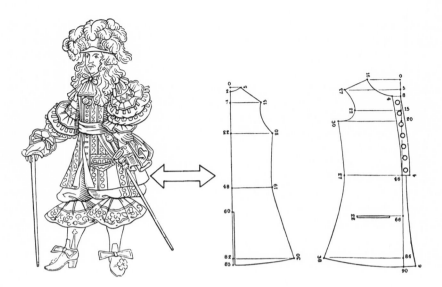

37. *Pattern for German doublet, second half of the sixteenth century*

purely theatrical and taken outside of the theatre, it loses its magic at once. It dies as a plant dies when uprooted. . . . Each separate costume we create for a play must be exactly suited both to the character it helps to express and to the occasion it graces. We shall not array Lady Macbeth in pale blue organdie or Ariel in purple velvet. Mephistopheles will wear his scarlet and Hamlet his solemn black as long as the theatre continues to exist. A Hamlet in real life may possess a wardrobe of various styles and colors. But in the theatre it is simply not possible for Mr. John Gielgud or Mr. Maurice Evans to say, "Tis not alone my tawny cloak, good mother, nor customary suits of tender green."

This is, essentially, a romantic conception of what the costume is or should be. Jones was, although the "most practical of dreamers," as Jo Mielziner has called him, basically romantic in his philosophy of theater.

There has been in recent years, however, a definite trend away from the romantic conception of costume design. More and more, dress for the stage is "selected" rather than designed, assembled rather than constructed. It is now a common practice for designers to use in a production old clothes found in secondhand stores and out of attics rather than constructing costumes from new fabric and then having them aged and broken down after their completion. Some designers will in fact, when designing costumes that are required to show great use and age, find their materials in old ready-made garments and then, after taking these garments apart, recut them into new patterns for costumes completely different from their original purpose and use.

During the past few years there has been a trend away from brightly colored elaborate costumes and toward simplification in cut and design, especially in German or German-inspired productions. At the same time, there has been a marked interest in the use of heavily textured materials and fabrics. Designers are also working with fewer colors—and those decidedly greyer in tone—and with a greater number of permutations of those colors. The cinema version of *Camelot* used a distinctly monochromatic palette while making great use of a variety of highly textured woven materials.

There has also been a corresponding interest in newer materials, not only synthetic fabrics, but plastics, metals, furs, and leather as well. The introduction of fiber glass cloth and strands, as well as other plastic impregnated materials that harden when exposed to chemical treatment, have opened up whole new vistas of possibilities in costume construction not feasible even twenty years ago.

But, if there is one major trend discernible in the progress of costume design during these past several decades, it is this: the costume designer has become less and less just a dressmaker and more and more a highly creative and independent artist whose techniques and artistry extend much further than just knowing how to sew a straight seam, cut a pattern, or dye a piece of cloth.

§7
"The Art of the Theatre: The First Dialogue"

By E. Gordon Craig

Although written in 1905, this chapter from The Art of the Theatre, *by Gordon Craig, still has power to influence the designer today; while styles and fashions have changed greatly, the conceptual basis of this statement still remains sound. Craig's designs, revolutionary in their day, are still not out of date now. And while the theater has changed greatly in almost every quarter, from then to now, much of what he has said still retains a certain freshness of expression and validity of viewpoint. Much has been made of his "impracticality"; but those who have attacked him have almost altogether mistaken his contribution to the art of scene design in their zeal to discredit his work. His defense will not be undertaken here; further study of Craig and his work will reveal the certain shortcomings he undoubtedly had as well as his positive virtues, of which there are many. What is important to note here, however, is the manner in which a highly gifted artist and an equally articulate writer can appeal to the highest instincts of the scene designer who aspires to the level of artist.*

D.R.P.

An Expert and a Playgoer are conversing.

STAGE-DIRECTOR: You have now been over the theatre with me, and have seen its general construction, together with the stage, the machinery for manipulating the scenes, the apparatus for lighting, and the hundred other things, and have also heard what I have had to say of the theatre as a machine; let us rest here in the auditorium, and talk a while of the theatre and of its art. Tell me, do you know what is the Art of the Theatre?

PLAYGOER: To me it seems that Acting is the Art of the Theatre.

STAGE-DIRECTOR: Is a part, then, equal to a whole?

PLAYGOER: No, of course not. Do you, then, mean that the play is the Art of the Theatre?

STAGE-DIRECTOR: A play is a work of literature, is it not? Tell me, then, how one art can possibly be another?

PLAYGOER: Well, then, if you tell me that the Art of the Theatre is neither the acting nor the play, then I must come to the conclusion that it is the scenery and the dancing. Yet I cannot think you will tell me this is so.

STAGE-DIRECTOR: No; the Art of the Theatre is neither acting nor the play, it is not scene nor dance, but it consists of all the elements of which these things are composed; action, which is the very spirit of acting; words, which are the body of the play; line and colour, which are the very heart of the scene; rhythm, which is the very essence of dance.

PLAYGOER: Action, words, line, colour, rhythm! And which of these is all-important to the art?

STAGE-DIRECTOR: One is no more important than the other, no more than one colour is more important to a painter than another, or one note more important than another to a musician. In one respect, perhaps, action is the most valuable part. Action bears the same relation to the Art of the Theatre as drawing does to painting, and melody does to music. The Art of the Theatre has sprung from action—movement—dance.

PLAYGOER: I always was led to suppose that it had sprung from speech and that the poet was the father of the theatre.

STAGE-DIRECTOR: This is the common belief, but consider it for a moment. The poet's imagination finds voice in words, beautifully chosen; he then either recites or sings these words to us, and all is done. That poetry, sung or recited, is for our ears, and, through them, for our imagination. It will not help the matter if the poet shall add gesture to his recitation or to his song; in fact, it will spoil all.

PLAYGOER: Yes, that is clear to me. I quite understand that the addition of gesture to a perfect lyric poem can but produce an inharmonious result. But would you apply the same argument to dramatic poetry?

STAGE-DIRECTOR: Certainly I would. Remember I speak of a dramatic poem, not of a drama. The two things are separate things. A dramatic poem is to be read. A drama is not to be read, but to be seen upon the stage. Therefore gesture is a necessity to a drama, and it is useless to a dramatic poem. It is absurd to talk of these two things, gesture and poetry, as having anything to do with one another. And now, just as you must not confound the dramatic poem with the drama, neither must you confound the dramatic poet with the dramatist. The first writes for the reader, or listener, the second writes for the audience of a theatre. Do you know who was the father of the dramatist?

PLAYGOER: No, I do not know, but I suppose he was the dramatic poet.

STAGE-DIRECTOR: You are wrong. The father of the dramatist was the dancer. And now tell me from what material the dramatist made his first piece?

PLAYGOER: I suppose he used words in the same as the lyric poet.

STAGE-DIRECTOR: Again you are wrong, and that is what every one else supposes who has not learnt the nature of dramatic art. No; the dramatist made his first piece by using action, words, line, colour, and rhythm, and making his appeal to our eyes and ears by a dexterous use of these five factors.

PLAYGOER: And what is the difference between this work of the first dramatists and that of the modern dramatists?

STAGE-DIRECTOR: The first dramatists were children of the theatre. The modern dramatists are not. The first dramatist understood what the modern dramatist does not yet understand. He knew that when he and his fellows appeared in front of them, the audience would be more eager to *see* what he would do than to *hear* what he might *say*. He knew that the eye is more swiftly and powerfully appealed to than any other sense; that it is without question the keenest sense of the body of man.

The first thing which he encountered on appearing before them was many pairs of eyes, eager and hungry. Even the men and women sitting so far from him that they would not always be able to hear what he might say, seemed quite close to him by reason of the piercing keenness of their questioning eyes. To these, and all, he spoke either in poetry or prose, but always in action: in poetic action which is dance, or in prose action which is gesture.

PLAYGOER: I am very interested, go on, go on.

STAGE-DIRECTOR: No—rather let us pull up and examine our ground. I have said that the first dramatist was the dancer's son, that is to say, the child of the theatre, not the child of the poet. And I have just said that the modern dramatic poet is the child of the poet, and knows only how to reach the ears of his listeners, nothing else. And yet in spite of this does not the modern audience still go to the theatre as of old to see things, and not to hear things? Indeed, modern audiences insist on looking and having their eyes satisfied in spite of the call from the poet that they shall use their ears only. And now do not misunderstand me. I am not saying or hinting that the poet is a bad writer of plays, or that he has a bad influence upon the theatre. I only wish you to understand that the poet is not of the theatre, has never come from the theatre, and cannot be of the theatre, and that only the dramatist among writers has any birth-claim to the theatre—and that a very slight one. But to continue. My point is this, that the people still flock to *see,* not to hear, plays. But what does that prove? Only that the audiences have not altered. They are there with their thousand pairs of eyes, just the same as of old. And this is all the more extraordinary because the playwrights and the plays have altered. No longer is a play a balance of actions, words, dance, and scene, but it is either all words or all scene. Shakespeare's plays, for instance, are a very different thing to the less modern miracle and mystery plays, which were made entirely for the theatre. *Hamlet* has not the nature of a stage representation. *Hamlet* and the other plays of Shakespeare have so vast and so complete a form when read, that they can but lose heavily when presented to us after having undergone stage treatment. That they were acted in Shakespeare's day proves nothing. I will tell you, on the other hand, what at that period was made for the theatre—the Masques—the Pageants—these were light and beautiful examples of the Art of the Theatre. Had the plays been made to be seen, we should find them incomplete when we read them. Now, no one will say that they find *Hamlet* dull or incomplete when they read it, yet there are many who will feel sorry after witnessing a performance of the play, saying, "No, that is not Shakespeare's *Hamlet.*" When no further addition can be made so as to better a work of art, it can be spoken of as "finished"—it is complete. *Hamlet* was finished—was complete—when Shakespeare wrote the last word of his blank verse, and for us to add to it by gesture, scene, costume, or dance is to hint that it is incomplete and needs these additions.

PLAYGOER: Then do you mean to say *Hamlet* should never be performed?

STAGE-DIRECTOR: To what purpose would it be if I replied "Yes"? *Hamlet* will go on being performed for some time yet, and the duty of the interpreters is to put their best work at its service. But, as I have said, the theatre must not forever rely upon having a play to perform, but must in time perform pieces of its own art.

PLAYGOER: And a piece for the theatre, is that, then incomplete when printed in a book or recited?

STAGE-DIRECTOR: Yes—and incomplete anywhere except on the boards of a theatre. It must be unsatisfying, artless, when read or merely heard, because it is incomplete without its action, its colour, its line and its rhythm in movement and in scene.

PLAYGOER: This interests me, but it dazzles me at the same time.

STAGE-DIRECTOR: Is that, perhaps, because it is a little new? Tell me what it is especially that dazzles you.

PLAYGOER: Well, first of all, the fact that I have never stopped to consider of what the art of the theatre consisted—to many of us it is just an amusement.

STAGE-DIRECTOR: And to you?

PLAYGOER: Oh, to me it has always been a fascination, half amusement and half intellectual exercise. The show has always amused me; the playing of the players has often instructed me.

STAGE-DIRECTOR: In fact, a sort of incomplete satisfaction. That is the natural result of seeing and hearing something imperfect.

PLAYGOER: But I have seen some few plays which seemed to satisfy me.

STAGE-DIRECTOR: If you have been entirely satisfied by something obviously mediocre, may it not be that you were searching for something less than mediocre, and you found that which was just a little better than you expected? Some people go to the theatre, nowadays, expecting to be bored. This is natural, for they have been taught to look for tiresome things. When you tell me you have been satisfied at a modern theatre, you prove that it is not only the art which has degenerated, but that a proportion of the audience has degenerated also. But do not let this depress you. I once knew a man whose life was so occupied, he never heard music other than that of the street organ. It was to him the ideal of what music should be. Still, as you know, there is better music in the world—in fact, barrel organ music is very bad music; and if you were for once to see an actual piece of theatrical art, you would never again tolerate what is today being thrust upon you in place of theatrical art. The reason why the public does not want it, not because there are not excellent craftsmen in the theatre who could prepare it for you, but because the theatre lacks the artist—the artist of the theatre, mind you, not the painter, poet, musician. The many excellent craftsmen whom I have mentioned are, all of them, more or less helpless to change the situation. They are forced to supply what the managers of the theatre demand, but they do so most willingly. The advent of the artist in the theatre world will change all this. He will slowly but surely gather around him these better craftsmen of whom I speak, and together they will give new life to the art of the theatre.

PLAYGOER: But for the others?

STAGE-DIRECTOR: The others? The modern theatre is full of these others, these untrained and untalented craftsmen. But I will say one thing for them. I believe they are unconscious of their inability. It is not ignorance on their part, it is innocence. Yet if these same men once realized that they were craftsmen, and would train as such—I do not speak only of the stage-carpenters, electricians, wigmakers, costumiers, scene-painters, and actors (indeed these are in many ways the best and most willing craftsmen)—I speak chiefly of the stage-director. If the stage-director was to technically train himself for his task of interpreting the plays of the dramatist—in time, and by a gradual development he would again recover the ground lost to the theatre, and finally would restore the Art of the Theatre to its home by means of his own creative genius.

PLAYGOER: Then you place the stage-director before the actors?

STAGE-DIRECTOR: Yes; the relation of the stage-director to the actor is precisely the same as that of the conductor to his orchestra, or of the publisher to his printer.

PLAYGOER: And you consider that the stage-director is a craftsman and not an artist?

STAGE-DIRECTOR: When he interprets the plays of the dramatist by means of his actors, his scene-painters, and his other craftsmen, then he is a craftsman—a master craftsman; when he will have mastered the uses of actions, words, line, colour, and rhythm, then he may become an artist. Then we shall no longer need the assistance of the playwright—for our art will then be self-reliant.

PLAYGOER: Is your belief in a Renaissance of the art based on your belief in the Renaissance of the stage-director?

STAGE-DIRECTOR: Yes, certainly, most certainly. Did you for an instant think that I have a contempt for the stage director? Rather have I a contempt for any man who fails in the whole duty of the stage-director.

PLAYGOER: What are his duties?

STAGE-DIRECTOR: What is his craft? I will tell you. His work as interpreter of the play of the dramatist is something like this: he takes the copy of the play from the hands of the dramatist and promises faithfully to interpret it as indicated in the text (remember I am speaking only of the very best stage-directors). He then reads the play, and during the first reading the entire colour, tone, movement, and rhythm that the work must assume comes clearly before him. As for the stage directions, descriptions of the scenes, etc., with which the author may interlard his copy, these are not to be considered by him, for if he is master of his craft he can learn nothing from them.

PLAYGOER: I do not quite understand you. Do you mean that when a playwright has taken the trouble to describe the scene in which his men and women are to move and talk, that the stage-director is to take no notice of such directions—in fact, to disregard them?

STAGE-DIRECTOR: It makes no difference whether he regards or disregards them. What he must see to is that he makes his action and scene match the verse or the prose, the beauty of it, the sense of it. Whatever picture the dramatist may wish us to know of, he will describe his scene during the progress of the conversation between the characters. Take for instance, the first scene in *Hamlet.* It begins:

Ber:	Who's there?
Fran:	Nay, answer me; stand and unfold yourself.
Ber:	Long live the king!
Fran:	Bernardo?
Ber:	He.
Fran:	You come most carefully upon your hour.
Ber:	'Tis now struck twelve; get thee to bed, Francisco.
Fran:	For this relief much thanks, 'tis bitter cold,
	And I am sick at heart.
Ber:	Have you had quiet guard?
Fran:	Not a mouse stirring.
Ber:	Well, good night.
	If you do meet Horatio and Marcellus,
	The rivals of my watch, bid them make haste.

That is enough to guide the stage-director. He gathers from it that it is twelve o'clock at night, that it is in the open air, that the guard of some castle is being changed, that it is very cold, very quiet, and very dark. Any additional "stage directions" by the dramatist are trivialities.

PLAYGOER: Then you do not think that an author should write any stage directions whatever, and you seem to consider it an offence on his part if he does so?

STAGE-DIRECTOR: Well, is it not an offence to the men of the theatre?

PLAYGOER: In what way?

STAGE-DIRECTOR: First tell me the greatest offence an actor can give to a dramatist.

PLAYGOER: To play his part badly?

STAGE-DRECTOR: No, that may merely prove the actor to be a bad craftsman.

PLAYGOER: Tell me, then.

STAGE-DIRECTOR: The greatest offence an actor can give to a dramatist is to cut out words or lines in his play, or to insert what is known as a "gag." It is an offence to poach on what is the sole property of the playwright. It is not usual to "gag" in Shakespeare, and when it is done it does not go uncensured.

PLAYGOER: But what has this to do with the stage-directions of the playwright, and in what way does the playwright offend the theatre when he dictates these stage directions?

STAGE-DIRECTOR: He offends in that he poaches on their preserves. If to gag or cut the poet's lines is an offence, so is it an offence to tamper with the art of the stage-director.

PLAYGOER: Then is all the stage direction of the world's plays worthless?

STAGE-DIRECTOR: Not to the reader, but to the stage-director and to the actor—yes.

PLAYGOER: But Shakespeare—

STAGE-DIRECTOR: Shakespeare seldom directs the stage-manager. Go through *Hamlet, Romeo and Juliet, King Lear, Othello,* any of the masterpieces, and except in some of the historical plays which contain descriptions of possesions, etc., what do you find? How are the scenes described in *Hamlet?*

PLAYGOER: My copy shows a clear description. It has "Act I, scene i. Elsinore. A platform before the Castle."

STAGE-DIRECTOR: You are looking at a late edition with additions by a certain Mr. Malone, but Shakespeare wrote nothing of the kind. His words are "Actus primus. Scæna prima." . . . And now let us look at *Romeo and Juliet.* What does your book say?

PLAYGOER: It says: "Act I, scene i. Verona. A public place."

STAGE-DIRECTOR: And the second scene?

PLAYGOER: It says: "Scene ii. A street."

STAGE-DIRECTOR: And the third scene?

PLAYGOER: It says: "Scene iii. A room in Capulet's house."

STAGE-DIRECTOR: And now, would you like to hear what scene directions Shakespeare actually wrote for this play?

PLAYGOER: Yes.

STAGE-DIRECTOR: He wrote: "Actus primus. Scæna prima." And not another word as to act or scene throughout the whole play. And now for *King Lear*.

PLAYGOER: No, it is enough. I see now. Evidently Shakespeare relied upon the intelligence of the stage-men to complete their scene from his indication. . . . But is this the same in regard to the actions? Does not Shakespeare place some descriptions through *Hamlet*, such as "Hamlet leaps into Ophelia's grave," "Laertes grapples with him," and later, "The attendants part them, and they come out of the grave"?

STAGE-DIRECTOR: No, not one word. All the stage directions from the first to the last, are the tame inventions of sundry editors, Mr. Malone, Mr. Capell, Theobald and others, and they have committed an indiscretion in tampering with the play, for which we, the men of the theatre, have to suffer.

PLAYGOER: How is that?

STAGE-DIRECTOR: Why, supposing any of us reading Shakespeare shall see in our mind's eye some other combination of movements contrary to the "instructions" of these gentlemen, and suppose we represent our ideas on the stage, we are instantly taken to task by some knowing one, who accuses us of altering the directions of Shakespeare—nay more, of altering his very intentions.

PLAYGOER: But do not the "knowing ones," as you call them, know that Shakespeare wrote no stage directions?

STAGE-DIRECTOR: One can only guess that to be the case, to judge from their indiscreet criticisms. Anyhow, what I wanted to show you was that our greatest modern poet realized that to add stage directions was first of all unnecessary, and secondly, tasteless. We can therefore be sure that Shakespeare at any rate realized what was the work of the theatre craftsman—the stage-manager, and that it was, part of the stage-manager's task to invent the scenes in which the play was to be set.

PLAYGOER: Yes, and you were telling me what each part consisted of.

STAGE-DIRECTOR: Quite so. And now that we have disposed of the error that the author's directions are of any use, we can continue to speak of the way the stage-manager sets to work to interpret faithfully the play of the dramatist. I have said that he swears to follow the text faithfully, and that his first work is to read the play through and get the great impression; and in reading, as I have said, begins to see the whole colour, rhythm, action of the thing. He then puts the play aside for some time, and in his mind's eye mixes his palette (to use a painter's expression) with the colours which the impression of the play has called up. Therefore, on sitting down a second time to read through the play, he is surrounded by an atmosphere which he proposes to test. At the end of the second reading he will find that his more definite impressions have received clear and unmistakable corroboration, and that some of his impressions which were less positive have disappeared. He will then make a note of these. It is possible that he will even now commence to suggest, in line and colour, some of the scenes and ideas which are filling his head, but this is more likely to be delayed until he has re-read the play at least a dozen times.

PLAYGOER: But I thought the stage-manager always left that part of the play—the scene designing—to the scene painter?

STAGE-DIRECTOR: So he does, generally. First blunder of the modern theatre.

PLAYGOER: How is it a blunder?

STAGE-DIRECTOR: This way: A has written a play which B promises to interpret faithfully. In so delicate a matter as the interpretation of so elusive a thing as the spirit of a play, which, do you think, will be the surest way to preserve the unity of the spirit? Will it be best if B does all the work by himself? or will it do to give the work into the hands of C, D, and E, each of whom see or think differently from B or A?

PLAYGOER: Of course the former would be best. But is it possible for one man to do the work of three men?

STAGE-DIRECTOR: That is the only way the work can be done if unity, the one thing vital to a work of art, is to be obtained.

PLAYGOER: So, then, the stage-manager does not call in a scene painter and ask him to design a scene, but he designs one himself?

STAGE-DIRECTOR: Certainly. And remember he does not merely sit down and draw a pretty or historically accurate design, with enough doors and windows in picturesque places, but he first of all chooses certain colours which seem to him to be in harmony with the spirit of the play, rejecting other colours as out of tune. He then weaves into a pattern certain objects—an arch, a fountain, a balcony, a bed—using the chosen object as the centre of his design. Then he adds to this all the objects which are mentioned in the play, and which are necessary to be seen. To these he adds, one by one, each character which appears in the play, and gradually each movement of each character, and each costume. He is as likely as not to make several mistakes in his pattern. If so, he must, as it were, unpick the design, and rectify the blunder even if he has to go right back to the beginning and start the pattern all over again—or he may even have to begin a new pattern. At any rate, slowly, harmoniously, must the whole design develop, so that the eye of the beholder shall be satisfied. While this pattern for the eye is being devised, the designer is being guided as much by the sound of the verse or prose as by the sense or spirit. And shortly all is prepared, and the actual work can be commenced.

PLAYGOER: What actual work? It seems to me that the stage-manager has already been doing a good deal of what may be called actual work.

STAGE-DIRECTOR: Well, perhaps; but the difficulties have but commenced. By the actual work I mean the work which needs skilled labour, such as the actual painting of the huge spaces of canvas for the scenes, and the actual making of the costumes.

PLAYGOER: You are not going to tell me that the stage-manager actually paints his own scenes and cuts his own costumes and sews them together?

STAGE-DIRECTOR: No, I will not say that he does so in every case and for every play, but he must have done so at one time or another during his apprenticeship, or must have closely studied all the technical points of these complicated crafts. Then will he be able to guide the skilled craftsmen in their different departments. And when the actual making of the scenes and costumes has commenced, the parts are distributed to the different actors, who learn the words before a single rehearsal takes place. (This, as you may guess, is not the custom, but it is what should be seen to by a stage-director such as I describe.) Meantime, the scenes and costumes are almost ready. I will not tell you the amount of interesting but laborious work it entails to prepare the play up to this point. But even when once the scenes are placed upon the stage, and the costumes upon the actors, the difficulty of the work is still great.

PLAYGOER: The stage-director's work is not finished then?

STAGE-DIRECTOR: Finished! What do you mean?

PLAYGOER: Well, I thought now that the scenes and costumes were all seen to, the actors and actresses would do the rest.

STAGE-DIRECTOR: No, the stage-manager's most interesting work is now beginning. His scene is set and his characters are clothed. He has, in short, a kind of dream picture in front of him. He clears the stage of all but the one, two, or more characters who are to commence the play, and he begins the scheme of lighting these figures and the scene.

PLAYGOER: What, is not this branch left to the discretion of the master electrician and his men? *

STAGE-DIRECTOR: The doing of it is left to them but the manner of doing it is the business of the stage-manager. Being, as I have said, a man of some intelligence and training, he has devised a special way of lighting his scene for this play, just as he has devised a special way of painting the scene and costuming the figures. If the word "harmony" held no significance for him, he would of course leave it to the first comer.

PLAYGOER: Then do you actually mean that he had made so close a study of nature that he can direct his electricians how to make it appear as if the sun were shining at such and such an altitude, or as if the moonlight were flooding the interior of the room with such and such intensity?

STAGE-DIRECTOR: No, I should not like to suggest that, because the reproduction of nature's lights is not what my stage-manager ever attempts. Neither should he attempt such an impossibility. Not to *reproduce* nature, but to *suggest* some of her most beautiful and most living ways—that is what my stage-manager shall attempt. The other thing proclaims an overbearing assumption of omnipotence. A stage-manager may well aim to be an artist, but it ill becomes him to attempt celestial honours. This attitude he can avoid by never trying to imprison or copy nature, for nature will be neither imprisoned nor allow any man to copy her with any success.

PLAYGOER: Then in what way does he set to work? What guides him in his task of lighting the scene and costumes which we are speaking about?

STAGE-DIRECTOR: What guides him? Why, the scene and the costumes, and the verse and the prose, and the sense of the play. All these things, as I told you, have now been brought into harmony, the one with the other—all goes smoothly—what simpler, then, that it should so continue, and that the manager should be the only one to know how to preserve this harmony which he has commenced to create?

PLAYGOER: Will you tell me some more about the actual way of lighting the scene and the actors?

---

* Why waste time talking to so stupid a man as this "Play-goer"? asked a charming lady—and would not wait for an answer. The reply is obvious: one does not talk to wise people—one listens to them.

STAGE-DIRECTOR: Certainly. What do you want to know?

PLAYGOER: Well, will you tell me why they put lights all along the floor of the stage—footlights they call them I believe?

STAGE-DIRECTOR: Yes, footlights.

PLAYGOER: Well, why are they put on the ground?

STAGE-DIRECTOR: It is one of the questions which has puzzled all the theatre reform gentlemen, and none has been able to find an answer, for the simple reason that there is no answer. The only thing to do is to remove all the footlights out of all the theatres as quickly as possible and say nothing about it. It is one of those queer things which nobody can explain, and at which children are always surprised. Little Nancy Lake, in 1812, went to Drury Lane Theatre, and her father tells us that she also was astonished at the footlights. Said she,

> And there's a row of lamps, my eyes!
> How they do blaze—I wonder why
> They keep them on the ground.
> —*Rejected Addresses*

That was in 1812! and we are still wondering.

PLAYGOER: A friend of mine—an actor—once told me that if there were no footlights all the faces of the actors would look dirty.

STAGE-DIRECTOR: That was the remark of a man who did not understand that in place of the footlights another method of lighting the faces and figures could be adopted. It is this simple kind of thing which never occurs to those people who will not devote a little time to even a slight study of the other branches of the craft.

PLAYGOER: Do not the actors study the other crafts of the theatre?

STAGE-DIRECTOR: As a rule—no, and in some ways it is opposed to the very life of an actor. If an actor of intelligence were to devote much time to the study of all the branches of the theatrical art he would gradually cease to act, and would end by becoming a stage-manager—so absorbing is the whole art in comparison with the single craft of acting.

PLAYGOER: My friend the actor also added that if the footlights were removed the audience would not be able to see the expression of his face.

STAGE-DIRECTOR: Had Henry Irving or Eleanora Duse said so, the remark would have had some meaning. The ordinary actor's face is either violently expressive or violently inexpressive, that it would be a blessing if the theatres were not only without footlights but without any lights at all. By the way, an excellent theory of the origin of the footlights is advanced by M. Ludovic Celler in *Les Decors, les costumes et la mise-en-scène au XVII siècle.* The usual way of lighting the stage was by means of large chandeliers, circular or triangular, which were suspended above the heads of the actors and the audience; and M. Celler is of the opinion that the system of footlights owes its origin to the small plain theatres which could not afford to have chandeliers, and therefore placed tallow candles on the floor in front of the stage. I believe this theory to be correct, for common sense could not have dictated such an artistic blunder; whereas the box-office receipts may easily have done so. Remember how little artistic virtue is in the box-office! When we have time I will tell you some things about this powerful usurper of the theatrical throne—the box-office. But let us return to a more serious and a more interesting topic than this lack of expression and this foot-light matter. We had passed in review the different tasks of the stage-manager—scene, costume, lighting—and we had come to the most interesting part, that of the manipulation of the figures in all their movements and speeches. You expressed astonishment that the acting—that is to say, the speaking and actions of the actors—was not left to the actors to arrange for themselves. But consider for an instant the nature of this work. Would you have that which has already grown into a certain unified pattern, suddenly spoiled by the addition of something accidental?

PLAYGOER: How do you mean? I understand what you suggest, but will you not show me more exactly how the actor can spoil the pattern?

STAGE-DIRECTOR: *Unconsciously* spoil it, mind you! I do not for an instant mean that it is his wish to be out of harmony with his surroundings, but he does so through innocence. Some actors have the right instincts in this matter, and some have none whatever. But even those whose instincts are most keen cannot remain in the pattern, cannot be harmonious, without following the directions of the stage-manager.

PLAYGOER: Then you do not even permit the leading actor and actress to move and act as their instincts and reason dictate?

STAGE-DIRECTOR: No, rather must they be the very first to follow the direction of the stage-manager, so often do they become the very centre of the pattern—the very heart of the emotional design.

PLAYGOER: And is that understood and appreciated by them?

STAGE-DIRECTOR: Yes, but only when they realize and appreciate at the same time that the play, and the right and just interpretation of the play, is the all-important thing in the modern theatre. Let me illustrate this point to you. The play to be presented is *Romeo and Juliet.* We have studied the play, prepared scene and costume, lighted both, and now our rehearsals for the actors commence. The first movement of the great crowd of unruly citizens of Verona, fighting, swearing, killing each other, appals us. It horrifies us that in this white little city of roses and song and love there should dwell this amazing and detestable hate which is ready to burst out at the very church doors or in the middle of the May festival, or under the windows of the house of a newly born girl. Quickly following on this picture, and even while we remember the ugliness which larded both faces of Capulet and Montague, there comes strolling down the road the son of Montague, our Romeo, who is soon to be lover and the loved of his Juliet. Therefore, whoever is chosen to move and speak as Romeo must move and speak as part and parcel of the design—this design which I have already pointed out to you as having a definite form. He must move across our sight in a certain way, passing to a certain point, in a certain light, his head at a certain angle, his eyes, his feet, his whole body in tune with the play, and not (as is often the case) in tune with his own thoughts only, and these out of harmony with the play. For his thoughts (beautiful as they may chance to be) may not match the spirit or the pattern which has been so carefully prepared by the director.

PLAYGOER: Would you have the stage-manager control the movements of whoever might be impersonating the character of Romeo, even if he were a fine actor?

STAGE-DIRECTOR: Most certainly; and the finer the actor the finer his intelligence and taste, and therefore the more easily controlled. In fact, I am speaking in particular of a theatre wherein all the actors are men of refinement and the manager a man of peculiar accomplishments.

PLAYGOER: But are you not asking these intelligent actors almost to become puppets?

STAGE-DIRECTOR: A sensitive question! which one would expect from an actor who felt uncertain about his powers. A puppet is at present only a doll, delightful enough for a puppet show. But for a theatre we need more than a doll. Yet that is the feeling which some actors have about their relationship with the stage-manager. They feel they are having their strings pulled, and resent it, and show they feel hurt—insulted.

PLAYGOER: I can understand that.

STAGE-DIRECTOR: And cannot you also understand that they should be willing to be controlled? Consider for a moment the relationship of the men on a ship, and you will understand what I consider to be the relationship of men in a theatre. Who are the workers on a ship?

PLAYGOER: A ship? Why, there is a captain, the commander, the first, second, and third lieutenants, the navigation officer, and so on, and the crew.

STAGE-DIRECTOR: Well, and what is it that guides the ship?

PLAYGOER: The rudder?

STAGE-DIRECTOR: Yes, and what else?

PLAYGOER: The steersman who holds the wheel of the rudder.

STAGE-DIRECTOR: And who else?

PLAYGOER: The man who controls the steersman.

STAGE-DIRECTOR: And who is that?

PLAYGOER: The navigation officer.

STAGE-DIRECTOR: And who controls the navigation officer?

PLAYGOER: The captain.

STAGE-DIRECTOR: And are any orders which do not come from the captain, or by his authority, obeyed?

PLAYGOER: No, they should not be.

STAGE-DIRECTOR: And can the ship steer its course in safety without the captain?

PLAYGOER: It is not usual.

STAGE-DIRECTOR: And do the crew obey the captain and his officers?

PLAYGOER: Yes, as a rule.

STAGE-DIRECTOR: Willingly?

PLAYGOER: Yes.

STAGE-DIRECTOR: And is that not called discipline?

PLAYGOER: Yes.

STAGE-DIRECTOR: And discipline—what is that the result of?

PLAYGOER: The proper and willing subjection to rules and principles.

STAGE-DIRECTOR: And the first of those principles is obedience, is it not?

PLAYGOER: It is.

STAGE-DIRECTOR: Very well, then. It will not be difficult for you to understand that a theatre in which so many hundred persons are engaged at work is in many respects like a ship, and demands like management. And it will not be difficult for you to see how the slightest sign of disobedience would be disastrous. Mutiny has been well anticipated in the navy, but not in the theatre. The navy has taken care to define, in clear and unmistakable voice, that the captain of the vessel is the king, and a despotic ruler into the bargain. Mutiny on a ship is dealt with by a court-martial, and is put down by very severe punishment, by imprisonment, or by dismissal from the service.

PLAYGOER: But you are not going to suggest such a possibility for the theatre?

STAGE-DIRECTOR: The theatre, unlike the ship, is not made for purposes of war, and so for some unaccountable reason discipline is not held to be of such vital importance, whereas it is of as much importance as in any branch of service. But what I wish to show you is that until discipline is understood in a theatre to be willing and reliant obedience to the manager or captain no supreme achievement can be accomplished.

PLAYGOER: But are not the actors, scene-men, and the rest all willing workers?

STAGE-DIRECTOR: Why, my dear friend, there never were such glorious natured people as those men and women of the theatre. They are enthusiastically willing, but sometimes their judgement is at fault, and they become as willing to be unruly as to be obedient, and as willing to lower the standard as to raise it. As for nailing the flag to the mast— this is seldom dreamed of—for *compromise* and the vicious doctrine of compromise with the enemy is preached by the officers of the theatrical navy. Our enemies are vulgar display, the lower public opinion, and ignorance. To these our "officers" wish us to knuckle under. What the theatre people have not yet quite comprehended is *the value of a high standard and the value of a director who abides by it.*

PLAYGOER: And that director, why should he not be an actor or a scene-painter?

STAGE-DIRECTOR: Do you pick your leader from the ranks, exalt him to be captain, and then let him handle the guns and the ropes? No; the director of a theatre must be a man apart from any of the crafts. He must be a man who knows but no longer handles the ropes.

PLAYGOER: But I believe it is a fact that many well-known leaders in the theatres have been actors and stage-managers at the same time?

STAGE-DIRECTOR: Yes, that is so. But you will not find it easy to assure me that no mutiny was heard of under their rule. Right away from all this question of position there is a question of the art, the work. If an actor assumes the management of the stage, and if he is a better actor than his fellows, a natural instinct will lead him to make himself the centre of everything. He will feel unless he does so the work will appear thin and unsatisfying. He will pay less heed to the play than he will to his own part, and he will, in fact, gradually cease to look upon the work as a whole. And this is not good for the work. This is not the way a work of art is to be produced in the theatre.

PLAYGOER: But might it not be possible to find a great actor who would be so great an artist that as manager he would never do as you say, but who would always handle himself as actor, just the same as he handles the rest of the material?

STAGE-DIRECTOR: All things are possible, but firstly, it is against the nature of an actor to do as you suggest; secondly, it is against the nature of the stage-manager to perform; and thirdly, it is against all nature that a man can be in two places at once. Now, the place of the actor is on the stage, in a certain position, ready by means of his brains to give suggestions of certain emotions, surrounded by certain scenes and people; and it is the place of the stage-manager to be in front of this, that he may view it as a whole. So that you see even if we found our perfect actor who was our perfect stage-manager, he could not be in two places at the same time. Of course we have sometimes seen the conductor of a small orchestra playing the part of the first violin, but not from choice, and not to a satisfactory issue: neither is it the practise in large orchestras.

PLAYGOER: I understand, then, that you would allow no one to rule on the stage except the stage-manager?

STAGE-MANAGER: The nature of the work permits nothing else.

PLAYGOER: Not even the playwright?

STAGE-DIRECTOR: Only when the playwright has practised and studied the crafts of acting, scene-painting, costume, lighting, and dance, not otherwise. But playwrights, who have not been cradled in the theatre, generally know little of these crafts. Goethe, whose love for the theatre remained ever fresh and beautiful, was in many ways one of the greatest of stage-directors. But, when he linked himself to the Weimar theatre, he forgot to do what the great musician who followed him remembered. Goethe permitted an authority in the theatre higher than himself, that is to say, the owner of the theatre. Wagner was careful to possess himself of his theatre, and become a sort of feudal baron in his castle.

PLAYGOER: Was Goethe's failure as a theatre director due to this fact?

STAGE-DIRECTOR: Obviously, for had Goethe held the keys of the doors that impudent little poodle would never have got as far as its dressing-room; the leading lady would never have made the theatre and herself immortally ridiculous; and Weimar would have been saved the tradition of having perpetrated the most shocking blunder which ever occurred inside a theatre.

PLAYGOER: The traditions of most theatres certainly do not seem to show that the artist is held in much respect on the stage.

STAGE-DIRECTOR: Well, it would be easy to say a number of hard things about the theatre and its ignorance of art. But one does not hit a thing which is down unless, perhaps, with the hope that the shock may cause it to leap to its feet again. And our Western theatre is very much down. The East still boasts a theatre. Ours here in the West is on its last legs. But I look for a Renaissance.

PLAYGOER: How will that come?

STAGE-DIRECTOR: Through the advent of a man who shall contain in him all the qualities which go to make up a master of the theatre, and through the reform of the theatre as an instrument. When that is accomplished, when the theatre has become a masterpiece of mechanism, when it had invented a technique, it will without any effort develop a *creative art* of its own. But the whole question of the development of the craft into a self-reliant and creative art would take too long to go thoroughly into at present. There are already some theatre men at work on the building of the theatres; some are reforming the acting, some the scenery. And all of this must be of some small value. But the very first thing to be realized is that little or no result can come from the reforming of a single craft of the theatre without at the same time, in the same theatre, reforming all the other crafts. *The whole renaissance of the Art of the Theatre depends upon the extent that this is realized.* The Art of the Theatre, as I have already told you, is divided up into so many crafts: acting, scene, costume, lighting, carpentering, singing, dancing, etc., that it must be realized at the commencement that ENTIRE, not PART reform is needed; and it must be realized that *one* part, one craft, has a *direct* bearing upon each of the other crafts in the theatre, and that no result can come from fitful, uneven reform, but only from a systematic progression. Therefore, the reform of the Art of the Theatre is possible to those men alone who have studied and practised all the crafts of the theatre.

PLAYGOER: That is to say, your ideal stage-manager.

STAGE-DIRECTOR: Yes. You will remember that at the commencement of our conversation I told you my belief in the Renaissance of the Art of the Theatre was based in my belief in the Renaissance of the stage-director, and that when he had understood the right use of actors, scene, costume, lighting, and dance, and by means of these had mastered the craft of interpretation, he would then gradually acquire the mastery of action, line, colour, rhythm, and words, this last strength developing out of all the rest. . . . Then I said the Art of the Theatre would have won back its rights, and its work would stand self-reliant as a creative art, and no longer as an interpretative craft.

PLAYGOER: Yes, and at the time I did not quite understand what you meant, and though I can now understand your drift, I do not quite in my mind's eye see the stage without its poet.

STAGE-DIRECTOR: What? Shall anything be lacking when the poet shall no longer write for the theatre?

PLAYGOER: The play will be lacking.

STAGE-DIRECTOR: Are you sure of that?

PLAYGOER: Well, the play will certainly not exist if the poet or playwright is not there to write it.

STAGE-DIRECTOR: There will not be any play in the sense in which you use the word.

PLAYGOER: But you propose to present something to the audience and I presume before you are able to present them with that something you must have it in your possession.

STAGE-DIRECTOR: Certainly; you could not have made a surer remark. Where you are at fault is to take for granted, as if it were a law for the Medes and Persians that that *something* must be made of words.

PLAYGOER: Well, what is this something which is not words, but for presentation to the audience?

STAGE-DIRECTOR: First tell me, is not an idea something?

PLAYGOER: Yes, but it lacks form.

STAGE-DIRECTOR: Well, but is it not permissible to give an idea whatever form the artist chooses?

PLAYGOER: Yes.

STAGE-DIRECTOR: And is it an unpardonable crime for the theatrical artist to use some different material to the poet's?

PLAYGOER: No.

STAGE-DIRECTOR: Then we are permitted to attempt to give form to an idea in whatever material we can find or invent, provided it is not a material which should be put to better use?

PLAYGOER: Yes.

STAGE-DIRECTOR: Very good; follow what I have to say for the next few minutes, and then go home and think about it for a while. Since you have granted all I asked you to permit, I am now going to tell you out of what material an artist of the theatre of the future will create his masterpiece. Out of ACTION, SCENE, and VOICE. Is it not very simple?

And when I say *action,* I mean both gesture and dancing, the prose and poetry of action.

When I say *scene,* I mean all which comes before the eye, such as the lighting, costume, as well as the scenery.

When I say *voice,* I mean the spoken word or the word which is sung, in contradiction to the word which is read, for the word written to be spoken and the word written to be read are two entirely different things.

And now, though I have but repeated what I told you at the

beginning of our conversation, I am delighted to see that you no longer look so puzzled.

§8
"The Building or the Theatre"

By Sean Kenny

The theatre has become a thing outside of life. Too far outside. It's a mediocre, minority, closed-group activity. It has nothing to do with people having bread or finding things that are exciting. In economically developing countries, people are finding, for the first time, that they can have things other than necessities. They can go places, do things, that weren't available to them before. If the theatre is to be an art form of our time, it must take these new excitements of ordinary people and develop them into a new voice. A new voice: a new theatre.

People are deserting the old form, the old theatre, because it's rubbish. There's nothing to it. We have to forget about eighteenth-century drawing room behavior and all that nonsense. Let's relegate Chekhov, Ibsen, and Shakespeare to their proper place: a museum theatre that would show how things were written and done in the past; how dancers, singers, and actors can interpret a life, a situation, a problem of another time. In art, people take a seventeenth-, eighteenth-, or nineteenth-century painter and consider his work a comment on things as and when he saw them—not a comment on today. But we in the theatre are still painting eighteenth-, seventeenth-, even fifteenth-century paintings and we call them modern. What we call Modern Theatre is Theatre of Yesterday. We go on using it because we've developed no alternative. It's as though there were no more movies and we kept showing Charlie Chaplin and the Marx Brothers, saying: this is good cinema and this is the only cinema.

Our civilization is becoming more and more a civilization of action. People don't want to sit down, like coy Victorians, to watch a semi-risque story and giggle. They want to take part; they want to do something; they want to shout, to answer back, to rebel and to acclaim. I think these people would want to take part in a new theatre, a theatre that would be theirs and theirs to enjoy.

They'd want to take part in a theatre that reflects what's really happening in this world. At the moment, we have culture salesmen, amateurs who peddle culture to the masses, proclaiming life is an extension of art, art is all. They say to the factory workers: this is what you've missed. But those characters in the factory are bored. What the hell do they know about Picasso? What do they care about folk-lorists or old musical instruments?

I'm not advocating a socialistic, comment-message-ridden theatre. I want a theatre of excitement. A theatre where you don't have to wear furs, eat chocolates, and read programs. A theatre where you can go and have a ball, where you can drink, where you can do what you bloody well like: dance and jump around and sing.

This theatre, like a baseball bat, would hit you over the head with ideas. It would offer new breakaways, show new break-throughs, suggest how there can be more to life. It would show us how to be more individual—not better, not good, but more individual; it would tell us how to release the emotions half-hidden within ourselves. It would be a place for man: for each and every one of us.

I realize this sounds anarchistic, but in order to prepare the ground for a new theatre, we have to break down all the old barricades, the old ways of doing things. We have to get rid of and destroy, once and for all, the Victorian Birdcage. We have to destroy the idea that theatre is designers, is theatre managers, is committees, is directors, is buildings.

Theatre is simply a playwright and a group of actors who want to tell a story before an audience. It doesn't require a building. A building can be a great liability.

People who want to build a theatre think first of all of the structure. They don't think of the heart of the matter, the powerhouse behind it: the group of people who will be the theatre. At meetings of theatre people, everybody discusses the building and the stage as if theatre originates with these inanimate elements. They debate three-cornered versus four-cornered, five-cornered, in-the-round, in-the-square, or upside down. If we could find a good, well-designed stage, they feel, we'd have the answer. They are just evading the real issue: what is theatre, what does it talk about, what's doing in our world today? Tackling this does not require a building; any place would do, any street corner, any parking lot. If the people were inventive enough, they would send somebody down the street for a couple of beer barrels and a plank, and have him stand on it.

New theatres, in almost all cases, are not being built by the people. City halls are building them, and the structures they turn out have nothing to do with true theatre. They are badges of culture: symbols of how well we live and how well we conserve and publicize our culture. They are part of the prevailing cultural supermarket—the Museum of

Modern Art sells over the counter—and have no value to anyone but status-seekers, people who put badges on their walls.

Speaking of myself as a designer, I don't think I set out to change the theatre or to make it into something different. I wanted to find out exactly what could be done with it, as it was and as it is, and how far it could be stretched. But the nature of a designer's role limits his ability to influence the theatre. He is an outside man; he is not, and cannot be, too involved.

We designers spend most of our time arranging wallpaper, chairs, and settees, odd bits of things here and there, that are supposed to make some kind of comment on the story. But to me, design in the theatre is basically a waste of time. A designer can't change anything about the theatre as it is now, unless he stops being a designer and writes a story. Short of that, there is nothing more he can do in the existing theatre; he's just a prop man.

But the designer could do something for a new theatre. He could find a very good square, a good space where the theatre could begin again, where he would say to the actors and the playwright: here is a good place to tell your story in—not a building inside which you can tell it, but a place. It would be marvelous if this place could be found, but I suspect it will have to be different from what we have now.

The new theatre will begin almost as the old began; someone will go to a small town with a group of actors and give a performance. In the prairies, in the mountains, it doesn't matter. There, like a dance, or a song, or a ballad that evolves into a story, theatre will emerge. And it will attain real significance when it succeeds in attracting the people in the streets and the children.

Our best hope for a new theatre may lie in the children themselves, for children have an idea of excitement beyond themselves. If, instead of erecting stages in gymnasiums, the schools were to give platforms, chairs, and materials to the children and let them do whatever they want, we might hear the beginnings of a voice called theatre. The children, as they grow up, might suddenly discover that there is one particular way in which they speak best of all, a way important to us. Tomorrow's audience, tomorrow's playhouse, tomorrow's playwrights, could be born in the schools. Just find a thousand acres, plunk the children in the middle with wood, nails, canvas—whatever they want— and say: now, you speak. It might be worth trying.

My feeling on theatre design, on problems of visual concept, is this: to hell with national theatres, to hell with provincial theatres, and to hell with Lincoln Center. Let's just have airplanes, trains and buses.

Let's have squares and fields. But let's not build reinforced concrete theatres until we begin to find out which direction, which way our theatre is going to go.

Theatre should be like a floating crap game. It should be able to change its arrangement, to change its environment, to change its whole influence, in relation to the things around it. Reinforced concrete foundations are a yoke. They won't let you move; they won't let you change. We are building theatres at this moment, designed for the next 80 or 90 years—however long they stand up—that are impossible to change. We are forced to exist inside them; we have to behave inside the architecture. This can't be theatre. We need structures we can knock holes in; we need to be able to move walls out entirely. The trouble with our theatre today is that if you push out the walls, the roof will fall in.

If this is a beginning period, a beginning time, then we need a beginning shape, and the only thing that we can have at this time is some kind of space tent or something, so that we can move in whatever direction our new theatre wants to go.

We need frames that can be changed; we need places where people can find their own physical ease for watching, sitting, lying, standing, whatever it is. We need a new kind of space into which a director and a group of actors and a playwright can come and say: well, we'll put a platform here, and orchestra there, some of the audience here so they'll look like the Roman soldiers we're short of. The entire space could be designed, for each particular performance, for each particular story. The entire space should be always fluid, always flexible. A space that you couldn't even call a theatre, because it wouldn't exist until those boys came in and started to do something. Only then would it become a theatre.

All a painter asks for is a clean white canvas. We need a clean white canvas place, in which we can begin to tell a new kind of story. There should be no architectural statements made before we begin, no statement at all. We can do anything with whatever media we want to use: lighting projection, sound, everything in the world. But first we need this new kind of space.

In the new theatre the designer would be part of a cooperative team altering the place to suit the play. In some cases the designer might say to the director and the actors: you don't need anything from me, you don't need anything for this play; just play it with two chairs—the ones you're sitting on right now.

And there are people who go in this direction, people like Little-wood, Wells, Guthrie, and Svoboda. There are lots of people who have ideas; individuals who really want to speak out, who want to reorganize, who want to adjust and say: let's go in a new direction. But control of the theatre is in the hands of the wrong people, the direction is in the hands of old critics.

John Whiting, while he was writing *The Devils,* asked me to help him place the scenes. The only thing I could say to John at that stage was—don't write *any* place. If you can, think in terms of a cinema idea, a television idea, because it should be possible to do anything, to create any place. It doesn't always have to be "enter down left and cross to fireplace"; these sorts of things don't have to happen in the theatre. And so a lot of the stage directions in *The Devils* simply come out: two men are walking, two men are talking. My advice to writers is to start where you want to; go ahead and write—the man jumps out the window onto the back of a white horse and the white horse, chased by ten more horses, runs away through the audience. There should be a freedom about writing for the stage. Why set handcuffs on the theatre?

Lorca said the theatre must impose itself on the audience. It has to; the reason we're doing it in the first place is for an audience, not for ourselves. We do it initially to make a life for ourselves, but we do it finally and eventually for an audience.

Any dissatisfaction that I'm talking about, anything I'm complaining about, is inside the theatre. The trouble lies not with the audience but with how *we* are doing it. We're not doing it well.

I know that design can help change the theatre, can help change its direction. But all I can do right now is voice my frustration and say that it's no good. From now on, I refuse to work in the theatre as it is, unless to change its direction. I don't mean that tomorrow every theatre has to be popular or I won't work in it; I mean that its direction must change to have reference to me in our time. There are things happening in our time that ought to have something to do with the theatre and theatre with them. Tomorrow we'll be on the moon; we can't do Molière on the moon.

A good parallel to the problem of theatre design is: How do you design a church for 1967? Now, it would be impossible to design a church for 1967 without first examining how religion relates to life in 1967. You couldn't possibly just design a church. You would have to find out the *meaning* of religion in ordinary life, how it affects people, everyday problems, and excitements. It should be impossible to examine the idea of designing a new theatre without finding out what theatre has to do with everyday life, what place it occupies in the lives of people today. The question of place relates closely to the questions of the physical thing called theatre: the physical building, the space it stands in, where it is, how we approach it, how we go to it. We should all be concerned with asking and finding answers.

Suggested Reading

Appia, Adolphe. *Music and the Art of the Theatre.* Coral Gables, Fla.: University of Miami Press, 1962.

Aronson, Joseph. *The Encyclopedia of Furniture.* New York: Crown Publishers, 1959.

Bellman, Willard F. *Lighting the Stage: Art and Practice.* San Francisco: Chandler Publishing Company, 1967.

Chippendale, Thomas. *The Gentleman and Cabinet-Maker's Director.* New York: Dover Publications, 1966.

Clay, James H., and Krempel, Daniel. *The Theatrical Image.* New York: McGraw-Hill, 1967.

Craig, Gordon. *On the Art of the Theatre.* Boston: Small, Maynard, 1924.

Hainaux, Rene. *Stage Design throughout the World Since* 1935. New York: Theatre Arts Books, 1957.

——. *Stage Design throughout the World Since* 1950. New York: Theatre Arts Books, 1964.

Jones, Robert Edmond. *The Dramatic Imagination.* New York: Theatre Arts Books, 1941.

Larson, Orville, ed. *Scene Design for Stage and Screen.* East Lansing: Michigan State University Press, 1961.

Macgowan, Kenneth, and Melnitz, William. *The Living Stage.* Englewood Cliffs, N.J.: Prentice-Hall, 1964.

Mielziner, Jo. *Designing for the Theatre: A Memoir and Portfolio.* New York: Atheneum, 1965.

Miller, William J. *Modern Playwrights at Work.* New York: Samuel French, 1968.

Motley. *Designing and Making Stage Costumes.* New York: Watson-Guptill Publications, 1964.

Nutting, Wallace. *Furniture Treasury.* New York: Macmillan Co., 1961.

Pilbrow, Richard. *Stage Lighting.* London: Studio Vista, Ltd., 1970.

Praz, Mario. *An Illustrated History of Furnishings.* New York: Braziller, 1964.

Simonson, Lee. *The Stage Is Set.* New York: Atheneum, 1965.

Sitwell, Sacheverell. *Great Houses of Europe.* New York: G. P. Putnam's Sons, 1961.

Yarwood, Doreen. *The English Home.* London: B. T. Batsford, Ltd., 1956.

PART 2 Creative Research

Like architecture, the theater is receptive to all the other arts, indeed it could hardly exist without recourse to several among them, but it does not consist of any of them in particular.

Etienne Gilson

The greatest natural genius cannot subsist on its own stock; he who resolves never to ransack any mind but his own will soon be reduced from mere barrenness to the poorest of all imitations. It is vain to invent without materials on which the mind may work and from which invention must originate. Nothing can come of nothing.

Sir Joshua Reynolds

§9
The Nature of Research

No matter how creative the individual designer may be, the art of scene design cannot be pursued without frequent recourse to research. In the producing theater the importance of this multifaceted, many-leveled activity should not be minimized; it is as important that the designer be adept in finding appropriate source materials that will aid him, as well as to know what and how much to take from those sources, as it is that he be able to paint set sketches or draft working plans. Yet there is a vast difference between mere research, that is, finding something that relates to the design requirements in a vague way, and creative research which seeks to find exactly the *right* thing. The first type of activity is satisfied with a superficial representation of period detail

99

alone; the hundreds of costume movies of the last forty years are ample testimony to the essentially unthinking and inartistic manner in which research can be done. Creative research, on the other hand, is much more concerned with what these details mean or originally meant and to what extent they assist the designer in clarifying the underlying themes of the production. Yet how does one know what to select and how does he know what he selects is *right*? For, out of a world of possibilities, the designer must finally make a limited number of selective judgments.

How precise, then, should the designer be when considering the details that go into a production? Several years ago a design student selected *Hamlet* as a project; the scene where Polonius is stabbed through the arras in the Queen's bedchamber was under discussion. What about the design of this curtain, he was questioned. "Well," he said, with a look of slight impatience, "I haven't really picked one out yet or designed it. Just a tapestry." He was asked if the selection of this tapestry—or his design—might in any way help reinforce the scene. Was it possible, perhaps, to tell something about the Queen? After all, she probably did choose this tapestry to decorate her room. What sort of things does she select? Or isn't it possible that, somehow, this tapestry might subtly underscore, even intensify the feelings of the audience who will witness the cold-blooded murder of a harmless old man as he hides behind the hanging? The student thought about these possibilities. (He also admitted that he had not considered the selection of the room's furnishings very carefully.) Finally, at a later time, he came to the conclusion that although the tapestry needn't be greatly symbolic in any way, consideration of those questions might help him recognize the right tapestry when he did start his research or give him initial ideas for its design.

Everything man fashions—his houses, works of art, the clothes he wears, the tools he makes in order to create the objects he needs or wants, even the institutions that mold his social life—speaks a silent language not easily comprehensible and has a story to tell that superficial investigation will not reveal. Simple research will isolate these things so that they may be named and categorized: creative research, on the other hand, not only does this, it also deals with their interpretation and meaning—it hears and translates that silent language into practical information. The artist must learn to see in more than one dimension. He must see *through* the surface of things, opaque as that surface often is.

I recall the time when Jones was supervising the execution of the stage setting for the seventeenth-century Spanish room in *The Buccaneer*. A week earlier he had completed his design, and on this particular day the crew of fine scenic artists in Bergman's Studio was executing the set on the paint-frame below Jones's studio. Bobby couldn't bear the idea that they would think of their work as simply the job of executing a large painting; so he scurried out with me to gather up bits and pieces of what he called "living things" which related to the setting: a lovely antique bench of the period with the patina of age and the beauty of line that he loved so much; a swatch of antique yellow satin, with some black lace and a huge artificial red flower; a yard or two of heavy gold lace; one lovely Spanish Renaissance tile. These things he placed on the floor beside the setting on which the painters were at work, because Jones wanted—for himself and for all who were working with him—to be conscious of the relations of this painting to its final achievement and appearance on the stage. . . .

Robert Edmond Jones could be described as a dreamer, but he was also a doer. Idealist he was, but certainly he cannot be dismissed as a mere visionary. A prophet, yes, but at the same time a most practical craftsman. [Jo Mielziner, "Practical Dreams," in *The Theatre of Robert Edmond Jones* by Ralph Pendleton]

This, then, is the crux of our problem when we endeavor to do more than mere literal research. As Jones wrote in 1941, "we may fairly speak of the art of stage designing as poetic, in that it seeks to give expression to the essential quality of a play rather than to its outward characteristics." Although these words come from a time which had a view of theater somewhat different from the one we profess today, yet the essential truth and good common sense of Jones's view still applies, is still valid. In the final analysis, creative research is a means to the poetic art of scene design that Jones felt was so important. What he sought then, although much has changed in theater since, is still basically what we seek now, what we as designers still attempt to do.

John Ruskin, the noted nineteenth-century art critic, once wrote:

Great nations write their autobiographies in three manuscripts, the book of their deeds, the book of their words and the book of their art. Not one of these books can be understood unless we read the two others, but of the three the only trustworthy one is the last. [Kenneth Clark, *Ruskin Today*]

It is an accepted principle of most historians that all activities of an age reflect either directly or indirectly the spirit of the time. Music, philosophy, religion, and political theory, as well as architecture, sculpture, and painting all exercise influences one on the other and interrelate to such an extent that the theatrical use of any one element cannot help but call a knowledge of the others into question. Not even so great an artist as Michelangelo, despite his personal genius and singularity, can be fully understood without consideration of his close working relationship to the Church and the doctrines of the day. Nor could the Church itself be fully understood without examining its relationship to the secular, political milieu of late Rennaissance Italy. To comprehend the visual image of a period along with the myriad facets of that image—and this is the designer's ultimate aim—he must also understand the forces that had molded the people who in turn determined the character of the age in which they lived. It is a common fault of young designers to limit their research into a period too narrowly; the veteran artist seeks his images and concepts from behind the surfaces, from the obscure, out-of-the-way nooks and crannies of the past. Simple research, that which stops at surface examination, can be carried out by the most uninterested of workers; creative research, that which goes into the deeper layers of what is being examined and seeks to understand more than a cursory glance can reveal, is a highly personal activity and the necessary business of an artist; discovery of a fact may be important but understanding and interpreting the forces that created that fact is essential if the resultant findings are to have any real worth to the designer. It was precisely in this area—the difference between these two ways of approaching research—that the designers of most nineteenth-century productions fell short; they were more than conscientious and meticulous in reproduction of historical detail, but contemporary drawings and early photographs reveal that what they produced would have been more serviceable for Madame Tussaud's Wax Museum than it was for a living theater. Accuracy of detail alone is not sufficient to insure that the contemporaneity of the past can be evoked.

In speaking of the craft of poetry, Dylan Thomas once pointed out that, "the best craftsmanship always leaves holes and gaps in the works of the poem so that something that is not in the poem can creep, crawl, flash, or thunder in." Creative research is not altogether unlike this; often a designer feels he is looking for something (having read and studied a playscript or libretto) the nature of which he is not quite sure. Often the most knowledgeable and experienced designer cannot with absolute certainty always know just what this unknown quantity he is looking for is until it is found. And it is quite possible that he overlooks what he needs by looking too hard. As Jean Dubuffet, the French painter has noted:

> I am obsessed by the idea that there is something both false and unprofitable in looking at things too closely and too long. It is not normal for a human being to stare at objects for the sole purpose of inspecting them and making an inventory of their constituent parts. Such a position in our relation to them seems to me to destroy completely (if not to empty them of all content) the mechanisms of communication that exist between man and the objects around him, the way he perceives them and the way they affect him. Man sees things without trying to see them. While he is looking at one thing he sees another as though obliquely. . . .
>
> . . . I must say my feeling is—always has been—very strong that the key to things must not be as we imagine it, but that the world must be ruled by strange systems of which we have not the slightest inkling. This is why I rush towards strange things. I am quite convinced that truth is strange; it is at the far end of strangeness that one has a chance to find the key to things. [Peter Selz, *The Work of Jean Dubuffet*]

But what do these words mean to the scene designer? Is this type of research valid, this philosophy of vision acceptable or usable to him; is it even employable in the practical world of theatrical production? Yes, it may very well affect the manner in which the designer approaches his research chores. And yet this does not mean to infer that research is wholly an intuitional activity or that the designer merely goes to the library or his files methodically examining everything in sight until some psychic bell rings; there are methods and principles of research that will both expedite much of the guesswork and still leave room for the "strange systems" alluded to by Dubuffet to do their work. As Ben Shahn, another famous painter, has pointed out in his book, *The Shape of Content:*

> The subconscious may greatly shape one's art; undoubtedly it does so. But the subconscious cannot create art. The very act of making a painting is an intending one; thus to intend and at the same time relinquish intentions is a hopeless contradiction, albeit one that is exhibited on every hand.

What Shahn says about painters applies equally well to designers; one must trust his intuition to a great extent but never use intuition as an excuse for not digging into a problem of research.

The subject of the following section is, primarily, spelling out some very broad and general principles of research in outline form. These principles are intended not so much for the mature designer as they are for the student with little experience in any sort of research. It is expected that as the student designer grows more proficient in his craft and art, as he becomes more knowledgeable in the whole field of theater, he may vary this initial approach radically, creating his own methods of gathering necessary materials and information; certainly no two designers ever work in exactly the same manner; nor, for that matter, does the individual designer work the same way during his whole career, especially not in this broad but extremely sensitive area.

For our immediate purposes, principles of research will be divided into two basic units: external research and internal research. The first category will include all those elements of information pertinent to but not actually found in the written script; the second category will deal with items of information that are stated explicitly in the text or may be gleaned from close investigation of it. In some cases this division, it should be expected, will result in a certain amount of overlapping; the need for research, moreover, varies considerably from script to script. A large part of the designer's research, especially the completely visual aspect of it, is comparatively easy to understand even for the beginning designer. The understanding of what lies below the surface of an object or detail, the forces that molded it and, incidentally, how it might be used in a design, is not as easily grasped. Even the order and pattern of the research process might greatly change from production to production. Only experience can speed up the process or give assurance to the designer that his choices are right or that his design will be artistically valid. Still, most designers who have worked in the theater for any length of time become intuitive in this area and develop a *feel* for these substrata of a historical period or a geographical location. Thus they are able to imbue their settings with the spirit of a past age or a sense of locale without copying blindly the exterior trappings or the minutiae of a time or place.

The following outline of research principles is necessarily sketchy; still, it may prove useful as a general guideline and as a checklist of possible leads to follow in seeking out that illusive spirit of a past age or of an unfamiliar place. But while the basic nature of these principles seems to be purely factual and "scientific," keep in mind this observation of the painter Jean Hélion: "The artist is born with a definite feeling that Unity exists throughout the incongruous, and that we do not see it only because the links are hidden, or missing, or misunderstood."

§10
External Research

1. Date of the Play

A. Date of the play's composition. No matter when the date of the play's action, it is always a sound idea to examine the time when the play was actually written. In some cases, as with some of Shakespeare's plays, this date may be unknown or disputed. Still, no matter when an author sets the action of his play, some of his own time will undoubtedly creep into the fabric of the text; it is well to pinpoint that time as exactly as possible.

B. Date of the play's action. This date, along with the above, gives the designer a specific period of time around which all his research will center. In many instances, an author, wanting to treat a contemporary problem, will choose a time with similarities to his own so that he may call attention to some topical point or thesis. Shakespeare, in his defense of and allegiance to the monarchy of his own age, used examples of corrupt governments and rulers from the past, both foreign and domestic, to demonstrate how fortunate his contemporary countrymen were to have the rule they had. (And to prove a point he is not above maligning unfairly men or groups who differed with him in opinion. Witness the unfair treatment he gives the characters Richard III and Joan of Arc.) A careful study of both dates, while these alone will not provide the only dates he will need, will give the designer an excellent starting clue for his further research.

2. Period of the Play

The period is a deceptive concept; periods don't actually exist. To assign a name and inclusive dates to a period of time is dangerous in that it leads to thinking that the past does divide itself into convenient compartments of time, which is not true, and is dangerous also in that the inhabitants of any particular period become stereotyped images rather than living people. More is always left out of this stereotype than is included; sometimes very important things are omitted simply because they don't "fit" the stereotype. Still, many books and articles have been written and visual materials compiled on the assumption that a span of time can be separated from others and given an appropriate name and character. But the designer should never be misled into thinking he can get all his material in one source or from one period only. To understand the romantic era, for instance, it is imperative to examine the eighteenth-century culture against which it revolted. Certainly all periods have their roots in those that preceded them. The astute designer is prepared to trace these roots as carefully and as far back as they extend; quite often he finds the meaning of something, incomprehensible in itself, easily understood when traced to its beginning.

3. *The Geographical Factors in Stage Design*

It is self-evident that the geographical location of a play will dictate much of the detail of its setting. Even when a play is produced in a style other than realistic, there is usually some attempt to manifest the geographical spirit of the actual place. This might show only in the basic colors of the production—golden yellow and brown for the desert, cold blues and greens for northern climates. (This was especially true in the recent cinema version of *Othello* with Laurence Olivier; texture and colors, with a minimum of historical detail, allowed the designer to give the viewer an accurate sense of place and time without making imitative pictures of Venice and Cyprus "as it really was.") Geographical location, moreover, has an altering influence on similar styles of decoration and fashion, even though the differences may go unnoticed to the casual eye. Recent large scale studies and publications such as *The Age of Expansion,* edited by Hugh Trevor-Roper, deal with particularly limited spans of time, in this case 1559 to 1660, and are able to clearly show the difference in developments in the arts, sciences, politics and religious activities of various countries during this period. It is possible to see in Trevor-Roper's study deviations both great and small as each individual country is examined, and this can be of immense value to the designer. While material can sometimes be found altogether, as in the case of the English historian's book, more often than not, the designer must compile such information from various sources. Temperaments and points of view that emerge out of climate and geographical location—not only of the characters who inhabit a play but of the authors too—are so enmeshed in the work that ignorance of these qualities and the underlying reasons for them could lead to serious dislocations of visual ideas. The sense of environment is important to a play but it is not always easy to distill from visual material alone.

Yet it is not often possible for a designer to go directly to a place and study firsthand the country from which he must draw material. Travel books are helpful, especially pictorial ones, and most designers maintain files and personal materials on various countries in their permanent collection of sources. Still, one can sometimes miss important points without firsthand knowledge. The young designer should be constantly on the lookout for writers who have been places and have written about their travels. Very often, this reportage, along with picto-rial materials, can be extremely valuable to the designer who has not had the opportunity to travel extensively. One of the best examples in support of this recommendation is Henry Miller's great account of his first visit to Greece in the late 1930s. When Miller speaks of Greece in the *Colossus of Maroussi,* it is of a Greece he saw in more than one time dimension. And while he was looking at the country as it existed then, he is also able to see what it was—an ancient Greece. But at the same time he perceives a living world and not just a dead past. While there is not one reference to a single production of a Greek play, any designer reading Miller's book could not help having his visual imagination stimulated and influenced by it. The same would hold true of Mary McCarthy's *The Stones of Florence,* a book that combines visual materials with perceptive observations. A sound principle of research, therefore, is that a designer may often be inspired by writings not directly related with his project.

4. *The Artistic Climate of the Time*

In any period of history, the various artistic endeavors will reflect, better than any other form of record we have, the form and texture of the time. During the austerely religious period that followed the fall of decadent Rome, one might expect the simple but powerful Gregorian chant, massive cathedrals and the sculpture of saints and martyrs. By the same token, it is reasonable to expect to find the spiritual lightness of the eighteenth century mirrored in the music of Mozart, the paint-ings of Watteau and Fragonard, and the excessively mannered busts of Bernini. Perhaps the arts are the most faithful lens we have to see into the past. Many times history, recorded only in words, can barely hint at what the arts can make very plain. Still, some arts are more useful to the designer than others. Architecture and sculpture very often show how a man would like to be; it shows what he aspires to rather than what he is. Painting, on the other hand, while it too has often been used to glorify both men and gods, tends to capture the more human side of man. Painters, even when they are thinking least about the present moment, cannot keep it out of their work. For this reason, the painter-draftsman, with his more quickly accomplished works, is proba-bly of more value to the scene designer than any other group of artists, even though a designer cannot exclude thorough study of them as well.

5. *The Religious Climate of the Time*

The religious philosophy of some periods has been their guiding force and all other activities have stemmed from it or have been affected by it. The ceiling of the Sistine Chapel, one of the great monuments of Western art, was a commission of the Church. Even the placement of each individual panel was dictated and supervised, along with the particular subject matter for each, by Church officials, not by Michelangelo. When religion has been a prime factor in the structure of a period, it usually is so strong that not to consider it as a molding force of the visual elements of the time, both spiritual and secular, is to miss the point entirely. A play such as Arthur Miller's *The Crucible* (although he was also dealing with the state of America in the twentieth century) or John Whiting's *The Devils* requires a thorough study of Church doctrines during the seventeenth century as they relate to witchcraft and Satanism. The Whiting play, in fact, is almost impossible to produce without an intense examination of Aldous Huxley's book, *The Devils of Loudun,* on which the play is based. Even when religion does not play a prominent part in the structure of a work, it is sometimes much easier to understand the characters of a play if their beliefs are given attention; a designer's job, as stated before, is not so much to reproduce the minutiae of the past as it is to capture the spirit of it.

6. The Political Climate of the Time

Since a great many plays concern or have political happenings current at the time of the play's composition, it is sometimes necessary to delve into the political history of the period to make any sense of the play itself. *Danton's Death* by George Büchner written in the early part of the last century and the *Marat/Sade* of Peter Weiss in our own day, both deal with the French Revolution and the forces that motivated it. And while both plays have different motivations and purposes (the Weiss play, for instance, deals more with the present day than it does with the past), it is not possible to intelligently produce either play without a comprehensive understanding of the political events that brought that revolution about. Although this area of research may be of more direct use to the director and actor, the designer cannot completely ignore or remain ignorant of what those events were or how they came about.

7. The Author's Commentary on His Own Time

Most works of art are, either consciously or unconsciously, evaluations made by their creators on the institutions and concepts he comes in contact with during his everyday life. The stage has often been used as a platform for the expounding—sometimes subtly, sometimes not—of ideas and philosophies. Sheridan, Shaw, and Brecht, to name but a few, have strong opinions concerning contemporary figures and their behavior. If the designer is not aware of the author's state of mind, he might very well misunderstand the author's intention and create settings that defeat rather than aid the playwright's purpose. Usually the author is fairly explicit in exposing his ideas through the medium of the play; in *School for Scandal,* Sheridan attacks not only a few isolated characters, but a whole level of society whose behavior he found particularly offensive (the fabrication and perpetuation of scandalous stories, often gratuitously and always maliciously). And, on at least one occasion Shaw's thoughts concerning a play (*Androcles and the Lion*) exceed in length the play itself. Sometimes, however, the designer must turn to other writings by the same author or about the author to answer questions concerning the play.

8. *Style of Production of the Play as Originally Produced*

The theater of any period had some singular style of production which employed the accepted conventions of the day. Today, in many instances, in order to recapture some of the original force of a work, it is produced with what are now outmoded conventions. But, even when the play is presented with modifications of those original conventions, a thorough knowledge of those conventions is essential. Much research has been done on all the important plays of the past still being produced today and much information has been unearthed concerning theaters in which the plays were performed, details of setting, lighting practices (if any), and mode of costume. It is sometimes almost a necessity to understand fully, if not reproduce exactly, the basic format of the original production in order to secure the results the author desired. During the last part of the nineteenth century Shakespeare was given such extravagantly designed productions that the plays scarcely survived the scenic devices superimposed on their dramatic structures. In these plays scenes were altered or transposed to such an extent (in many cases important ones simply cut) in order to facilitate scene changes, that little or no regard was paid to the integrity of the play's internal structure. Research since that time has shown, oddly enough, that the simple, often crude Elizabethan theater was, from what little we do know of it, not only an almost ideal form in which to produce the plays of the period, but actually determined to a great extent the writing of them.

These, then, are some of the basic investigations a designer must make in seeking material about a production. Just when the external research must be done may change with different projects (as well as how much). In one production he may find one category important to explore, another useless; in another production, just the reverse might be true. Keep in mind, therefore, that any sort of research is rarely—if ever—a straight-line activity; jumping from group to group, from fact to fact, sometimes working forward, sometimes backtracking, is all part of the technique.

For a moment, examine the following engraving (fig. 38). It shows a London street in the middle 1880s. This engraving contains a great amount of visual material observed firsthand and recorded meticulously. Looking at this drawing closely it is almost impossible not to be puzzled about some of the things it contains, curious about the smaller details of the buildings, the street, and the activities of the people in those buildings and on the street. We can see, too, so much more from the high angle the artist has chosen and can thus determine not only how the place *looked,* but how it was *used* as well. Research materials, such as this picture, that show the activity of human beings, are much more valuable to the designer than pictures of isolated buildings, empty rooms or details taken out of their human context. At another time these things might need be examined and assessed, but it is very important at any stage of research that the designer never forget the actor—the human aspect. Even on working drawings, many designers always place a simple line drawing of a human figure to remind him of the human scale.

One of the most beneficial things that can happen to a designer when he is working in the initial stages of research is to get sidetracked. There are several reasons for this diversion; often he is exposed to the possibility of material, "happy accidents," that simply do not fall within the scope or follow the logical pattern of research. Another possible reward is to make discoveries that may not be useful at the present time or for the immediate project, but that will be useful at another time. There are very few professional designers who will not admit that many times what they need specifically in a design they find accidently. Artwork has sometimes been compared to night vision; during the daylight hours we can see an object directly in front of us without difficulty whereas in the dark our eyes are so constructed that one is able to see the object in front of him only by looking to the side of it. As a matter of fact, as Jean Dubuffet noted, it is possible to look too hard for something and in that way miss it altogether.

Quite often, too, the necessary information the designer is seeking comes in an aggregate form, that is, hidden among things not important, much in the manner in which we looked at the engraving of the London street. Keep in mind, therefore, that the best historical research materials are often the richest in detail. This means that the designer's task is not only to find such a source (that is scarcely half the job), but to be able to interpret and understand, emotionally as well as

38. A London Street, *by Gustave Doré*

intellectually, what he needs from it. Designing is often much like re-fining gold: there is always more dross than anything else and the pro-cess of refining is tedious.

§11
Internal Research

1. *Explicit Directions Written by the Author*

These directions are usually the minimum amount of information to denote entrances and exits or necessary physical actions to clarify di-alogue references. But stage directions are not all the same type nor do all convey the same kind of information. In most past periods of the-ater, stage directions actually written as part of the scripts have been scanty or nonexistent. On the other hand, it is a practice of today's playwrights to give elaborate and lengthy directions to supplement the dialogue. Some producers of plays, both directors and designers, make it a practice to remove or ignore all written directions when they study the playscript; they do not wish to be too influenced by the author's in-structions because they feel that he, the playwright, is not necessarily the final arbiter in actually bringing the work to the stage. (While most playwrights do not like this practice on the part of their co-workers, some have seen the wisdom of if it and have said so in print.) Most directors and designers, in defense of this attitude, think that the better the playwright has done his work in the text the less he will need to explain it in a stage direction. Here is a brief outline of the various types of stage directions a designer might encounter in a script. While it is not, perhaps, necessary to ignore completely stage directions any-more than it is necessary to blindly try to follow their advice, it is im-perative for the designer to know precisely what these directions at-tempt to say and then make an evaluation as to how far they should be observed or disregarded.

A. *Factual descriptions.* Shakespeare wrote very few directions; most of the directions that are found in his work have been supplied by later editors of his plays. Most plays, in fact, until about the last one hundred fifty-odd years, have little more than act and scene divisions and one or two-word locale references. Since that time, however, the pendulum has swung the other way. It is now a common practice to write lengthy stage directions. George Bernard Shaw's directions were, for instance, often long and carefully worded essays to give background material primarily concerning the characters in his plays. Often he would also discuss the setting where these characters lived since he felt that that too revealed a great deal about what they were or had become because of this environmental influence. Most playwrights working today, while not writing as voluminously as Shaw, present their directions more or less in this manner.

B. *Poetic descriptions.* Some authors, not many though, attempt to give the reader hints concerning the mood of the play by evocative and poetic descriptions (although not in verse form) of locales and characters. Perhaps Tennessee Williams is one of the best examples of a writer who uses this device. Take the beginning of *The Glass Menagerie* for instance:

> The Wingfield apartment is in the rear of the building, one of those vast hive-like conglomerations of cellular living-units that flower as warty growths in overcrowded urban centers of lower middle-class population and are symptomatic of the impulse of this largest and fundamentally enslaved section of American society to avoid fluidity and differentiation and to exist and function as one interfused mass of automatism.
>
> The apartment faces an alley and is entered by a fire escape, a structure whose name is a touch of accidental truth, for all of these huge buildings are always burning with the slow and implacable fires of human desperation.

While this is not poetry, its intention is poetic. Eugene O'Neill did much the same thing in his earlier plays, but in a colder prose form. Both try to give more than just a factual account of the places where the action of the play takes place and a keener insight into the people who inhabit these places. Jo Mielziner, in speaking of Williams's practice of writing directions in this manner, has said:

> If I were teaching an advanced course in scene design, I think I might ask the students to read the production notes that Tennessee Williams writes for almost all his plays. After reading his notes in the early script for *Summer and Smoke,* I felt that it would be truly difficult to design a setting for this play that was poor in concept. It might be inadequate in execution, but the extraordinarily knowledgeable and sensitive eye of the dramatist created a picture that even a mediocre designer could not spoil.

C. *Stage directions in acting editions of plays.* Most young students in the theater are surprised to learn that many of the directions in a published version of a Broadway success were not written down by the author but by the production's stage manager. He usually does this on the instructions of the director, since it is the function of the stage manager to compile and record the official prompt script. This prompt-script, later used as the basis for the published version of the play, usually gives detailed information about all entrances, exits, directions of movements, and, quite often, key words that indicate interpretations and vocal timings. The author's original directions and admonitions often get cut, inverted or swallowed up in general process of rehearsal and tryouts in front of test audiences. These scripts also contain detailed lists of properties, sound and light cues, costume plots, and floor plans for a particular production. In most cases, although there is a tendency especially among amateurs to regard this information as somehow sacrosanct, it can be and should be completely disregarded or at least carefully scrutinized.

2. Deductive Evidence Gained from Direct and Indirect References by Characters in the Play

It is often possible to glean information about a play's setting by careful study of oblique remarks made by the characters in their dialogue. It seems to be characteristic of well-written plays that the deductive evidence is of greater value to the designer in his research than explicit directions or descriptions. One of the drawbacks of seeking information by deduction is that, unless the contributing factors which lead to the deduction are fairly specific and easy to interpret, the resulting information may be subject to wide interpretation. (The design and use of the Elizabethan stage is one of the best examples of the confusion that can result from interpretative study of internal evidence.) Nevertheless, the deductive process is one most followed by almost all artists and is the area in which the designer can make his greatest contribution to the production. It is this deductive process that is the primary focus of most of the ensuing sections of this book.

§12
Historical Accuracy

In the late nineteenth century there was an intense desire in the theater to dress the stage and actor with settings and costumes as correct in period detail as was possible to determine from research. To our eye the results of this activity, if we accept the visual materials which have come down to us as representative, have a certain quaint but essentially moribund charm. Part of this feeling can be explained by the time lapse between then and now; styles and customs of the past have always seemed slightly humorous. Yet much of the strangeness associated with these settings and costumes stems from a lack of understanding on the part of the designers of the period that accuracy of detail alone does not, cannot in fact, insure that the intangible spirit of the original will automatically be recreated in the reproduction. All too often, when we study a costumed actor (and we have had photographs of actors for over a hundred years) what we see is a real person in a mode of dress he did not ordinarily affect, not a believable character wearing appropriate clothes; what he was *not* is more evident than what he was supposed to be. The same relationship (or lack of it) doubtlessly held true for the actor's involvement with his scenic environment. Even though the theater has developed in many directions since then, the desire to be *real* and *accurate* is still a dominant attitude in production today. It is unfortunate that we unquestioningly accept accuracy as a true test of theatrical accomplishment; this attitude is slowly changing but it is apparently too deeply embedded in both producers and audience to disappear quickly or altogether.

Many student designers follow a fairly consistent pattern of development in regard to the problem of historical accuracy in design. There is at first an almost total disregard of any research at all. This cavalier approach is often replaced (after it is discovered that research need not be an unavoidable chore when inspiration fails) by an intense insistence on complete accuracy. There is a third period—which engenders an attitude that comes only with maturity and experience—that can only be described as one where the designer allows himself to be *consciously anachronistic,* to combine periods or use a detail from one period out of its time. The reasons for doing this cannot be completely or logically explained; it is a practice, however, that many designers follow. Peter Brook, the eminent English director who often works either very closely with a designer or designs his productions himself has said this on the subject in his book, *The Empty Space:*

> One of the pioneer figures in the movement towards a renewed Shakespeare was William Poel. An actress once told me that she had worked with Poel in a production of *Much Ado about Nothing* that was presented some fifty years ago for one night in some gloomy London Hall. She said that at the first rehearsal Poel arrived with a case full of scraps out of which he brought odd photographs, drawings, pictures torn out of magazines. "That's you," he said, giving her a picture of a

debutante at the Royal Garden Party. To someone else it was a knight in armour, a Gainsborough portrait or else just a hat. In all simplicity, he was expressing the way he saw the play when he read it—directly, as a child does—not as a grown-up monitoring himself with notions of history and period. My friend told me that the total pre-pop-art mixture had an extraordinary homogeneity. I am sure of it. Poel was a great innovator and he clearly saw that consistency had no relation to real Shakespearian style. I once did a production of *Love's Labour's Lost* where I dressed the character called Constable Dull as a Victorian policeman because his name at once conjured up the typical figure of the London bobby. For other reasons the rest of the characters were dressed in Watteau-eighteenth-century clothes, but no one was conscious of an anachronism. A long time ago I saw a production of *The Taming of the Shrew* where all the actors dressed themselves exactly the way they saw the characters—I still remember a cowboy, and a fat character busting the buttons of a pageboy's uniform—and that it was far and away the most satisfying rendering of this play I have seen.

This third period can only be reached by going through the second (and few designers ever completely fall out of love with the past and the desire to render it faithfully on a stage). Let us assume, then, that the student designer is currently approaching or is in the second phase of this development, that he has learned research can be an engrossing activity as well as a necessary part of his work. He will, almost certainly, find that many plays which demand extensive research quite frequently contain puzzling questions seemingly with no logical solutions. For a moment, therefore, let us examine one such question which quite possibly might arise from a study of the play *Hamlet*.

Suppose that a director and designer agreed to produce *Hamlet* as much in period as possible, that is, as close as possible to the time when the story was intended to occur. If the play were *Julius Caesar,* the problem would not be too difficult; the facts and dates for the original story are well documented. *Hamlet,* however, is a very different case; we know a great deal less about who Hamlet really was (if he existed at all) and about the period in which he was supposed to have lived. Shakespeare probably wasn't too certain about these facts himself. Still, if we desire to be "historically correct," we must at least attempt to obtain as much information as possible from examination of the internal evidence of the play before starting our search for external material.

In other words, what did Shakespeare himself know and how much has he told us in the play?

In 1874, E. W. Godwin (the father of Gordon Craig) published an article in the British journal, the *Architect,* called "The Architecture and Costume of Shakespeare's Plays." In this essay he attempts to determine the historically correct period in which this play, *Hamlet,* should be set; the date around which he centers his research is about 1012. How did he arrive at this explicit time? He uses as his prime clue a reference made by Claudius in act 3, scene 1, to the "neglected tribute" that England owes the then more powerful Denmark. Following his research, Godwin notes that the last time England was under such an obligation to Denmark was about the first decade of the eleventh century. He believes, therefore, that this is the right and proper time to set the action of the play, the scenery and costumes to be designed accordingly. Having once made this decision, he then proceeds to provide a highly detailed analysis of the locales needed, descriptions of the architectural features of the period (along with information concerning building materials and finishing techniques) and, most specific of all, a minutely detailed account of the dress of the time. The primary source for his findings was, according to him, a manuscript now in the Bodleian library, that contained many illuminations showing contemporary scenes. It is difficult to quarrel with the facts as Godwin presents them; his research is thorough and carefully documented. But does this settle the question of when and how the play should be set if one wants to be completely "accurate"? For a number of reasons the answer must be no.

If one assumes that Shakespeare must have known something of the past history of England and Denmark in order to include such a fact as "neglected tribute" why not then accept the contention that what he said is what he meant, that he wanted the play to be considered as taking place in the time period to which the reference alludes? And if we do give Shakespeare the benefit of the doubt for knowing what he is writing about there seems to be no *reason* for not accepting Godwin's research as not only historically correct but also right and, consequently, the way the play should be set. Yet in the same play that gave us this information there are other remarks that shed doubt on the correctness of this decision.

In the second scene of the first act, this passage occurs:

KING: For your intent
        In going back to school in Wittenberg,
        It is most retrograde to our desire:

> And we beseech you, bend you to remain
> Here, in the cheer and comfort of our eye,
> Our chiefest courtier, cousin, and our son.
> QUEEN: Let not thy mother lose her prayers, Hamlet;
> I pray thee, stay with us; go not to Wittenberg.

Surely Godwin read this passage. And it could also be assumed that he must have been aware of the fact—since his reasoning for the chosen time of the play's action was based on a much more obscure piece of knowledge—that the action could also be dated, using this reference as proof, no earlier than 1502, the year Wittenberg university was founded. Nor would it be reasonable to assume that Shakespeare thought that that university had been in existence for five hundred years.

What do these contradictory "facts" tell us? Karl Elze, the nineteenth-century German critic thinks that Shakespeare's reason for using Wittenberg as Hamlet's school was that, "Shakespeare had to send the *Dane* Hamlet to some *northern* university, and probably none other was so well known to him or to his audience as Wittenberg." In other words, the decision to use this particular school was more an expedient measure than anything else, not a deeply considered point of reference; certainly it does, however, indicate to us that Shakespeare considered Hamlet a Renaissance figure rather than a medieval one. The play fits much more the sixteenth century than it does the eleventh in spite of the fact that the legend has its roots in the latter. Godwin probably was aware of the possibilities but chose to ignore them in order to satisfy his desire to be "historically accurate." This same problem will face the designer of today many times during his career.

In the cinema version of *Camelot,* all the designers knew that they were working with a legend that supposedly took place before the sixth century A.D. Nevertheless, they consciously used design elements which spanned a time period of over nine hundred years. One complete scene, for instance (the "Lusty Month of May" song and dance sequence), took its entire visual motivation—setting, costume, atmosphere—from Botticelli's *Primavera,* a painting created in or around 1477. The designer often uses an anachronistic detail (or as in this case, a whole series of details) not through ignorance but from the need to reinforce a theme or bridge a gap in understanding that may be caused by differences in time.

Interpretation of a play is rarely in the hands of the designer alone, nor are even all the visual aspects of the production. While he has the prime responsibility for the way it appears to an audience, his decisions are almost always the product of more than one mind, more than the reflection of a single artistic sensibility. Jan Kott, in his book *Shakespeare Our Contemporary,* sums up the problem that interpretation precipitates when the members of a production ask themselves the question, "How are we going to set this play, in what style and period?"

> *Hamlet* cannot be played simply. This may be the reason why it is so tempting to producers and actors. Many generations have seen their own reflections in this play. The genius of *Hamlet* consists, perhaps, in the fact that the play can serve as a mirror. An ideal *Hamlet* would be one most true to Shakespeare and most modern at the same time. Is this possible? I do not know. But we can only appraise any Shakespearean production by asking how much there is of Shakespeare in it, and how much of us.
>
> What I have in mind is not a forced topicality, a *Hamlet* that would be set in a cellar of young existentialists. *Hamlet* has been performed, for that matter, in evening dress and in circus tights; in medieval armour and in Renaissance costume. Costumes do not matter. What matters is that through Shakespeare's text we ought to get at our modern experience, anxiety and sensibility.
>
> There are many subjects in *Hamlet.* There is politics, force opposed to morality; there is discussion of the divergence between theory and practice, of the ultimate purpose of life; there is tragedy of love, as well as family drama; political, eschatological and metaphysical problems are considered. There is everything you want, including deep psychological analysis, a bloody story, a duel, and general slaughter. One can select at will. But one must know what one selects, and why.

"But one must know what one selects, and why." This could very well become the touchstone of the designer's philosophy of interpretation.

The past cannot be re-created, only evoked. If there is one thing to be learned from the Belasco experiments which finally made visual authenticity the only standard in scene design, it is that following this practice (although few do today) almost always produces the opposite effect desired; the minuteness of detail, out of context as it must always be in the theater, puts the attention of the audience in the wrong place—on the setting, not the performer seen within it. What is more, it provokes the audience into a situation detrimental to the total production: the more "real" the setting, the more intense the desire on the part of this audience to discover its secret, that is, seek out the unreality they know is there. Given time they will; this cannot be done, however, except at the expense of the actor and the play.

§13
Research into Designs

The young designer might well ask, "When do I do the exterior research, when the interior?" The answer is, there is no possible way to determine an absolute and definite priority. Nor will it take the student designer long to realize that research on an actual project doesn't lend itself to easy categorization or a fill-in-the-blanks approach. When he comes face to face with the myriad paths that lead to the research material he needs for his design, the steps are not always clearly or logically defined, the road not marked, and directions on how to get to the information he wants are often vague and confusing. Perhaps the only real hard and fast statement that can be made about the whole process is that one thing found almost invariably gives rise and meaning to what follows—sometimes, but not always. Research, as stated earlier, lies not so much in the ability to assemble a number of clear, independent and unrelated watch-part facts into a predetermined form as in the careful and often tedious tracking of a *feeling* (for want of a better word) through an uncharted labyrinth of information, some of which is spectacular and visually exciting but not really useful or appropriate to the design, some of which is deceptively simple but useful and necessary. Many designers, while not always admitting it aloud, are not altogether sure of what they are looking for; sometimes it takes time for them to give meaning and importance to what at first is the vaguest of feelings that what they have found is, indeed, important. But part of the artist's working technique and function is to recognize the useful and correct detail even when it is accidently encountered, even if he has no *real* reason for feeling as he does. This does not mean the designer-researcher is nothing more than a supersensitive but unthinking receiving machine which merely absorbs and then proceeds to capitalize on its accidental finds; rational selection, careful tracking of clues, and the ability to reject the easy solution are also fundamental parts of his working procedure. The point to be made here is, however, that an openly inquisitive nature is as important as skill in painting or a working knowledge of stagecraft techniques and practices. This type of curiosity and interest in the search for the "right" way is in itself a highly important and integral part of the designer's artistic apparatus even though it is not as wholly predictable or as completely under his rational control as is skillful brushwork or perfect drafting technique.

In most instances, the designer is working from two poles, from opposite points in a spectrum of factual possibilities and production needs. On the one hand, he is concerned with the "facts," that information he gains from study of historical or documented materials. This information will, of course, influence his designs no matter how abstractly or theatrically he uses it (fig. 39). On the other hand, he is working also from the interior needs of the production (both factual and symbolic) and especially with the needs of the performers themselves (both physical and psychological [fig. 40]).

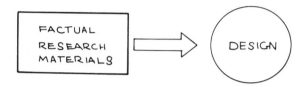

39. *Design process diagram*

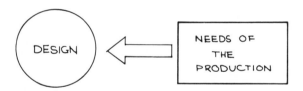

40. *Design process diagram*

Before proceeding to the next section, let us try to understand just what is happening in the designer's mind—on both the conscious and subconscious levels—during this period of gestation. Figure 41 is a diagram that attempts to show how this process operates. Perhaps it will clarify—if only a little—the uniqueness of the designer's purpose. The forces and influences that affect the stage-setting design include:

A. The written script—the needs of the production (the actor's, director's and technician's needs). This we determine in large part from our internal research.

B. Factual material concerning period, etc.—this we determine from investigation as outlined in "External Research."

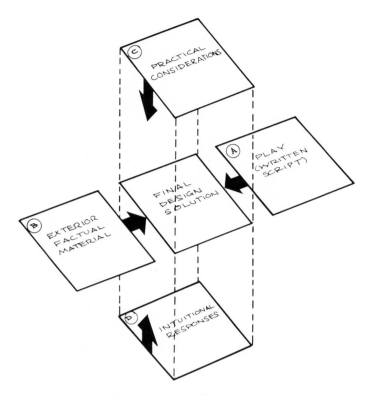

41. *Forces and influences that affect the stage-setting design*

These were discussed in detail in an earlier section. They play a great part in the designer's conscious logical work pattern. But, as every working designer knows, these are not the only materials that condition how he works or what he must eventually accomplish. He must also realize that there are:

C. Practical considerations—limitations of budget, inadequacies of stage facilities, time deadlines, and (not least in every producing organization), oppositions from others concerned with the production. These are all present-oriented problems and also tend to be limiting in nature.

But, although these three categories comprise the rational and logical part of the designer's task, there is one more area to be considered and this, in large part, determines the artistic value of the designer's accomplishment:

D. Intuitional responses and decisions—this area is primarily past-oriented; it is made up of personal preferences, a backlog of known facts, previous solutions to design problems (other scene designs), and prejudices. This area, depending upon the bent of the individual artist, may be traditional and conservative in nature or radical and revolutionary. This area, being subconscious for the most part, is the most difficult one for the designer to bring into use let alone master.

It is easy to understand, therefore, that the design of a stage setting can never be a simple straight-line accomplishment as the solving of a problem in mathematics might be. And, of course, one should expect the use of these areas in the design process to assume different proportions with different projects; the work done on and the thinking behind *The Odd Couple* will have little in common with the effort expended on *Macbeth*.

(One of the best explanations of how the artist's mind works and of the very nature of artistic creation itself, is contained in *The Hidden Order of Art,* by Anton Ehrensweig, published by Weidenfeld & Nicolson, London. This is a difficult book to read but is nevertheless highly recommended to any student deeply concerned with his own conscious and unconscious processes as well as those of artists working in other fields. This book belongs in the serious designer's permament library and can be read many times with profit.)

§14
The Designer's Library

In the Introduction to this book, mention has already been made of the need for the designer to possess a library of research materials and pertinent texts. The list of suggested readings at the end of each section, it was noted, comprise the basis of this library, hopefully the nucleus of a larger more comprehensive one.

Most designers are (or soon become) avid collectors of books and printed materials. Of course this is understandable since the mature designer not only uses this material directly in his work, but also allows it to trigger his imagination. (Imagination, which is an indisputable part of the designer's art, has a voracious appetite and needs constant feeding. There is no doubt that many designers develop early this craving to collect visual materials.)

The designer today, however, is much more fortunate than those who started even fifteen years ago; the printing of low and medium priced paperback art books had had a tremendous growth during this period. At the same time, there has been a phenomenal interest in printing visual subject matter that would not have had a market before this period. Pictorial records of private and public buildings, detailed studies of architecture, furniture, etc., are being brought to the general public in a diversity unparalleled in printing history. One of the most helpful developments, especially to the scenic designer seeking a more comprehensive understanding of not only a period or a style but the social and economic reasons behind them, is the fairly recent emergence of a number of books that deal with a relatively brief period but present the various activities of the period in visual terms and in great depth. These books "show" history rather than just describe it in words; they not only trace political history but also take into consideration the social trends and demonstrate how, in any one age, different countries reacted to and produced variations on prevalent styles. Many of these books, it must be admitted, are expensive, but the designer should consider them extremely wise investments. And while the acquisition of books, even the lower priced ones, will always be an expense, the practice of buying them on a regular basis somehow seems the easiest and least expensive way to acquire a library. (Any book the designer buys to use in his work is, by the way, tax deductible, as are his art materials.) A personal library is, and I think there are few designers who will not corroborate this, a positive means by which the artist continues to grow in his profession.

§15
A Filing System for the Scene Designer

Another source of visual materials (and an extremely important one) is the collection of loose materials—single photographs, clippings from magazines, brochures, etc. Most designers, in addition to their libraries, also maintain extensive file collections. These files are as important to a designer's efficient operation and productivity as is the dictionary or encyclopedia to a research scholar. But the designer cannot purchase this system ready-assembled as he might a set of books; he must, rather, build it up slowly and over a long period of time. Many designers have collections accumulated over years. No designer is capable of storing in his mind all the images, bits of visual information, sources of supply, all those innumerable items which he needs in his day-to-day operation. Much of this material has a short-lived general exposure, in magazines and newspapers for example, which makes it imperative that the designer keep his eye open and his scissors handy at all times. A file system, therefore, is the only effective method of

42. *Suzanne Lalique's design for Molière's* Le Bourgeois Gentilhomme

keeping track of all the various pieces of information that constantly present themselves to the designer's attention.

(The designer in New York City is especially fortunate since the New York Public Library maintains an extremely large picture and clipping collection; most professional designers make extensive use of this service.)

Just how directly this visual information can be used varies greatly from production to production and each designer ultimately must decide how much or how little of an original source to use. Some designers are very eclectic while others rely heavily on an already existing image. This is undoubtedly true of Susanne Lalique's famous design for *Le Bourgeois Gentilhomme* (fig. 42). Although she simplifies the structure of the room considerably and lightens the tonality, this design still owes a great deal to an actual room in Danzig, Germany, built around 1660 (fig. 43).

Below is a suggested list of file folder headings that should be sufficient for the beginning theater artist. A good file system, like a good personal library, conscientiously kept and periodically consulted and

43. *German room, from* Deutsche Wohn-Und Festraume Aus 6 Jahrhunderten. *Courtesy of Verlag Von Julius Hoffmann, Stuttgart*

revamped, will save the designer many hours of outside research away from his studio and keep him constantly on the alert for new visual and technical information. Of course, as this system grows, it will be necessary not only to add new headings, but to subdivide and refine those already in existence.

Many designers, in addition to the file headings, also open a separate file for each production they design. They begin this file at the start of the project and add to it all the information they collect during the time they are actively engaged in the production. In this file one might expect to find not only initial ideas, sources, and working drawings but also photos of the production, lighting cue sheets, property plots, costs and estimates, notes and communications with the director, reviews, etc.

File Folder Headings

Source   1—Interiors (broken into periods and styles)
Source   2—Architecture (broken into periods and styles)
Source   3—Architectural Detail
Source   4—Exteriors and Vistas
Source   5—Trees and Plants
Source   6—Furniture (broken into periods and styles)
Source   7—Ornament and Decoration
Source   8—Windows and Doors
Source   9—Machines, Factories, Etc.
Source   10—Set Ideas (photos and drawings with striking images, rough-idea sketches)
Sculpture
Paintings
Materials 1—Paint
Materials 2—Fabric
Materials 3—Wood
Materials 4—Miscellaneous (new materials, plastic, etc.)
Stage Equipment and Hardware
Working Drawings 1—Flats
Working Drawings 2—Profile Pieces
Working Drawings 3—Plastic Pieces (3-dimensional)
Working Drawings 4—Properties and Furniture
Working Drawings 5—Floor Plans
Light 1—Instruments, Control, and Support
Light 2—Color Mediums
Light 3—Projection of Scenery Data
Light 4—Light Plots
Properties 1—Historical Visual Materials
Properties 2—Sources (catalogues, dealers)
Properties 3—Construction and Materials
Properties 4—Property Plots
Costume 1—Materials

Costume 2—Construction
Costume 3—Accessories
Costume 4—Sources (catalogues)
Special Effects (fire, fog, rain, snow, etc.)
Photo 1—Set
Photo 2—Models
Photo 3—Costume
Photo 4—Miscellaneous
Stagecraft Procedures
Scene Painting Techniques
Stages and Auditoriums
Scene Designs (by other designers)
Scene Designer's Articles
Production Articles

§16
"Stage Design for the Epic Theatre:
An Evaluation of Caspar Neher"

By Bertolt Brecht

We often begin rehearsing without any knowledge of the stage designs, and our friend merely prepares small sketches of the episodes to be played (for instance, six people grouped around a working-class woman, who is upbraiding them). Perhaps we then find that in the text there are only five people in all, for our friend is no pedant; but he shows the essential, and a sketch of this sort is always a small and delicate work of art. Whereabouts on the stage the woman is to sit, and her son and her guests, is something we find out for ourselves, and that is where our friend seats them when he comes to construct the set. Sometimes we get his designs beforehand, and then he helps us with groupings and gestures; not infrequently also with the differentiation of the characters and the way they speak. His set is steeped in the atmosphere of the play, and arouses the actor's ambition to take his place in it.

He reads plays in a masterly fashion. Take just one example. In *Macbeth*, Act I, scene vi, Duncan and his general Banquo, invited by Macbeth to his castle, praise the castle in the famous lines:

> This quest of summer,
> The temple-haunting martlet does approve,
> By his loved mansionry, that the Heaven's breath
> Smells wooingly here . . .

Neher insisted on having a semi-dilapidated grey keep of striking poverty. The guests' words of praise were merely compliments. He saw the Macbeths as petty Scottish nobility, and neurotically ambitious.

His sets are significant statements about reality. He takes a bold sweep, never letting inessential detail or decoration distract from the statement, which is an artistic and an intellectual one. At the same time everything has beauty, and the essential detail is most lovingly carried out.

With what care he selects a chair, and with what thought he places it! And it all helps the playing. One chair will have short legs, and the height of the accompanying table will also be calculated, so that whoever eats at it has to take up a quite specific attitude, and the conversation of these people as they bend more than usual when eating takes on a particular character, which makes the episode clearer. And how many effects are made possible by his doors of the most diverse heights!

This master knows every craft and is careful to see that even the poorest furniture is executed in an artistic way, for the symptoms of poverty and cheapness have to be prepared with art. So materials like iron, wood, canvas are expertly handled and properly combined, economically or lavishly as the play demands. He goes to the blacksmith's shop to have the swords forged and to the artificial florist's to get tin wreaths cut and woven. Many of the props are museum pieces.

These small objects which he puts in the actor's hands—weapons, instruments, purses, cutlery, etc.—are always authentic and will pass the closest inspection; but when it comes to architecture—i.e. when he builds interiors or exteriors—he is content to give indications, poetic and artistic representations of a hut or a locality which do honour as much to his imagination as to his power of observing. They display a lovely mixture of his own handwriting and that of the playwright. And there is no building of his, no yard or workshop or garden, that does not also bear the fingerprints, as it were, of the people who built it or who lived there. He makes visible the manual skills and knowledge of the builders and the ways of living of the inhabitants.

In his designs our friend always starts with "the people themselves" and "what is happening to or through them." He provides no "decor," frames and backgrounds, but constructs the space for "people" to experience something in. Almost all that the stage designer's art consists in he can do standing on his head. Of course Shakespeare's Rome was different from Racine's. He constructs the poets' stage and it glows. If he wants he can achieve a richer effect with a varied structure of different greys and whites than many other artists with the entire palette. He is a great painter. But above all he is an ingenious storyteller. He knows better than anyone that whatever does not further the narrative harms it. Accordingly he is always content to give indications wherever something "plays no part." At the same time these indications are stimulating. They arouse the spectator's imagination, which perfect reproduction would numb.

He often makes use of a device which has since become an international commonplace and is generally divorced from its sense. That is the division of the stage, an arrangement by which a room, a yard or a place of work is built up to half height downstage while another environment is projected or painted behind, changing with every scene or remaining throughout the play. This second milieu can be made up of documentary material or a picture or a tapestry. Such an arrangement naturally gives depth to the story while acting as a continual reminder to the audience that the scene designer has built a setting: what he sees is presented differently from the world outside the theatre.

This method, for all its flexibility, is of course only one among the many he uses; his settings are as different from one another as the plays themselves. The basic impression is of very lightly constructed, easily transformed and beautiful pieces of scaffolding, which further the acting and help to tell the evening's story fluently. Add the verve with which he works, the contempt he shows for anything dainty and innocuous, and the gaiety of his constructions, and you have perhaps some indication of the way of working of the greatest stage designer of our day.

When I eventually realized how indispensable an imaginative, experienced stage director is to a production, I began to read a script as though I were going to direct it myself. This did not turn me into a director, but it did make me a better designer. It gave me a kind of inner eye, a necessity for all artists.

Jo Mielziner

In the last analysis the designing of stage scenery is not the problem of an architect or a painter or a sculptor or even a musician, but of a poet.

Robert Edmond Jones

Stage sets, theatre must be ignored. All the great playwrights thought outside the theatre. Look at Aeschylus, Sophocles, Shakespeare.

Antonin Artaud

§17
A Note: An Explanation
Concerning Explanations

The following section contains a number of written explanations whose purpose is to expose the reasoning behind scene designs as they were realized on the stage. They were recorded here in order to reveal not only the thinking process which informed those designs, but to demonstrate that there can be a logical approach to the art of scene design as well as an intuitive one.

It might be wise to draw the attention of the student designer to the fact that it will be a rare instance when, at some point during the production of a play, he does not have to defend in some manner, usually verbally, his decisions, explaining how and why he has created a particular design. Such explanations are a customary as well as necessary part of the planning of any production (although they would not be presented, as here, in written form). Naturally it should be expected that the designer will most likely present his ideas in visual terms; but he must also be prepared to communicate in words, when called upon, the reasons behind those ideas. How well the designer uses words varies from person to person; many competent artists find it difficult to "talk" a design without extensive use of pen and pencil. Quite possibly, the real test of a design (apart from its final realization on the stage) lies more in this form of communication than in words or theories. Nevertheless, discussion of the design concept—what it means and how it furthers the aims of the production as a whole—is usually the only sure way the director can determine if he is understanding the designer or, equally important, if the designer is understanding the director's point of view. The danger in talk, however, is that it can all too easily become an end in itself degenerating into vague rationalization which serves no real purpose in the creative process. Nevertheless, as most designers will admit, discussion of ideas is a positive activity which can, when both parties strive for honest exchange of viewpoints, produce results in production more satisfactory (and no less personal) than the efforts of either the designer or director alone.

The ability to explain underlying motives in a design is an important part of the student designer's development, not only so that he may inform others what he is trying to achieve but to make himself aware of these motives as well. Often he will not have a clear understanding of what these are until he has faced the challenge of explaining or defending them to another. It is during this formative stage, moreover, that he should be encouraged to make not only a genuine effort to improve his techniques of verbal communication but to learn the all-important difference between positive defense of an idea and self-protective rationalization. Most important of all, he must learn not to hide behind superficial theories. ("Truth is concrete," according to Bertolt Brecht and so is good theory.) Designers, like almost all other artists generally withdraw from discussions when their ideas or schemes are attacked or refuted; but by carefully thinking out what he will say and why he believes as he does, the designer will have a much better base from which he may present or defend a considered position or design.

From here on all that follows is pretty much a matter of individual critical and artistic judgment. What is presented does not purport to define any universal principles nor suggest that any such principles can be formulated out of these examples. Most of these judgments, although not all, were made by a single person, the author of this study; to that extent they represent a singular and limited point of view. (I prefer the open stage or variations of it even in the proscenium theater rather than strict proscenium theater productions, and this predilection will be fairly obvious.) No apology is made for this situation since a universal point of view isn't possible even if it were desired. It will be noticed too that, while these examples are not given as the final word on or the solution to the design problems inherent in them, what is shown by way of illustration is presented from a predominantly realistic point of view, although not necessarily a naturalistic one. The style of the designs is based less on personal expression (as the designs of Salvador Dali always have been), and more on actual observation of the world as it appears to the outer eye. In other words, the designs presented and discussed will be more likely to resemble figure 44 than figure 45.

While the first design is not an attempt to reconstruct in the theater a replica of an actual room as it might have existed in the O'Neill family home in Connecticut at the turn of the century—the locale and time

44. *Design for* Long Day's Journey into Night

45. *Design for* Three Blind Men

of O'Neill's biographical drama—it is certainly a more realistic representation than is the setting for the de Ghelderode play, which in no way tries to show how the countryside in the province of Brabant looked during the sixteenth century. The reason for this particular emphasis here is not a prejudice against imaginative designs; it is that, as interesting as they might be in themselves, they are too subjective, too personal to have much value in demonstrating the process of design which is our real focus. (Besides, there are many designs that simply cannot be "explained" but still may be artistically right for the productions they serve. The examples that were selected are those which allow discussion—if not final justification—of this design process rather than of the artistic merit of the individual designer or his results.) This process is, it is hoped, a fairly logical one (although it never can be that completely), at least to the degree that it might aid the student new to the study of stage design to gain some insight into the conceptual considerations that all designers—no matter how intellectual or intuitive—must face in the practice of their art. The prime reason for this book is to show that it is possible—perhaps even unavoidable—to study and build on this process. Intuition, personal insight, perception, difference in exposure, past experience—all valuable to the individual artist in guiding his work—are not our primary subjects here, although it will never be possible to preclude them altogether.

§18
From Text to Designs

We must now begin to consider the process by which the written words of the text engender visual ideas for the designer; the subjective limitless world of the imagination must begin to come to terms with the objective limits of the stage. This is an extremely critical juncture; it is the time when the designer must begin to direct his attention to the range of possibilities open to him and, more important, begin to make selections from and judgments on those possibilities. Yet the problem is never the same from production to production; some scripts tell more than others, some tell little at all, some tell on the wrong things (at least in their written stage directions). But formal research into period or decorative style, important as it will be at a later time, is not the primary focus at this point.

If, as will be suggested in the next few pages, the first reading of the play quite possibly is the single most influential creative act in designing (not all would agree with this contention completely however), then the step under consideration here (actually, not one simple step but a complex of related ones) is certainly next in importance since it will begin to define, no matter how crudely and tentatively, the outer boundaries of the design and will represent the designer's personal concepts—his intuitions and rational decisions—in their most fundamental form. Although an exciting step in the design process, it is also a formidable one. Quite possibly this is the period when the designer's intuitive powers operate most strongly; but, since in almost every instance, that is, at the beginning of every production, many more ideas and possible solutions will present themselves than the designer can ever use or fully investigate, it is potentially a dangerous period. Knowing what to reject, what to pursue and refine, is every bit as important as getting an idea in the first place; most designers, while they find this period to be an exciting one, also suffer anxiety as they explore the various possibilities open to them. And it is rare, most designers will assure you, when the first ideas and drawings prove to be the right and final ones. (The fact that young designers sometimes quickly do stumble onto a successful design is, and should be seen for what it is, an accident, not a method of work one should attempt to build a career on.)

Yet these initial visual thoughts do have some merit; they may very well contain in an unrefined form the seeds of ideas which will eventually prove useful in the final stages of the design. Also, during this period, the designer should trust least his painting and drawing skills. By this I mean, that he should not begin to "decorate" the scene by making detailed or finished sketches until he has determined the skeleton or dramatic structure of it. This framework can only be derived from a thorough analyzation and understanding of what the text does say, and, sometimes more important, what it leaves unsaid. It would be well to recall the words of Peter Brook quoted earlier:

> What is necessary, however, is an incomplete design; a design that has clarity without rigidity; one that could be called "open" as against "shut." This is the essence of theatrical thinking: a true theatre designer will think of his designs as being all the time in motion, in action, in relation to what the actor brings to a scene as it unfolds. . . . The later he makes his decisions, the better.

§19
Reading the Script: Some Initial Considerations

To read is to translate, for no two persons' experiences are the same. A bad reader is like a bad translator: he interprets literally when he ought to paraphrase and paraphrases when he ought to interpret literally. In learning to read well, scholarship, valuable as it is, is less important than instinct; some great scholars have been poor translators.

W. H. Auden, *The Dyer's Hand*

Playwrights, no matter how abstractly they work, almost always conceive of their characters as springing from and existing in a specific set of circumstances, in a particular kind of environment; in other words, their people live in a world that is real enough no matter how strange and foreign that world may be. Yet, in the playwright's art, many things must be sacrificed to the limitations of the play form. He cannot, as the novelist is able to do, give us detailed background data about the place where the people he is concerned with live or what this background is like. (While stage directions can tell a certain amount, the playwright is still much more limited in this respect than the novelist; the playwright also runs the risk of having his directions ignored by producers, a liberty most novel readers would probably never consider.) In some cases this situation doesn't really concern him all that much; a study of practically any playwright of the sixteenth or seventeenth century would bear this out. But when he does have definite ideas about the setting of his play, most playwrights find that the nature of play form is such that it restricts him almost completely to revealing this information to the audience in the theater through dialogue between the characters. Often we must piece out the necessary facts from oblique references. Even when the playwright does attempt to disclose pertinent information in stage directions, he not only is limited in space, he is powerless when others begin to interpret those directions to suit themselves.

Mordecai Gorelik, in his course the Scenic Imagination, maintains that one of the most creative acts a designer ever performs is the first reading of the play he is to design. First impressions may not always be workable or even accurate, but few will deny these first thoughts are extremely important and often make lasting marks on the creative mind, especially that part of the mind below the conscious level. Even though one's initial judgment may be later amended or reversed, those first impressions still have some elemental effect, still have weight. To a young designer, the reading of a play he is to design is usually an exciting and pleasurable experience, and he can not usually bring to it a backlog of hackneyed solutions to the problems it presents (nor often as much original imagination as he might like to believe). Later, as he reads more plays and designs more productions, he will begin to think in terms of former solutions; it is unavoidable. While this accumulated information and experience forms the basis of his knowledge and skill, it is not without its negative features; it can also be a danger to his continuing creativity. (Especially if he is seeking a "style" by which to identify himself.) This problem besets many artists in other fields but it is especially true for those in the theater where reliability is generally more trusted than creative originality. In the professional New York theater, for instance, more than one designer has been "typed" in much the same manner as actors: in the 1930s if one wanted a factory or run-down tenement building Howard Bay was the designer to get; if an elegant interior was needed, no one was better than Raymond Sovey, and so on and so forth. Still, to read the three hundredth play with the same kind of attention and response as one read the third is not possible even for the most creative designer. And yet, if he is to continue to develop new insights and renew his art with the passage of time, he must constantly keep this problem in mind. For once the designer loses the sense of excitement and challenge that an unfamiliar play, or even a familiar one, can produce, it is almost impossible to create a living design for it.

Many designers have also indicated that they believe this first reading should be done with little regard to the mechanical workings of the theater stage plant. This is not surprising since flats and backdrops and revolving stages have little place in the unlimited world of imagination. Important as the physical theater and its techniques are, they represent only the means by which the designer's visions are implemented, they should not be allowed to limit his thinking. It could be a great mistake by a designer to attempt visualization of the play on a stage during this important first reading. The world of imagination should not have a stage-right or stage-left orientation.

It might well be asked if all imagination—that process of seeing something in the mind—is not the same kind of activity. Perhaps it is in its most basic definition; but in the theater imagination must, by necessity, have a more specific function and more precise definition, especially when considered in relation to the designer's role. The methods by which imagination is brought to the stage, the very nature of it, differs greatly from how it is employed in poetry, painting, or music. This difference is a very practical one to the scene designer. In poetry or literature the object of the written word is most often to summon up images in the mind of a single person; the mind is the surface, the screen, on which these images find their form. No matter how vivid these mental images are to the individual, however, it is and always will remain a private "showing." No one can see these images but the person either reading the work or hearing it read.

The designer, on the other hand, does deal in imagery, but in a very special way. When he reads a play, it first exists, as with anyone else, only as a conceptual image, or rather, as a succession of images, since theater is, even in the mind, a time-space art and can never, as a painting or piece of sculpture can be, be seen all at once or contained in a single image. The difference between the function of the designer and the person who reads a play for his own pleasure and is accountable to no one for what he imagines is that the designer cannot stop there; he must create an outward manifestation of the images he perceives. His job is dependent on how well he is able to do this.

The business of the scene designer, then, is to make visible what at first exists nowhere but in the mind, and, difficult as this may be, it is complicated by the fact that he must also include in his visions those of the director and—when he writes specific directions in addition to the play dialogue—those of the playwright, bringing into some union what must be at first numerous incomplete and divergent ideas and points of view. But, to repeat, these images are set in motion, if not actually called into being, by the words of the text. While there seems to be less and less respect for the sanctity of the written script (most playwrights deplore the professional theater's treatment of their scripts—see *The*

Seesaw Log, by William Gibson, for one author's views on this subject—but find they are all but powerless to do anything about the situation) most designers and directors still attempt to present this text as they think the author would wish to have it interpreted.

But the designer of the mid-twentieth century has become less a reporter of the external appearance of environments and more a synthesizer of environmental qualities and, at times, a creator of totally new ones. *Waiting for Godot,* for example, requires the designer to provide a landscape that exists no place on earth; it is, rather, a landscape of the mind he is asked to create. Nor is this play unique in this respect. The designer has been required more and more not only to create places that were or could be found outside the theater, but also places that never could exist anywhere but in a theater.

The translation of words into images, subjective as this activity is, is the designer's primary purpose in the theater. It is the performance of this function which allows him to consider his contribution as a service on the same level as that of the director and actor. Yet student designers often have difficulty in explaining to others initial feelings and verbal reactions to the pervading qualitites they perceive in the scripts they are studying. Moreover, they tend to be too general in their descriptions of what and how they feel concerning mood and atmosphere, too fuzzy in their thinking and ability to communicate these impressions to another—the director, for instance. And for this very reason, they actually miss a great deal in the script which they would not miss if their communication skills were more refined. Ideas conveyed in words can and do produce concrete directions and results. Now, perhaps it is too much to ask of the designer, especially in his formative and training period, to be able to paint word pictures of what he "feels" ; nevertheless, attempting to find exact and specific words that somehow summon up images in the mind is a necessity, not only in dealing with others who are concerned with the visual aspects of the production, such as the director, but for himself as well; it helps him recognize what he is seeking when he does begin to search for objective correlatives of those abstract impressions and feelings.

One of the very first things I ask of students in our classroom discussions of their design projects is that they give the rest of the group the qualities of their selected plays in words that contain visual clues. At first they find it difficult; the words they often select are usually too abstract and general. (The real source of their difficulty lies in the fact, however, that they don't really think such an exercise is "serious.") Often the student will employ words like "colorful" or "old." When he is questioned further (and sometimes goaded) he will begin to narrow down his vision and bring a sharper focus to what he is trying to say; he has to think about what he is thinking about. He is forced to be less diffuse in his description and more specific. After some discussion he finds he can be much more precise in making others understand what he means. He also finds, as he does this, that his own understanding gains depth when he tries harder to make his feelings clear to others. After each student is subjected to this form of cross-examination, sometimes an ordeal, they almost all begin to see (from being on both sides of the fence—the one who explains and the one to whom something is being explained) that certain words are better than others, that some have more value, are more specific and precise than others. For instance, tinseled, sleazy, rickety, translucent, iridescent, mossy, gritty, metallic are better than colorful, heavy, dark, old, rich, grand.

Eventually the designer must make good the impressions and images he summons up in his discussions of his design concepts, but he should let himself range over a wide spectrum of possibilities during this phase. Notice how Robert O'Hearn, the designer of the Metropolitan Opera production of Richard Strauss's *Die Frau ohne Schatten,* gives his ideas (in the September 17, 1966 issue of *Opera News*), as to how he came to select the particular ideas and impressions he eventually incorporated into his designs:

> *Die Frau ohne Schatten* is one of the most difficult of operas to design, since it takes place not only in a fantasy world but in three fantasy worlds. It has not one but two stories to tell: the fairy-tale one we see and hear, and a very elaborate philosophical one running neck and neck with it. The real meanings are purposely hidden and the clues confused, so the designer must venture on a detective hunt. . . .
>
> . . . We decided that *Die Frau* should be placed in no specific country. Rather, the design should reflect the mood and meaning of each scene and world: a bluish icy-cold, glassy, jeweled world for the Empress, a warm red-earthy world of men for the Dyer and his steaming vats, a black-and-silver world of iridescent rock and winglike forms for the spirits. Also, water—physically and symbolically, the water of life—is important from the first utterance of the Nurse on and should be shown as shimmering light reflections from water, fountains and a tremendous real waterfall for the apotheosis. . . .
>
> In plot and mood the second act goes from light to darkness, the third from darkness to light. For the third act I planned a rainbow progression, starting with black and purple

for the grotto and going through blue to green to yellow green to golden yellow for the final burst of daylight and humanity.

. . . The architectural-research and mulling-over period. This meant dispensing with tempting Siamese and Indian temples, turning instead to enlarged photos of microscopic organisms and minerals, studies of jewels and branched quartz. We searched for unusual materials—transparent plastics, oily iridescent surfaces. . . .

The important Dyer's house went through about ten versions, from a darkly real Japanese interior to a sculptural abstraction something like the inside of a broken clay pot (or womb?) lit by a volcanic fireplace. In other words, relevant forms based on nature superseded real period detail to bring out the basic motives. The veined texture of the curved walls was suggested by a photo blow-up of the eye of a frog. . . .

. . . I tried to use in the model the unconventional materials of the real sets: plastics, crushed glass, jewels, crinkled metal-foil surfaces, etc.

§20
Environment: Creating a Living Atmosphere for the Actor

If it is true that the scene designer is, as Robert Edmond Jones has written, an "artist of occasions," it is equally true that he is an artist of environment. Although not quite the same, these two designations do work hand in hand; what is done is somehow caused by or reflected in where it is being done.

In the theater we think of environment in two major ways; first, its effect on a character or characters (and their reaction to it) and, secondly, its effect on an audience. Environment often is a means of delineating character or story. Playwrights are careful in the selection of an environment—not only the immediate locale but the surrounding area as well—but have limited resources to insure their personal wishes will be respected and observed; while some, as we have earlier noted, try to give this information in various forms of stage directions, their wishes concerning actions of the characters are more likely to be observed than the playwright's notes as to where those actions will be performed. They cannot, as the novelist does, "spell it out." A few have even admitted that it is not only out of their hands but outside their understanding: Michel de Ghelderode for one.

In the theater, the function of the environment does not have a single purpose. While the most important of these purposes is to provide an appropriate place for the action of the play to take place, an auxiliary function is to underscore the mood and atmosphere of those actions. The environment should rarely, however, do this in an overt fashion; certainly it should not, except in very special cases, do the business of the actor. That is, it should not tell the story or usurp the attention that is rightfully his. (I have seen many productions where the setting was so explicit and so overpoweringly atmospheric that the actors simply could not compete; visual reticence is not the least of the designer's virtues.) Environment in life outside the theater is often subtle, its effects not easily seen from day to day. It should be equally subtle when used in the theater no matter what the subject matter or what kind of play it serves. This does not lessen its importance to the production or to the actor; a strong production is usually one where all its constituent parts are in balance.

But what is environment in the theater? How is it brought into the design of a setting? For what purposes is it desired other than as visual background or to create what we call a mood? Two questions are always present when the designer begins to consider the environment. These are:

1. How will this environment help the actor to display more of his character's possibilities in terms of action than he could without it?

2. How will this environment increase the depth of visual understanding of an audience and thus deepen their total appreciation of the production?

Let us suppose that a script calls for an alley in a large city. The designer might create something that would look like figure 46. He is well aware of the fact, though, that the environment in this setting consists of two basic parts. Figure 47 shows the background portion of the set; its function is to provide a large part of the atmosphere of an alley by describing it visually, as it were, with brick walls. But all those things that an actor can make use of or that affect his movement (aside from the walls) have been removed.

Figure 48 shows exactly the opposite situation. Here all the things that affect the actor's movement are left and the walls are removed. It can be seen, however, that the sense of the environment still remains, perhaps more so than in figure 46. There is no doubt, either, that figure 47 is more important to the actor and that he will relate to it, quite possibly make use of it, much more than he would figure 46. Even

46. *Environment diagram with background and physical properties*

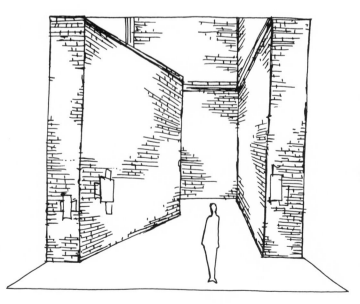

47. *Environment diagram with background only*

143

48. *Environment diagram with physical properties only*

visually figure 47 is more important than figure 46. If a choice had to be made between the two, as it would be necessary if this alley were to be put into an open stage form such as figure 49, there is little doubt which had to be cut out and which retained. But, in any form of staging—arena, three-quarter or proscenium arch theater—the principle exposed here would remain basically true; environment is not only visual, it is physical as well.

There are good reasons for considering the physical aspects of environment more closely today than even ten years ago. Until recently an actor's performance requirement had become almost entirely psychological and was structured along these lines:

1. Thought—analyzation of text and script directions to determine "inner motivation." The great emphasis put on this step was in reaction to the virtual thoughtlessness of the philosophy of acting during the nineteenth century which put its emphasis on individual bravura performance, beauty of voice and grandiloquent styles of delivery.

2. Verbal reaction—rehearsed and set in rehearsal to produce as little variation in performance as possible.

3. And, only after these two steps were assured, action.

The actor got his basic interpretation from paying more attention to the first two steps and then allowing the director to impose a pattern of

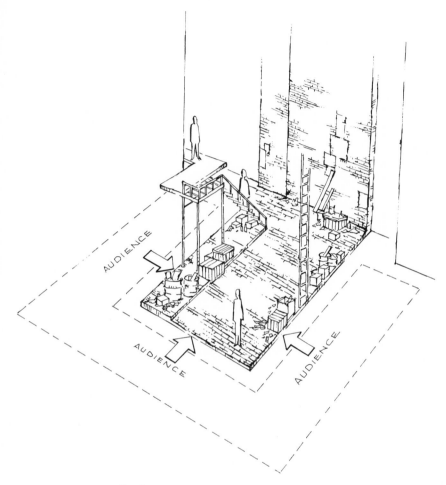

49. *Environment diagram developed for open stage*

action on him after he had mastered those. In actual life, words rise out of actions as well as actions resulting from words; in the theater, all too often, actions become secondary to the words. Still, this prevalent philosophy has resulted in the idea that the actor's primary function is to make his (and the playwright's) intentions plain through verbal communication whenever possible with action as an auxiliary adjunct to this performance. But now the trend in performance philosophy (and this has spread to any great degree only in the past decade) is to make movement and physical involvement with the scenic environment at least coequal in importance (if not more) with verbal utterance. And while this reversal of priorities is by no means universal, it has had a marked effect on actor's training programs throughout the whole world of theater. It is quite possible that the most significant companies of our period have created a whole new set of priorities unique in the theater history of Western civilization: (1) Physical action ⇄ verbal reaction; (2) and—in a poor second place—original meaning of the intent of the written text (if one exists).

The recent Peter Brook production of *A Midsummer Night's Dream,* for example, used circus equipment—notably trapezes—which the actors were required to use in the performance of their roles. (While this might seem to be a "stunt" device imposed on the play, it had a curiously appropriate application to this production; the circus elements used by Brook's performers helped to reveal a whole new aspect of this particular play.) What this trend plainly indicates (and it cannot be passed off simply as a fad) is that the actor is being forced—and is forcing himself—into a much more active relationship with the physical aspects of the stage.

The basic problem for the designer, therefore, is to bring two desires of the present-day theater together; that is, to create a scenic environment that not only shows abstract qualities of the production directly, but one that also makes these qualities (or the forms they assume) physically accessible to the actor so that he may use them or be channelled by them.

While the creation of an environment, as we have noted, is not restricted to naturalistic settings alone, for our purposes it is easiest to see and understand in that context; it is hard to conceive of *The Lower Depths,* for instance, in a setting that did not present graphically and explicitly to an audience the abject conditions of the people who must live there. Still, the fashioning of an environment on the stage is not limited to reproduction of accurate detail or completely factual documentation. Very often the designer must abstract the qualities of an environment for a design rather than creating a locale that might plausibly exist or pass for the actual place. The result might very well be, in fact, a creation that could exist nowhere but on a stage in a theater and still serve as an authentic environment for the play and the characters in it. As a matter of fact, it is impossible to lift a real locale, such as a room, from its natural context and put it on the stage without sacrificing some of its original form to the demands of the stage. For example, the house where Stanley and Stella live in *A Streetcar Named Desire* may very well be in or near the older part of New Orleans, the French

Quarter; and while this area still retains much of its original charm, the actual type of house where the play takes place is, in all probability, of the "shotgun" variety. These houses were built in the late nineteenth century and are designed strictly in the most economical manner—living room in the front, bedroom in the middle, kitchen and bathroom in the rear. They have little in common with much of the older architecture which often exists alongside these newer structures. Actually, there is no strictly residential section in the Quarter; warehouses and private houses coexist side by side (fig. 50).

Too often, though, the designer working on this play ignores this less romantic style of architecture because he becomes intrigued with the more interesting possibilities of the older buildings that exist in the Quarter. He selects the graceful wrought iron and interestingly weathered stone of these buildings in favor of the ill-kept rotting wood and mildewed wallpaper of the later structures. But it is precisely this sec-

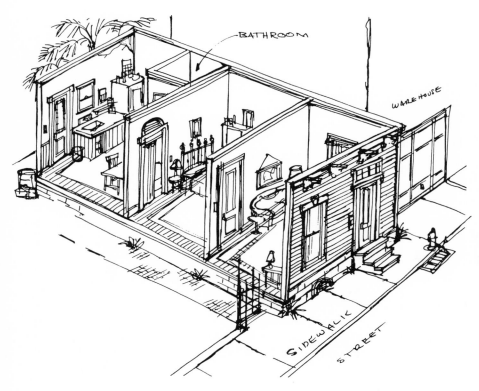

50. *New Orleans house*

ond type of building that creates a more accurate environment for this play to transpire in; the cramped rooms and cheapness of these houses figure greatly in Blanche's final downfall. She is extremely sensitive to her surroundings and this place where she now finds herself is an active force which helps to drive her mad.

Still, one cannot simply reproduce a facsimile of this house on the stage; there the features of the actual location (which quite possibly might also include elements of the older more romantic buildings surrounding this one house) must be taken apart, studied, and then reassembled to fit both the performer's needs in acting the play and the audience's view. Again, as we have said before, the resulting setting may be both a fitting and "real" environment for the play as well as a creation that belongs nowhere except in the theater (fig. 51).

If a designer does nothing more than reproduce without question or thought the findings of his research and documentation, then his designs will have nothing more than the antiquarian atmosphere of a museum, not that of a living and developing place where the characters of the play can live and move. If, on the other hand, he uses documen-

51. *Design for* A Streetcar Named Desire

tation in its proper role, that is to reinforce the intuitive solutions that he has distilled from study of the text, he will find that the specific needs of the play often will dictate much of what can be used and what may be disregarded. This ability to select, reject, and simplify is, if you study the body of work of a mature designer, something that grows over the years and is the hallmark of the disciplined artist. In *Designing for the Theatre,* Jo Mielziner takes himself to task for failure to select, reject, and simplify:

> As late as 1931, when I should have known better, I committed an equal offense against honest theatre with my settings for Schnitzler's *Anatol.* I looked upon this lush and lavish production of love and high life in old Vienna as a banquet table arrayed with tempting delicacies exclusively for me. Scene after scene offered an opportunity for elaborate pictorialization, and I seized each one greedily. It was one of the first times in my career that I received widespread praise from the critics, and there was applause from the audience every time the curtain went up on a new scene. But the fact was that my settings usurped attention that properly belonged to the script and the actors. The nine settings were nine separate and attractive pictures in which the scenes played, and played well, but there was no unity to the production. It would have been better to sacrifice the completeness or charm of an individual set in order to lighten the production, speed the changes, and bring harmony to the evening as a whole.

There has been a trend during the past two hundred years for the playwright to become increasingly more specific in his placement of action and in the description of the necessary details of the setting of his play. At one time, those in charge of creating a visual picture (scenery) for the stage merely provided the place described by the playwright and only that place. If the play required a front parlor, or a palace, or a garden, the designer would feel that he had fulfilled his obligation when he had provided the features specifically set down by the playwright. (Quite often he read not much more of the play than the directions at the beginning of acts or scenes.) During the fairly recent past, the designer's attention was focused on and ended at the boundaries set by the playwright and those things which lay inside those boundaries; if a room was desired, the designer considered his task completed after he had set the line of the walls, assured the placement of necessary objects within those lines and satisfied himself as to the correctness of the decor. Hardly any attention would be given to the world that lay outside and beyond the immediate area shown on the stage, that area which satisfied the minimum requirements of the script. ("What world?" the designer of eighty years ago would inquire. "The only 'world' behind the set is backstage!") If any of that other world were shown, it would usually be confined to only so much as could be seen through a window or open door; little opportunity for actions outside the room proper would be given the performers.

But then the cinema came into being and later television, both making it not only possible but also desirable to follow the action of a story through a succession of locales rather than confining it to one static place. The unlimited mobility of the camera literally opened up a whole world. Early writers for the film, even though they did not have sound, at first thought as stage playwrights but soon found that stage-writing technique was not at all suitable for the camera, simply did not work, and so began to develop scripts designed to capitalize on the possibilities of the camera's moving eye. In discovering what best suited the needs of that form, other playwrights, and some of these same film writers, began to see the possibilities of film technique on the stage. Many plays since then have been written under the influence of the film (*Death of a Salesman,* to mention but one) and have written into their structure techniques that are essentially cinematic; flashback, montage, cross-fading, all part of the moving picture, is now part of the stage. Cinematic technique in the live theater is now no longer new and some workers in legitimate theater (like Peter Larkin who has complained that many of today's playwrights would do better to stop writing movies for the stage and begin searching for a play form that more nearly suits the live theater) have been critical of this development. Now, in fact, there seems to be a trend away from plays whose form is cinematic.

Nevertheless, something has happened to the designer as a result of the development of the cinema and it is quite possible that this exposure—both to the film and to plays written under the influence of the film—cannot be altogether discounted or forgotten. Having been required to cope with this form of writing, he has begun to apply this same mode of thought to plays not specifically written with such treatment in mind. There is a great body of works, he reasons, written before the advent of the cinema which might also benefit from considering the settings of these plays in a larger visual context than heretofore imagined. Many of the plays might lend themselves to cinematic techniques better than the mode of production they have become associated with.

Let us consider for a moment how plays were produced just prior to the advent of the motion picture. In the last half of the last century almost all plays were given elaborate and cumbersome productions. Shakespeare, for instance, was produced quite literally; every scene was realized on the Victorian stage as completely as carpenters and (especially) painters were able. However, time required in shifting the scenery as well as limited stage space and expense meant that there had to be a priority applied to the settings. Big scenes and long scenes naturally received the most attention; the smaller ones were either incorporated into the larger ones, transposed, or, more likely, cut out entirely. The structure of the play was actually determined by the needs of the scenery, not the other way around. In the last years of the nineteenth century and during the first years of the present one, directors and designers began to see the error of this static approach to Shakespeare as well as to the theater in general. Figure 52 for instance, is a photograph of a setting produced in typical manner of the late 1800s.

Since that time, however, the static picture has given way to the fluid image; scenes no longer end with the lowering of the curtain, they

52. *Church scene for* Much Ado about Nothing. *George Alexander Productions, St. James Theatre,* 1898

dissolve into the next one. The curtain, in many cases, has disappeared altogether even in the proscenium theater. It has been conjectured that if Shakespeare were writing today, he might very well be working for the films or television rather than the stage. Although not a wholly valid assumption, it does point out one significant aspect of his technique of playwriting and that is that much of his effect depends upon a fluidity of action and a variation of locale that is similar to what we experience in the cinema. But while the camera has caused the stage to reevaluate its modes of presentation, something else more fundamental has been slowly eroding the old conceptions of what a stage setting should be, and, more importantly, what it should do.

As early as the first part of the nineteenth century, attitudes toward acting began to change; particularly the actor's involvement with his physical environment on the stage. The time when an actor need not concern himself about character until he has made an entrance, that is, comes into sight of the audience, has long since gone. Practically every serious actor working in the western theater spends much time "building a character"; he not only considers deeply what his inner motivations are while actually on the stage, he gives much thought to what the character has been doing before his entrance and as much effort in deciding what he will do once he has left the audience's immediate view. Undoubtedly some schools of acting have made too much of this practice; some actors, in reaction to the "method" philosophy (the deeply psychological approach to character development) contend that they do not to any great degree think of these characters when not on the stage or in a scene, but their performances often belie this denial (and sometimes unfortunately substantiate their claim). English actors, particularly those of older generations, are often notably antagonistic to this "inside-out" approach to theater. Laurence Olivier, speaking for more than one English actor, is outspoken in his mistrust of too much intellectual analyzation of the actor's motives or his psychological state of mind.

But is this kind of thinking which attempts to understand the past and future of the play the province of the actor or director only; is this extended view of the play, and the speculations it engenders, of no importance to the creative processes of the designer? It is probably every bit as important to the designer as it is to the actor to consider what the script does not say as well as what it specifically demands. Moreover, a great number of designers have come to believe that one of their chief functions is to assist, in whatever way they can, the actor to continue to "be" his character beyond the line set by the script's directions "enter" and "exit"; that in addition to creating the locale definitely needed for the play's primary actions—those stated or implied by the script—the designer must also consider the surrounding environment and, even though the playwright does not specifically call for it in his directions, in some instances provide for it. What is being advocated here, however, is not necessarily a matter of reproducing on the stage a naturalistic copy of a piece of the world outside the theater. The theater of today asks more of the designer (as well as the actor) than mere realism but, like many other artists, his experimental learning processes are often based in realistic observations.

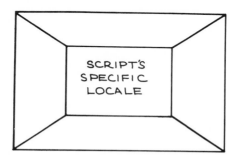

53. *Specific locale*

Until well into this century the designer's task was only to be responsible for a setting that showed a specific locale (fig. 53). In today's theater a play may often require that he be responsible for more than this limited and limiting view; it may ask that he provide a larger more comprehensive context in which the action of the play may develop. (Most of the plays of Tennessee Williams simply cannot be played in a single location; almost all require composite settings.) Even if not directly called upon to do so, the designer may decide to open up the setting (fig. 54).

But what is the import of these two diagrams? How does this concept of expanded interest and vision work? Let us take a look at a drawing made from research materials dealing with a Dublin street during the period that Sean O'Casey wrote *Juno and the Paycock,* the Dublin of the 1920s—the time of the "troubles." It shows a street with buildings that might very well contain an apartment similar to the one described in the script (fig. 55). Another view with a wall removed (Juno and her family live on the second floor) can be seen in figure 56.

The purpose of this inspection is to begin to understand better the relationship of the exteriors of the buildings (those were not difficult to

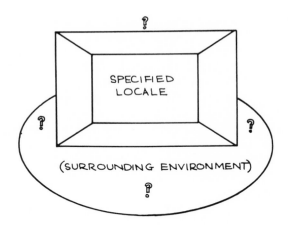

54. *Specific locale and surrounding environment*

find) with interiors (those are comparatively easy to research also).
What the designer must do for himself, however, is reconstruct—as it
has been done here—a view that combines both. That is not so easy to
obtain; and it is at this point that the designer's peculiar function
begins.

55. *Dublin street scene, 1922*

JUNO'S
APPARTMENT
WITH WALL
REMOVED

56. *Apartment building on Dublin street*

Copied from actual photographic sources contemporary with the play's action, matters of detail can be determined concerning the outward form of Juno's flat; it is easy to ascertain styles and details of architecture, building materials, and the effects of age (although not as clearly discernible here as in the photographs from which the drawings were made). However, what is more important is not only how this one building looks (its literal visual description) but how it fits into its greater context; equally important is the "feel" the designer develops by understanding how the particular place the author sets his action relates to its adjoining surroundings. It is quite possible the designer will find a need to employ this information in ways not envisioned by the author or at least not specifically noted by him in the play's specific written directions.

Let us take one example which might help to demonstrate why the designer might need to know more about the environment than would be shown or is evident in the immediate setting—Juno's apartment—or required by the author's explicit description of it:

O'Casey announced that he was going to write a play about a certain Johnny Boyle (an actual person with whom he was acquainted). Later, when he had finished *Juno and the Paycock,* this character, Johnny, had few of the lines in it and was not, apparently, a major character. But, if one examines the play closely, noting not only who speaks and how much, he will find that Johnny is an important structural device; he is not so much an active character as an important pivotal one, one around which the other characters of the drama gravitate and relate, even though the action of the play does not center on him. Indeed, much of the play's meaning and force depends upon and cannot be understood if his function is unclearly realized or presented; the designer can very much help the actor portraying Johnny (and thus the play as a whole) to expose what he thinks and how he feels. While part of the designer's task is to show how Juno has done the best she can to make this tenement flat a home for her family, it is also his obligation to show an audience what Johnny sees as he sits alone, crippled and broken in spirit, looking out of the second story apartment window. What does he see? Row after row of dirty, stained rooftops of other tenement buildings. Bleak structures crowding in on the place he lives, cutting him off from the active life he formerly led before his arm was blown off and his usefulness ended. Much of this play, even if it does not seem to deal directly with it, reveals the influence of the very atmosphere and nature of the neighborhood O'Casey knew and set his play. To concentrate only on the interior of the room where the main action of the play transpires is to ignore more than half of the world O'Casey wants to bring to the stage.

The important part which the visual atmosphere can play is not the only reason to consider what the surrounding environment is like nor the only possible advantage to be derived from exploration of the environment's possible uses. Expanding the limit of what the audience sees means that you also increase the possibilities of what the actor can use. Consider the scene where Joxer, the profligate crony of Captain Boyle, must hide to escape the wrath of Juno: not able to exit through the front door, and not able to escape through a back entrance (there is none), Joxer, on the advice of the Captain, decides to risk hiding on the small roof outside the window. Usually, once he is through the window, the actor is lost to the audience's sight. But, if this area is included in the designer's thinking, the audience will be able to see and appreciate Joxer's precarious position and obvious discomfort more than being told about it later. In a simple box interior (all that O'Casey asked for), these possibilities are lost both to the actor and the audience.

What the designer finds in his research, however, cannot always be used directly; more often than not he must take the elements of an original place apart, recompose and sometimes distort them in order that they may become useful in the final setting as it appears on the stage.

57. *Apartment window*

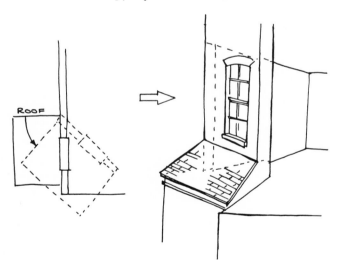

58. *Apartment window in two parts*

The window that might be used for Joxer's place of hiding may exist in an original building although not be completely usable as it is. The designer quite possibly might take a window (fig. 57) and twist it to allow the audience a better view of the outside (fig. 58). Or he might

59. *Apartment wall*

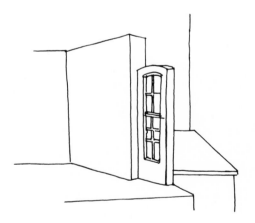

60. *Apartment wall removed*

take a wall (fig. 59) and cut it away, leaving the window, so that more of the outside will be exposed (fig. 60). Perhaps this is the window that Johnny sits at and looks out of; what he sees the audience sees too (fig. 61).

Already we begin to see that the needs of the actor in part determine the scenic requirement of the play; by providing a window seat we give Johnny an opportunity to stay at the window for a longer period of time than he might if he had to stand. And in a sitting posi-

61. *Cut-away wall*

tion he is also better able to show an audience an attitude of quiet despondency. O'Casey did not specifically ask for this scenic structure; but it is very possible the play will be just a little clearer and more meaningful for its inclusion.

These are but two isolated examples of how widening the scope of the locale—showing more than the author asks you to show—can have a specific usefulness to the actor in his attempts to create his character in a greater dimension. However, there is a danger for the designer when he creates a more comprehensive environment in which the characters of the play may live and move. He may succumb to the temptation of doing too much; with the very best intentions it is possible he may create an environment so elaborate and detailed that the effect becomes overpowering in which case the actors become part of his creation rather than he contributing to theirs. No matter how realistic the play, the designer and director must always take great care that they do not forget the higher purposes of the play in the reproduction of detail for its own sake, satisfying though this activity may be. Remember the warning of Robert Edmond Jones: "We may put aside once and for all the idea of a stage-setting as a glorified show-window in which actors are to be exhibited and think of it instead as a kind of symphonic accompaniment . . . as evocative and intangible as music itself." This is a criterion that applies to all designs regardless of style or period; the larger aims of the production must always be foremost in the designer's thoughts and work. Perhaps it would not be unwise to remember, at this point, the old adage that, *What does not help hinders*.

Figure 62 is a line drawing of an actual production of *Juno and the Paycock* that puts into practice some of the ideas just discussed. The designer and the director, it can be seen, decided to show more than the author dictated. The method used to arrive at this result was, essentially, to find and study research sources that allowed the designer to see the larger area where O'Casey's specific locale might be set. Both director and designer wanted to provide a setting that would aid the actor in showing more than they are usually given opportunity or scope to do and, at the same time, to give the audience a better look at just how this specific flat fitted into a larger more understandable context. By showing both inside and outside, it was possible to see just how much Juno had overcome the harshness of a hostile world.

62. *Design for* Juno and the Paycock

While this way of seeing is not a formalized method or system, it does bear a more detailed examination. Therefore, we will now take another example to show in more detail how this concept works. And since this method of approaching the design is based on the assumption that reconstruction of the larger picture can be helpful to the designer in several ways, not merely as literal documentation alone, let us give this activity a name. Since it is predicated on seeing the environment from a distant perspective and then progressively moving in, let us call this activity an "overview."

§21
The Overview: *Madame Butterfly*

Although it is not necessary in every work to know in precise detail the complete lay of the land surrounding the locale being represented, in some instances it is not time wasted to consider the larger area of which the specific place (that which shows in the setting on the stage) is a smaller part. The overview is, in operation, much like a camera panning from a great height and distance down and into the actual spot where the action is to take place.

As an illustration of this process let us examine the opera *Madame Butterfly,* by Giacomo Puccini. Puccini himself had a fairly keen sense of direction and is, in this opera in particular, much more consistent and logical in designation of locations than most opera composers. Only once in the text, however, does a character (the American counsel Sharpless) refer directly to key landmarks. But since this one reference is quite specific and detailed, it makes it necessary for anyone involved in making decisions concerning the design of the setting to make clear judgments as to these locations. He must consider not only Butterfly's house in relation to its immediate environment, but also its relationship to the nearby city of Nagasaki, the points of the compass (since times of day complete with setting and rising suns are integral parts of the opera's action and development), the location of the harbor where important events take place although not seen by the audience, and to the open sea which Butterfly watches for the better part of three years. The overview is a means by which some of these decisions can be realized. At this stage of planning a production it is important that both designer and director work very closely. Of course, it should be understood that no amount of research would turn up the exact place Puccini had in mind since this work was modeled not on a real occurrence but on another stage work, *Madame Butterfly,* by John Luther Long and

David Belasco. Therefore, in order to reconstruct this larger picture, the designer and director must first search the text carefully for points of reference and possible clues to physical relationships that might correspond to actual similarities in and around the actual city of Nagasaki. There are a number of references in the text that help to some degree. To list a few:

1. The house is away (how far?) from Nagasaki, but close enough to walk to or determine a ship's flag in the Nagasaki harbor with a small telescope.

2. The city is below the level on which the house stands. The American counsel complains of the steep climb, but remarks on the splendid view one gets from this vantage point. It is possible, we can deduce from his remarks, to look down into the harbor and to see out into the open ocean.

3. The house is fairly isolated inasmuch as Butterfly sees very few people during a three-year period and it is apparently not on any main path or road.

4. The house is surrounded by a fairly extensive garden since at one time during the course of the opera Butterfly and her maid must gather a great number of flowers quickly.

These are but a few of the clues derived from the text. This information, along with drawings and photographs of actual scenes in and around Nagasaki, serve as a start in making a simplified long-range view of the general area (fig. 63). But what value does this drawing have for the designer? So far we have nothing we can put on the stage. Several things are clearer, however; these being the basic relationship of the house to town, harbor, and sea. It is also now possible to establish the very important directions of north, south, east, and west. (Times of day, as earlier stated, figure importantly in the action of the opera and much of the action is linked to these time changes.) Even at this point we can see, knowing practically nothing about the finished design, that if Butterfly is looking toward the harbor she is looking north and that the sun will rise on her right and set on her left. We know that if she has her back to the harbor, land is to her left and the open sea lies around her. (Even now we begin to perceive certain internal relationships to the story; she is isolated from the city, that is, cut off from all past life and family, yet she can see down into the town where those who were dear to her live and where her own past life was spent.) This sort of orientation is especially helpful to the director and actor since it gives them a "world" in which the arbitrary directionless world of "upstage," "off-right," and "downstage-center" becomes one in which realistic and meaningful relationships may be established. (There might

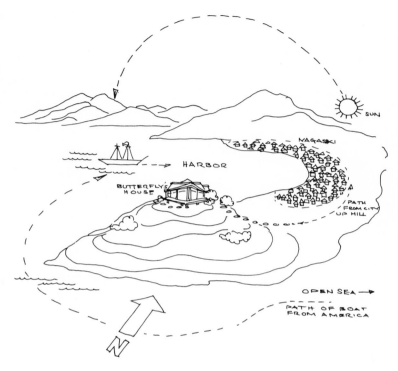

63. Area around Butterfly's house

even be a special case made for working in this manner on this particular opera since, although highly romantic in conception, its basic idiom is realism.) The primary objective, however, is to increase the visual understanding of the designer.

The next step in this process is to "pan-in," to take a closer look at the focal point of this general view. This is, of course, Butterfly's house and its immediate surroundings. We now begin research into the actual materials that will show Japanese architecture and, more important for the moment, how it relates to its exterior setting. Figure 64 is a drawing (actually made from the period the opera is set in) that gives a closer view of the area we wish to study. Still, a set cannot be designed from this picture although it might help to clarify a few more points and questions. At this same time, we also need to begin study of plans of domestic architecture and individual houses in more detail (fig. 65) or perhaps pictorial views of this architecture (fig. 66).

These items, considered by themselves, do not help much; they

64. *Japanese landscape from* Landscape Gardening in Japan *by Josiah Conder. Courtesy of Dover Publications, Inc.*

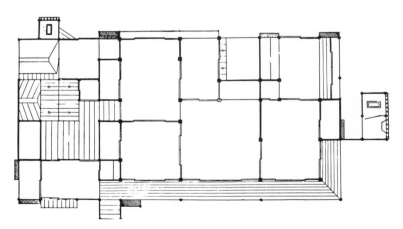

65. *Drawing of Japanese house plan from* Landscape Gardening in Japan *by Josiah Conder. Courtesy of Dover Publications, Inc.*

66. *Drawing of Japanese house from* Landscape Gardening in Japan *by Josiah Conder. Courtesy of Dover Publications, Inc.*

must be incorporated into a drawing that will allow the designer to study the possibilities of the first general overview at closer range. While figure 64 was more pictorial, figure 67 is more helpful in plan. This is not a floor plan for a setting on the stage however. Nor do we, at this point, have an audience orientation, an angle at which the designer wishes to compose his setting for the view of an audience. There are still too many questions that must be answered, too many possibilities that must be explored before that decision can be reached and the design finalized. But, even now, it can be seen that this process—zeroing in from a distance—is more comprehensive and artistically productive than simply putting together a set composed of flats and platforms like a jigsaw puzzle. This is not the time for stagecraft. The designer-artist, whenever possible, lets the setting design itself, that is, evolve out of the research materials he uncovers as this data comes into contact with his imagination and his awareness of the requirements of the

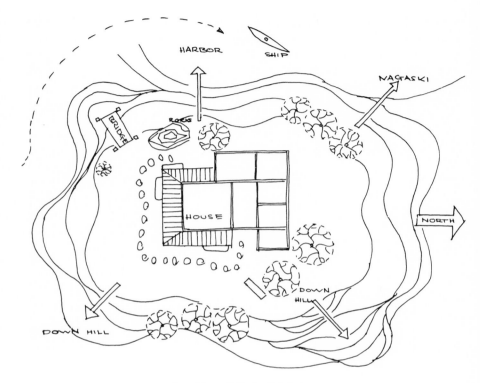

67. Plan of Butterfly's house

script. What we are attempting to show here, then, is a technique (although not complete in itself or automatically productive) that will most effectively allow this to happen. And while this procedure may seem arbitrary and a matter of cut-and-dried research technique, the designer will soon find that he is never relieved of the need to make subjective judgments that are, for want of a better word, artistic in nature.

As we proceed in our design, in our use of this technique, we must think progressively smaller and in a more detailed manner; having seen and comprehended the larger picture, we are free to let our eye become more selective and study the various elements of the total at closer hand. For instance, our plan shows a porch outside the house but it does not reveal anything about it in any great detail. Part of the problem now becomes more specific; not only do we need to find a more detailed view of this porch, we want to know how it fits into the architectural scheme of the house and gain some idea of the manner in which it relates to the area surrounding the house as well. Figures 68 and 69 are two such detail drawings that answer some of these questions. From these two drawings (both taken from *Landscape Gardening in Japan,* by Josiah Conder, a Dover paperback book), it is possible to determine a number of useful pieces of information that will have a direct bearing on the final design:

1. Construction and design of the porch itself.
2. Landscape features immediately around the house.

68. *Detail of Japanese house from* Landscape Gardening in Japan *by Josiah Conder. Courtesy of Dover Publications, Inc.*

69. *Detail of Japanese house and landscape features from* Landscape Gardening in
Japan *by Josiah Conder. Courtesy of Dover Publications, Inc.*

3. Construction and design of the house.
4. An indication (although not completely clear) of materials
   (wood, bamboo, stone, tile) used in the house and in the land-
   scaping.
5. An indication of the native vegetation and, more important, the
   manner in which natural features are manipulated into an esthetically pleasing union with the architectural structures.

While these details are by themselves helpful, the advantage we gain by
working from the larger view to the smaller is obvious; our understanding of the total is more complete than if we started with these details alone and tried to incorporate them into a setting without a firm
knowledge and understanding of their relationship to the total picture,
the complete environment.

It should be understood, however, that this approach to the design
of a setting leaves out more than half of the work the designer must accomplish if he is to really make a contribution to the production as a
whole; what he has not done is to consider just how this information
will be used by the director and the performer. Nor is it suggested that

this particular approach will be applicable or useful in all productions. It would certainly be foolish to make any general principle concerning all operas or how they should be produced as it would concerning all plays; while opera in general seems to have more inherent limiting factors in it, no one approach could ever serve for all. Figure 70 is a design based on the materials and observations revealed or "explained" by implementation of the overview principle.

This is, by necessity, a quick and sketchy accounting of how the overview process works; there are many important steps—mostly subjective—that are left out. Recounting them here would only take up space and be too specific to be useful to anyone else, especially if he were designing this particular opera. However, the usefulness of such a technique and procedure can be seen even at this stage and with the limited exposition it has received here. It should also be pointed out that many designers are able to accomplish this total understanding without going through the complete process in a formal manner as outlined here; some are able to jump directly to the last stages of design with the same depth of understanding that another could only at-

70. *Design for* Madame Butterfly

tain by doing the whole process step by step. The reasons for this are manifold; but the greatest reason this might be true would depend on the individual designer's previous experience, not only in the actual design of scenery for the stage, but in his exposure to information through travel and allied studies—art history, architecture. Travel gives the designer a firsthand understanding obtainable in no other way, although the study of photographs, books, artworks cannot be discounted.

§22
Research into Action: *Romeo and Juliet*

"Suit the action to the word, the word to the action." Shakespeare gave this advice to the players in *Hamlet,* but he meant it for all players everywhere, and while he didn't have the scene designer in mind, nevertheless, that advice holds equally well for him as it does the actor. But before we can determine what these actions in *Romeo and Juliet* are and just what the designer's responsibility to the production is in this regard, we must find out something about where they happen.

Actually there are, at the beginning of our research, two Veronas, not one. There is the Verona that can be discovered by factual research and there is the Verona of Shakespeare's mind. Just how alike or how different are they? A great part of our job (but not all) is to find out how much of one is in the other. At the end of our work there will be a third Verona, the one we must create on the stage. We must also insure that that Verona will be every bit as vital, an as equally *living* place as the originals, no matter what style we impose on the production, no matter how much or how little our Verona owes to those other two. Above all, it must be a place where action is possible.

Keep in mind, however, that what will be presented in this example has, to some extent, been put into a logical sequence (although not completely), even though the import of the actual research was not as quickly or easily perceived or organized as it might appear. What is important to note, then, is the clearly exposed principle that the research process does not follow a single line of development from conception to final resolution. In fact, no final resolution will be offered here and it really wouldn't be worth much if it were—what is demonstrated is not *how* this play should be designed but the means by which one designer did arrive at a solution he considered workable. And, what is even more important to note and comprehend is that the final design will always be in great part the result of many digressions, intuitional judgments, some incorrect assumptions, and numerous back-trackings; in other words, what we have is a voyage of exploration with all the attendant dangers such an expedition might entail. At any one moment in the creative process, the artist is working on more than one level and in more than one way. It can be a dangerous terrain.

> Two households, both alike in dignity,
> In fair Verona, where we lay our scene
> From ancient grudge break to new mutiny,
> Where civil blood makes civil hands unclean.
> From forth the fatal loins of these two foes
> A pair of star-cross'd lovers take their life;
> Whose misadventures piteous overthrows
> Do with their death bury their parents' strife.
> The fearful passage of their death mark'd love,
> And the continuance of their parents' rage,
> Which, but their children's end, nought could remove
> Is now the two hours' traffic of our stage;
> The which if you with patient ears attend,
> What here shall miss, our toil shall strive to mend.

The first four lines of the prologue give us an overall view of the city—again, to use the terminology of the cinema—from a long shot. Shakespeare's purpose is not only to tell us where this play will take place but to give us a more total physical context in which to understand it: a place where, for some very particular reasons, the inhabitants are at war with each other. The second four lines "pan in" to call our attention to a particular event (the story of Romeo and Juliet) that occurs within this particular context. The third four lines tie these two, the city, and its feuding troubles together, and then, with a short apology customary in the Elizabethan theater that says, "if you didn't get or understand the point of what this whole thing is all about, don't worry; we will work very hard to *show* you," he sets you down squarely in the middle of the situation he has just been describing—a city street of Verona. Shakespeare was an able dramatic craftsman; he didn't waste words nor did he waste time establishing what he considered to be environmental conditions necessary to the progress of the story. We would do well to heed this careful path he has led us on. We find, by following these strong clues, that the city itself is a very real and active force in the structure of the play, almost an actor in its physical presence and hostile nature. Before making any drawings or decisions, though, we must set up an order of things to do, a priority of activities:

A. We must read the play. (If for the first time, just for the plea-sure of reading an unfamiliar work. For the time being, theater does not exist.)

B. Having read the play, even once, certain things are evident and understandable, much more probably not. Certain questions will imme-diately want to be answered:

1. Where did the play take place?
2. When?
3. What was this place, Verona, like then?
4. Where can I go to find out some answers to these questions?

These questions can only be answered by doing a little preliminary research concerning the play itself, the structure of the Italian city states of the sixteenth century, and the nature of not only cities during that period but of Verona in particular. (Although not a large country, the cities of Italy have always been highly individual places each with its own interests and unique features; no designer in America would think of considering Boston as the same kind of city or having the same fea-tures as New Orleans, but all too many tend to think of all cities in another country or in other times as being essentially alike.)

First, let us set a probable date for the play's action. Shakespeare got his plot from a story by Luigi da Porto, of Vicenza. The Italian novel that contained the story did not appear until some years after the death of da Porto and was first printed in 1535, and since da Porto died in 1529, it is probable that the story could be historically placed around 1526. There is good reason to believe that Shakespeare's play was first produced between July of 1596 and April 1597, and it was, in all probability, costumed in contemporary English dress. This informa-tion helps us orient our research problem to a period of time and the possibility of at least two primary approaches to the visual design of the play: England at the end of the sixteenth century or Italy during the first quarter of the sixteenth century. And our first problem is not to confuse the two.

Now let us take a brief look at the primary locale of the scenes in the play, the city of Verona. During the investigation of this play we will, time and time again, return to study the city itself and to the ques-tion of how it relates to the play in general, but now all we want is some general information; we really don't know what we want or need at this stage.

Verona was an important Renaissance city. But before that it was a medieval city. (Perhaps Shakespeare had visited it at one time or an-other, we really don't know. But he certainly knew of it by report if not from firsthand.) All medieval cities were similar in some respects while being quite different in others. One of the important similarities, at least for our purpose, is that they were all walled cities. Why is this fact important? Most designers know that, given a number of facts, certain ones seem to have an importance more felt than understood; the fact that Verona is a walled city is just such an example as will be demonstrated later. So, let us start our investigation of this particular city at this point, that is, at the city wall.

In *Medieval Cities*, by Howard Saalman, the following information can be found:

> The walls of medieval cities were subject to an immutable law regarding their dimensions: they invariably followed the *smallest* possible perimeter! Every extension of the town diameter—every extra foot of wall—implied greater building costs, greater maintenance expenses, and a larger garrison for adequate defense. The attitude of the medieval man on the street regarding expenditure of public funds on enlarging the walls may be summed up with equal simplicity: as long as *his* house and *his* ship, *his* parish and *his* church were contained within the walls, then the wall was quite big enough.

The selfish attitude displayed during that period of time does not seem to have changed by the time of *Romeo and Juliet*. Not only was there an attempt to keep out those not contained with the walls, even those within the city were also constantly at war with one another; the feud between the Montagues and Capulets had its origin in the historical one (nor was it an uncommon occurrence) between the families of Montecchi and Cappelletti. A question we might begin wondering about is *why* did they fight, what was the real basis of the feud and was the city itself to blame in any way? Already we can begin to relate a little to what we know of the city; some of its problems we ourselves face today. Again Saalman provides relevant comment:

> The story of medieval cities is of people trying to get *into* town, not out of it. . . . Only in the city were there the conditions and facilities for an existence based on the production and exchange of goods and services as opposed to the life of baron, soldier, and serf on the land outside. . . . The closer you could get to the center of the city which, with its crossing roads, was the hub of the most intense urban activity, the better!

The walls of Verona were built much earlier than the time of Romeo and Juliet, so it is reasonable to assume that the town was beginning to suffer the pangs of urban areas that outgrow their hard limits—the city walls—and cannot expand those limits easily. Let us listen to Saalman once more:

> Space within the walls was limited. Two inherently different interests were competing for this space: private and public interests. . . .
> Perhaps the most essential difference between public and private space within a city is their relative penetrability. . . . Private space, whether it be enclosed or open, is impenetrable. It cannot be used, crossed, or entered except by consent of the owner.

Now we are beginning to acquire information that has some bearing on our own problems in this particular play; a number of important scenes in *Romeo and Juliet* deal with situations that require someone to gain access to or escape from a confined area. And several also deal with people in places where they shouldn't be. Perhaps it would be well to list some of the scenes that depend on the closing up or closing off of a space in order to keep out or keep in a character in the play.

1. The balcony scene is the first scene that comes to every mind and it deals with confinement of Juliet (one of Capulet's family—whom he thinks of as part of his goods and possessions to be disposed of as he sees fit) from the rest of the world. She even asks Romeo, fearfully, how he was able to penetrate the security of the private garden surrounding the house. His reply: "On love's light wings did I o'er perch these walls, / For stoney limits cannot hold love out." In other words, he had to climb the wall, and, discounting his poetic fervor due to his youthful passion, it probably wasn't all that easy. (One production comes to mind where Romeo had some difficulty in getting on top of a wall—actually to hide from the band of friends looking for him—and then disclosed himself to Juliet from that position. When he came to the above mentioned lines, he gave them as if the scaling of the wall were an easy and insignificant accomplishment. The laughter from the audience was desired from the performer; it gave the youthful ebullience so often lacking in performances which only stress the formal poetry of the play.)

2. The second most important scene, in many respects, is the tomb scene. Its quality of confinement is especially horrible, so much so that Shakespeare carefully describes it before we actually see it; Juliet tells

us directly of her fear of being too long in the locked tomb and the consequences that might result. (This speech contains many good images that might help in the visualization of the tomb):

> How if, when I am laid into the tomb,
> I wake before the time that Romeo
> Come to redeem me? There's a fearful point!
> Shall I not then be stifled in the vault,
> To whose foul mouth no healthsome air breathes in,
> And there die strangled ere my Romeo comes?
> Or, if I live, is it not very like,
> The horrible conceit of death and night,
> Together with the terror of the place,—
> As in a vault, an ancient receptacle,
> Where for these many hundred years the bones
> Of all my buried ancestors are pack'd;
> Where bloody Tybalt, yet but green in earth,
> Lies festering in his shroud; where, as they say,
> At some hours in the night spirits resort;—
> Alack, alack, is it not like that I
> So early waking, what with loathsome smells,
> And shrieks like mandrakes' torn out of the earth,
> That living mortals, hearing them, run mad—
> Or, if I wake, shall I not be distraught,
> Environed with all these hideous fears?
> And madly play with my forefathers' joints,
> And pluck the mangled Tybalt from his shroud,
> And in this rage, with some great kinsman's bone,
> As with a club, dash out my desperate brains?

3. The first time Romeo sees Juliet is at a private ball given by Juliet's father. Romeo is a gate-crasher and is almost thrown out by Tybalt when he is discovered.

4. One of the worst punishments that a dweller of a Renaissance city could receive was not death but perpetual banishment. Romeo was not alone in intense devotion to his home city and his great distress at being physically shut out of it. It may have been a small place, relatively speaking, but it was the whole world to him.

These, then, are necessary elements of the plot's construction that deal directly with enclosure; much of Shakespeare's imagery either directly or indirectly alludes to these restraining structures. If, however, one were to seek the dominating image in this play, it would be found to be, as Caroline Spurgion has pointed out in her admirable study, *Shakespeare's Imagery* (a book that should be in every designer's permanent library), light in various forms. It is certainly true that the designer must be keenly aware of this dominance and the special poetic atmosphere these images impart to the play. But the prevalence of light images—or rather light (usually faint or brief in duration) set against a vast dark void—is more symbolic in nature rather than accurate descriptions of actual situations or things found in the literal world of this play. As designers we must also be aware of that imagery which summons up the concrete detail and which aids us to create the objective world where the characters of the play live and move. And the single most important element in that world is the wall. *Romeo and Juliet* gets its very special atmosphere precisely from the environment out of which the characters have evolved; so basic and integral are the functions of this one element—the wall—to the total picture that to disregard its purposes is to practically misinterpret the entire play.

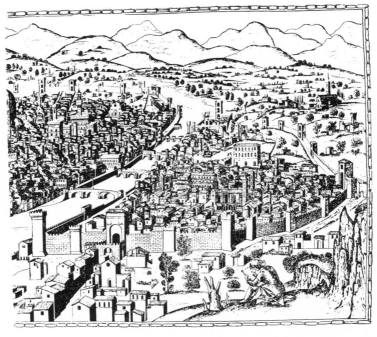

71. *Sixteenth-century Italian city. Courtesy of Istituto Geografico Militare, Florence, Italy*

Now let us begin a more detailed study of the city in relation to the space it encompasses. A contemporary view of an Italian Renaissance city (ca. 1470) gives us a fairly accurate idea of what Verona might have looked like (fig. 71). While this is not Verona it does have many features in common with it. And when we represent this diagrammatically (fig. 72), it can be seen even in this simple diagram that within the confines of the city lie not one area but many—spaces within spaces, or rather, walls within walls, and all crowding one another.

Now let us select the two spaces that concern us most directly—the larger confined area within the city wall and the smaller independently controlled spaces—the houses of Montague and Capulet. This also can be represented diagrammatically (fig. 73). "Two households both alike

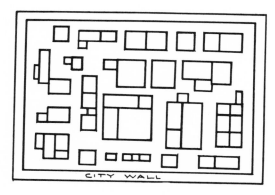

72. *Diagram of Italian city*

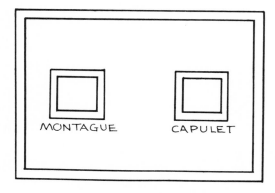

73. *Montague and Capulet households*

in dignity" (i.e., power, wealth, position in the city). We now have a simple geometric image of the situation that exists when the play begins. However, there is more to the situation than is told by this diagram alone. The influence and the power of the respective houses is maintained and guarded by members of the family (families were large and had fierce loyalties to the family name) and retainers who also tended to adopt their masters' viewpoints and allegiances. They carry this allegiance with them when they leave home base and enter into the areas common to the city's general population. For this reason, the influence of the Montagues extends a little farther than their own personal property and neighborhood. The same can be said for the house of Capulet. Our diagram might take on this added dimension (fig. 74).

We can see immediately that the situation lends itself to disputation through overlapping spacial claims. Indeed, the very first scene of the play is a confrontation between factions of the two rival houses in just such an instance. Although they are both on "neutral ground," the basis of the scene's action is to determine who has the preeminent right to the space at that moment. Actually it is a kind of game; but it is a deadly one. In many of these encounters, the confrontation begins as a type of schoolboy daring and ends in deadly seriousness; Mercutio is finally killed in such a fray. And it is not until the very last moment before he dies that he himself sees the senselessness of the whole foolish situation. A designer might very well wonder just what Mercutio *sees* in those last moments of his life. Examine that scene for a moment:

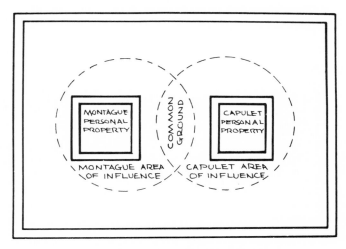

74. *Montague and Capulet influence*

Tybalt is in the act of baiting Romeo, who, now in love with Juliet, does not want to fight with her cousin. Mercutio takes Romeo's remarks for cowardice and challenges Tybalt himself.

MERCUTIO: Tybalt, you rat-catcher, will you walk?
TYBALT: What wouldst thou have with me?
MERCUTIO: Good king of cats, nothing but one of your nine
lives, that I mean to make bold withal, and, as
you shall use me hereafter, dry-beat the rest of
the eight. . . .
TYBALT: I am for you.   (Drawing.
ROMEO: Gentle Mercutio, put thy rapier up.
MERCUTIO: Come, sir, your passado.   (They fight.
ROMEO: Draw, Benvolio; beat down their weapons.
Gentlemen, for shame, forbear this outrage!
Tybalt, Mercutio, the prince expressly hath
Forbid this bandying in Verona streets.
Hold, Tybalt! good Mercutio!   (Exeunt Tybalt
and his Partisans.
[Mercutio has been stabbed at this point.]
MERCUTIO: I am hurt;
A plague o' both your houses! I am sped:

What was a moment before just a joke and a game has now turned sour and serious. For a second time, a character in the play has made an allusion to the rival houses as being equally matched; the Chorus speaking of their official recognition as important families, Mercutio now implying they are to be cursed for their equally unbending wilfulness and pride.

For a moment, put yourself in his place, with life's blood flowing out and a premonition that death is near. Take a good look around the street and try to see what he is seeing for the last time: narrow dirty streets, ancient walls much used and many times repaired, yellowed and dirty from men and dogs having made water on them for hundreds of years, windows and doors locked and barred, and, only by looking straight up can a little of the sky be seen. This is a far cry from the romantic image of Romeo in the moonlight under Juliet's balcony. Yet it is the very same play. All too often a designer will concentrate only on the attractive scenes of this play and completely ignore the more brutal and repellent aspects of it. But Shakespeare meant us to know that side of the story as well or else he would not have been so careful to provide the many details that clearly show the cruel and ugly side of life in Verona.

Let us consider this aspect of Verona. The first scene of the play is the occasion of a fight similar to the one in which Mercutio is provoked and slain. And like this scene, it also takes place in a street somewhere in the city. Two men of the house of Capulet are walking along with no real purpose or destination in mind. (Their aimlessness helps the playwright underscore the mindless way in which the various brawls in the play get started.) Very early in their discussion they allude to walls and the use of them when walking in the street. (This banter is based on the symbolic nature of walls as well as the actual physical properties of them.)

> SAMPSON: I will take the wall of any man or maid of Montague's. [Keeping next to the wall on a street was the pedestrian's safest way to keep from getting soiled either by being splashed from the dirty streets or by being hit from slop jars being emptied from second story windows. To "take the wall" could also be an insult; ordinarily to yield it would be considered courteous, but, in this case, it would show cowardice.]
> GREGORY: That shows thee a weak slave; for the weakest goes to the wall. [He changes the meaning here somewhat—a favorite pastime in Shakespeare's day was wordplay.]
> SAMPSON: 'Tis true; and therefore women, being the weaker vessels, are ever thrust to the wall [this is an allusion to a sexual assault on women]: therefore I will push Montague's men from the wall [take the best place] and thrust his maids to the wall [sexually assault them].

This gives a pretty fair idea of how each side regarded the other. At best it is not a friendly atmosphere in Verona; but what is significant is that so early in the play an important clue is given the designer concerning some elements of the physical environment the play will demand.

A more complete diagram of this total environment may now be attempted (fig. 75). Keep in mind that these diagrams do *not* represent settings or scenery; their purpose is to help us understand the play in relation to its simplest physical needs (although psychological elements also play a part in these considerations). Once this stage has been reached, the designer must begin to "test" the rightness of his ideas and plans. He must begin to think about individual scenes and their needs in greater detail. By this time some investigation of actual ma-

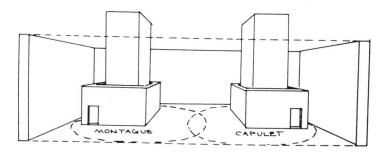

75. *Montague and Capulet environment*

terials from the period would be underway—paintings, photographs of architecture, etc. But what are we looking for? Right now we are primarily interested in buildings, walls, juxtaposition of structures which might show the overcrowded aspect of the Renaissance city. We might also begin to look for details of architecture—door and window design, treatment of building materials, techniques of building structure. But is that all we need? No, not quite.

So far we have been working from the outside in, that is, observing the overall environment rather than noting individual events within that environment, i.e., scenes from the play. (This is not entirely true, but the greater number of our observations have been basically external, not greatly concerned with specific actions.) Still, it would be safe to say at this point, that the main action of the play concerns itself with people getting into places where they are not supposed to be and getting out of places where they don't want to stay. The constant factor in both cases, then, is the wall both physical and psychological (the solid walls of the city and its buildings and the enmity that has built a wall of hate between the two families). And, in both cases, the function of these walls is to contain, repel or cut off.

We are now at the point where the attention and efforts of the designer must be more carefully focused, more specifically detailed and channeled. We are also at the point where the focus of attention must be directed to the internal needs of the play rather than only toward the external information we have so far uncovered. Thus far we have accomplished three important steps:

1. A reading of the play.
2. An attempt to see the "large picture"—the total background of the age, the locale, and nature of the people who have created this place and who in turn are influenced by it (and that, of course, cannot

be understood by examining *only* those directly involved, but those who lived before and left their mark).

3. A free and unstructured examination of several scenes (those considered important to the structure of the play because they contain information and, more important, significant actions or series of actions).

Until now there has been much jumping around in the play; the meanings of the play cannot be understood by examining each separately without regard to others. Cross-references are essential bits of information that help form the web by which the playwright holds his play together; the designer must be able to discern these threads and where they lead. But now we must begin to limit our focus and begin a more detailed study of a fewer number of scenes. (This is a natural development in the study of the play since, in examining a great number of scenes, we realize that some are more important than others and that some need more attention; it gives us a priority by which to scale and direct our work.)

One of the key or crucial scenes (and also probably the best known) in the play is the so-called balcony scene. Not only is this the most famous scene in the play, it is quite probably the most dangerous one, the one that has led more designers astray than any other.

Several years ago, a student picked this play as a subject for her term project. She labored mightily on it and performed all the exercises with diligence and with care. But her work did not progress and it seemed to lack something; she was not able to crystalize any concrete ideas for her designs. Part of the requirement for the project was to be able to give various oral reports on her research, the progress of ideas and, in general, explain to the rest of the class what she was doing (or was not able to do) to forward her work. In these discussions with the other members of the class, it became apparent that she was either sidestepping certain aspects of the play, wasn't herself aware of them or simply ignoring them. Her conception of Verona, it became more and more obvious, was more suited to the French Riviera of today than to a brutal Renaissance city of the early sixteenth century. (It was, for that matter, no different from the attitude displayed by George Cukor in his lush 1936 Hollywood version of this same play which starred Leslie Howard and Norma Shearer.) The people populating her play were, for the most part, good upstanding, clean-living, middle-class mannequins; at the very most, they were only actors in pretty costumes. In her findings there was not the slightest hint of a real world—no intrigue, no desire, only love of the purest kind, no dirty streets, and nobody, apparently, who ever sweated. It was all good clean fun—a little sad at the end, however. Finally, it was asked how she *saw* this play, through what lens did she view all those events of so long ago. Her actual reply, "Through the eyes of love"; that was her answer and only reason. Questioned more closely as to where she got this particular way of thinking about the play, what caused her to take this approach, she said, "From the garden scene—you know, the balcony scene. . . . This is about the most important scene in the play and so I just wanted to do the play through the eyes of Romeo and Juliet since they are also the most important people in the play and we have to see the way they do." It was pointed out that the scene *was* important, but that it was (1) a scene totally *different* from practically every other scene, and (2) in order for it to retain its individuality, it must be shown to be different by contrasting it to the others, not by making it exactly alike. Her attention was then called to a few other scenes unlike this one in order to point out some of the more brutal moments she had apparently missed in her reading. She was requested, in addition, to read to the rest of the class—slowly—Juliet's monologue describing the horrors of being locked up alive in the tomb, and then asked to give a visualization of what that tomb might look like according to the information Juliet imparts. She was also asked to describe a street brawl and what might happen to those involved in such an event. (It was apparent that nobody ever bled in her Verona either. Her reply to all these questions was, "You are always talking about horrible things and blood in these plays." We had been working on *Macbeth* too.) It became more and more clear that the play was still nothing more to her than words on a page, that her conception of the play was every bit as clean and sterile as that printed page from which she read. It was then pointed out that Shakespeare himself could not get more than four lines into the play without mentioning blood and that was just what he meant.

We have reached another juncture in our design process. Having assembled a certain amount of information, and having approached this information from a certain point of view (mostly exterior in nature) it is now possible to explore some practical possibilities that might lead eventually to the design of this scene.

Yet, while it is possible for the designer, at this stage, to create a design which will include all the foregoing considerations and give to the director a workable plan, rarely does this final step happen so quickly or effortlessly. On the contrary, usually another period of experimental work precedes the design concept and the finished working plans and sketches. It is during this second period that the designer will find it necessary to make a number of drawings, none complete in statement or complicated in execution. These pictures are, actually, less than pictures and more a form of visual shorthand which the designer employs to make his ideas easier to understand both for himself and for the director. So, before we continue our design of a scene from *Romeo and Juliet,* let us look at the way this visual shorthand is accomplished. These drawings will be called action drawings, because that is precisely what they show—action.

Many designers foster germinal ideas for a scene design, especially in relation to the basic shape of the playing area, by "directing" scenes in their own imaginations—seeing the action of the characters in relation to each other and to their surroundings—and then setting down these observations and ideas in a series of quick sketches. These sketches are, unlike those of painters or draftsmen, meant to show *action* possibilities rather than *pictorial composition* or likenesses. Nor are they meant to show complete settings in a frame; they are, rather, fragments of a scene, not necessarily viewed from a single fixed point or an audience position. The term action drawing is the most appropriate description of this activity since, more than anything else, they are diagrams that chart movements of characters as they relate to each other and to the surrounding environment and especially to those objects or pieces of scenery necessary for motivation or for completion of actions. (These drawings differ from a director's blocking diagrams in one major way: while in the director's plan the exact shape of the playing area has been previously confirmed, along with everything contained within that area, in the designer's preliminary drawings, nothing is set for certain. He is, in fact, attempting to determine what the director will eventually use.) The primary purpose of these drawings is to clarify visually, for the designer, space relationship possibilities and to help him determine the physical needs of the actors as they perform a scene. Quite often the designer will make a number of these action drawings before he is able to determine a definite shape or pattern to a playing area. And he must consider not only the flat floor, but levels as well, since often actors must be given the possibility of moving up and down from the stage floor as well as around its surface. The concept behind this activity is not, as some designers apparently believe, to arbitrarily decide on a shape or form for the playing areas and then force patterns of movement into it, but, rather, to define the boundaries of this area *progressively* as the needs of the actors become evident through the investigation of successive actions.

These sketches should be done quickly, though not thoughtlessly. Only essentials should be included; in other words, only that space or those items directly needed or concerned with the actor in a limited sequence of actions should be put down and studied. It is a mistake to try to make one action drawing show too many movements. It is also more helpful for the designer to concentrate on high points of the scene first and then work backward to less important happenings. He will find that, by considering the actions of the performers as part of his design work—not only climactic moments but those of less importance as well—he is more able to assist the director in clarification of a scene which, in turn, might also help the actor to reinforce his own work.

In *The Theatre of Bertolt Brecht,* John Willett relates just how important the designer can be to the director (and also to the playwright) in planning and influencing action as well as creating a place where it will take place.

> Brecht was extremely sensitive to grouping and gestures, which in all the early rehearsals were designed simply to tell the story, in an almost silent-film way, and only later became refined and polished up. In this he depended often on his old friend and associate Caspar Neher, who would not only design the setting and the costumes but in dozens of sketches would suggest the action too: Puntila having his bath for example, or Matti haranguing a broom as he sweeps out the yard. . . .
>
> . . . In Brecht's theatre he (Neher) played a decisive part from school-days on, providing him with drawings and projections and teaching him to use the elements of scenery as if they were simply properties on a bigger scale. In his kind of setting every item that matters to the play is as authentic and tangible as it can be made, and all else is merely indicated: a real door, a real fence, a real streetlamp, standing solid and fit for use on an otherwise almost empty stage. . . .
>
> "But above all he is an ingenious story-teller. He knows better than anyone that whatever does not further the narrative harms it."
>
> And again, "in his design our friend always starts with 'the people themselves' and 'what is happening to or through them' " . . . he constructs the space for "people" to experience something in.

Neher did not think of these small drawings as "pictures." They were, rather, a means by which actions could be recorded for use on the stage. And if these drawings we will make do have any value, it will not be as pictorial statements. They are meant to show, rather, the actors in relations to each other and to their most basic environmental needs. For instance, if walls are needed, as in the following example, their decoration and style are not as important as a knowledge of the function they will serve. Although this decoration and style must be considered at some point, it is not important at the moment.

Earlier, the street brawls which occur periodically in the play were discussed in visual terms—but using words to describe the street and the events taking place on them, not with actual diagrams or pictures. Now we are going to show how the designer might develop these ideas into diagrams. Only three will be shown to illustrate the process, although it would be more likely that three dozen would be made rather than this few. But, before any diagrams are made, let us look at a pictorial view of a Verona street based on contemporary sources (fig. 76). In studying this drawing it is possible to see that it contains many features we might expect to show up in the final design. But just how usable is this information at this time? Can we simply copy this street with all its details and put it directly on the stage? Perhaps we could; the Hollywood approach to scene design during the twenties and thirties of this century was essentially not much more than this—reproducing paintings in three-dimensional structures. What the actors were required to do was really not a consideration of any importance, at least not artistically, to the designer; he was more concerned with the looks of the setting than its potential service to the actor or to the drama. And, when presented any latitude of selection, the pretty picture always won the day; the 1936 cinema version of *Romeo and Juliet,* when compared with the more recent Zeffirelli production, shows this very clearly. But, while we must make use of pictures such as the street illustration at some time during our research, only certain features of it are of any great value to us at the present time. This street might very well be diagramed in this manner; we are not as interested in pictorial aspects of the locale as we are in its spatial qualities (fig. 77).

All we are interested in are the essential features of such a street, not all its outward details and surfaces. This is also true for the people who inhabit these diagrams; we are less interested in their costumes or external features than in their actions. These actions can be adequately expressed by the use of simple stick figures rather than elaborately drawn costumed ones (fig. 78). For our purposes, A is no more helpful than B.

Now, let us return to the construction of the diagrams:

1. SITUATION: Two retainers of the house of Capulet are walking along one of the narrow streets of Verona. They are boasting about what they would do should they encounter members of the rival house

76. *Italian city street*

of Montague. Suddenly, at the other end of the street, two servants of that house do appear. There is no escape for either pair (both pairs probably less brave than they would like to appear and would, if they could, avoid open conflict), the walls more or less channeling their pos-

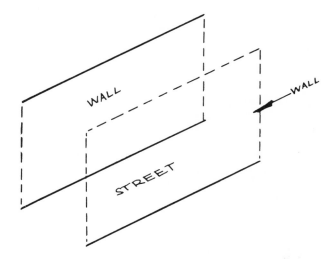

77. *Diagram of street*

78. *Figure in action*

sibilities of movement—either backward (retreat) or forward, almost certain conflict of some sort (verbal or physical). Figure 79 is a diagram of this moment when they first see each other.

2. SITUATION: Both parties have had to advance to save face. The men from the one house begin to bait the men of the other. The conflict is only on the verbal level at this point. Their actions quite pos-

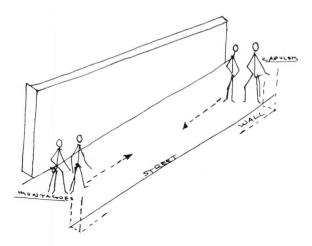

79. *Encounter of characters in street*

sibly are those similar to the combatants in a box ring or cockfight—
basically circular, while each takes the measure of the other, waiting for
the best time to strike. If possible, a fight is to be avoided. But this is
contingent on the assumption that one side will give way to the superi-
ority of the other (fig. 80).

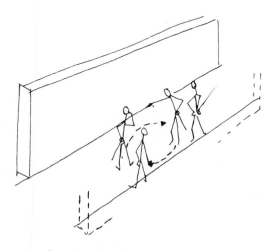

80. *Encounter of characters in street*

3. SITUATION: The two groups taunt each other until one person begins a physical attack. Very soon all four are fighting and in a few moments, others have come onto the street to join the fray. The fight becomes larger and involves more people until finally the two heads of the rival households appear. Our drawing at this point is not adequate—we need to have some idea of where these other people are coming from. The drawing must be extended to help us visualize the paths these other combatants might take to get to the area where the fight is taking place. In other words, we are extending our image to satisfy the need of the actors for an access to the place of action. So, our drawing must grow to include these areas as well as those first drawn. The acting space increases, therefore, as the need for it becomes evident. This is the organic way that stage space and the shape of the immediate acting area are determined (fig. 81).

The designer must make dozens of these drawings for each and every separate scene. At this stage, however, we are not too much concerned with the possible relationship of these individual spaces to each other. (Although they will, at a later stage in the design, have to be correlated, combined and given a priority, some scenes demand less space or definition, some more. The needs of some of these lesser scenes can be combined and then absorbed in the requirements of a more important scene.) The final design, while not evident now, will eventually be determined by just such ideas and drawings. At a later stage of work, specific plans must be made about the exact shape and size of the playing area, whether or not it has levels, and the appearance of the setting as a whole. But, for now, these decisions are still

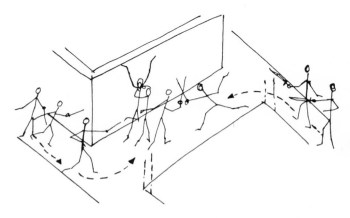

81. *Encounter of characters in street*

waiting to be resolved from future drawings. Making these action drawings is only a first step, but it is a most important and necessary one, especially for the student designer. In putting pencil to paper, the designer is beginning to build that important bridge that links the macrocosm of the playwright with the microcosm of the stage.

These, then, are the types of drawings the designer might make and show to the director or work out with him in conference. It is quite possible that the director will make some of these sketches himself, since the skill required for such work is negligible in terms of formal art training. It is a good practice to urge the director to make such drawings; if nothing else, it saves a great deal of time, especially if the director does have firm convictions concerning space utilization. And it is much easier, most designers will agree, to work with a director who is able to think in graphic terms, who has firm (not inflexible) ideas and is able to contribute his own ideas, as well as accept those of a designer, in visual form, rudimentary though they be.

At first glance this whole mode of thinking may seem to encroach on the director's territory and function; but, as it has been noted before, designing a set is to a large extent directing; the designer causes the actor to move in in certain ways and in predetermined directions even if they never exchange so much as one word. The wise director always takes advantage of this situation. It greatly accounts, in fact, for the desire of many directors to use designers with whom they are familiar or have worked successfully before; in such a collaboration, each not only knows the way the other thinks and works, he knows how to make the task of the other more meaningful and productive.

Most directors will admit that working with designers who evolve designs from the standpoint of action is easier than working with those who are only concerned with the visual aspects of the setting; some will even admit that, far from tying them down, the designer actively concerned with space and the actor's needs many times suggests ideas which they had not considered. Yet, by putting ourselves in the role of director or actor, we do not necessarily lose our own identities as scene designers; it merely give us a different and, quite possibly, more inclusive perspective. It also helps us to comprehend better the playwright's hidden reasons for selecting the particular place he has to set his play. While it is only possible for a scene designer to accomplish this understanding in a limited way, even the attempt to do so is a healthy attitude which will make him much more ready and willing to think first of the production as a whole and not just as an opportunity to exhibit his designs. Furthermore, if a sincere attempt is made by the designer to put himself in the place of the director and the actor, he will begin to develop that all-important inner eye without which no designer can hope to become an artist.

The most important thing for the designer to learn, although it may take years to attain, is how to design scenes that promote action, not pictures that promote scenery.

The greatest danger in the balcony scene, as we have noted before, lies in the possibility that the designer may see the whole production in terms of this one scene. It is quite appropriate that the audience be shown a garden that is unlike the city outside it—romantic and beautiful. The scene, however, virtually stands alone in the play in regard to the kind of romantic vision it represents. But to insist on and maintain this vision throughout the entire play, as is often the case, is wrong on at least two counts. First, it robs this scene of its uniqueness and, second, it does not allow the hard cruel background, which is much more the natural condition of the time and this play, to perform its proper role. Romeo and Juliet become much more important to us, their plight all the more pathetic, if we see them pitted *against* a physical situation that has little beauty or romance about it. Too many designers have forgotten the important fundamental principle of any art form that contrast in background gives importance to that which is placed before it.

Just how was this garden scene done on Shakespeare's own stage? To date no scholar has given a completely satisfying explanation of the means by which the action in the street just before the main portion of the scene is transferred into the garden itself; with the little actual knowledge we have of the workings of this stage, it is not clear whether this was done with some accepted convention (and there must have been many used in this form of theater) or by using an actual scenic device—not part of the permanent stage structure—that an actor could climb over and hide behind. Nothing in the various works that purport to explain the workings of Shakespearian stagecraft illuminates this particular scene; no one, although there have been many conjectural inquiries into this question, has been able to agree or to give a satisfactory explanation just what does really happen. (In the theater that uses scenery, such as the proscenium stage, it is not difficult to find ways of solving this problem; on the open stage, however, a workable solution would not be as easily found.)

It is interesting to compare the quarto of 1597 with more recent texts:

Quarto of 1597

NURSE: *Come your mother staies for you, Ille goe a long with you.*
          Exeuent.

Enter Romeo alone.

Ro: Shall I goe forward and my heart is here?
       Turne backe dull earth and finde thy Center out.
                   Enter Benuolio Mercutio
Ben: *Romeo,* my cofen *Romeo.*
Mer: Doeft thou heare he is wife,
       Vpon my life he hath stolne him home to bed.
Ben: He came this way, and leapt this Orchard wall.
       Call good *Mercutio.*
Mer: Call, nay Ile coniure too. . . .
Mer: . . . Come lets away, for tis but vaine,
       To seeke him heare that meanes not to be found.
Ro: He iefts at fcars that neuer felt a wound:
       But soft, what light from yonder window breakes?

   [And we then begin the garden scene proper. Here, now,
is the same scene from an accepted modern-day version of this
play.]

                   Modern Version
Nurse: Anon, anon!—
       Come, let's away the strangers all are gone.
                   Enter Chorus
       Now old Desire doth in his death-bed lie,
       And young Affection gapes to be his heir: . . .
       But passion lends them power, times means, to meet,
       Tempering extremities with extreme sweet.

                                       (*Exit Chorus*
                   ACT II
       Scene I. *A lane by the wall of Capulet's orchard.*
                   Enter Romeo, *alone*
Rom: Can I go forward when my heart is here?
       Turn back, dull earth, and find thy centre out. (*He
       climbs the wall, and leaps down within it.*
Ben: Romeo! my cousin Romeo! Romeo!
Mer: He is wise;
       And, on my life, hath stol'n him home to bed.
Ben: He ran this way, and leap'd this orchard wall:
       Call, good Mercutio.
Mer: Nay, I'll conjure too. . . .
Ben: Go, then; for 'tis in vain
       To seek him here that means not to be found.   (Ex-
       eunt.

Scene II. *Capulet's orchard*
Enter Romeo
ROM: He jests at scars that never felt a wound.
Juliet appears above, at a window.
But, soft! what light through yonder window breaks?

There are, as one can easily see, distinct differences between the earlier and later texts. Let us consider just what can be deduced from a study of these variations. First, a few of the more obvious differences should be noted:

1. In the quarto the action is continuous; there is no Chorus (which many feel was not even written by Shakespeare because of its lack of purpose and its generally inferior writing).

2. In the modern version editors have written in stage directions based on what they *thought* was occurring and they have broken the one scene into two (street-garden).

3. There is an interior reference to Romeo climbing over a wall. (And it had to be done on stage, there is no opportunity for him to leave the stage.)

4. Romeo has to be where he can hear what is said. The noted Shakespearian critic E. K. Chambers has surmised that Romeo is in the garden at the beginning of the scene and Mercutio and Benvolio are on the outside in the street.

> As there in no indication in the Qq and Fi of Romeo's entrance here, it is not impossible that in the old arrangement of the scene the wall was represented as dividing the stage, so that the audience could see Romeo on one side and Mercutio on the other.

R. G. White, another nineteenth-century scholar, has a more detailed explanation.

> From the beginning of this Act to the entrance of the Friar, there is not the slightest implication of a supposed change of scene, but rather the contrary; and the arrangment in question [Rowe's] seems to have been the consequence of an assumption that Benvolio's remark (II, i, 5) is made on the outside of the wall; whereas the text rather implies that the whole of this Act, from the entrance of Romeo to his exit after his interview with Juliet, passes within Capulet's garden; for after the stage direction, "Enter Romeo alone" (which has a like

particularity in all the old copies), Romeo says, "Can I go forward while my heart is here?"—not in the street or outside the wall, but *here,* in the dwelling-place of his love, which is before his eyes. After he speaks the next lines, the old copies (from the absence of scenery) could not direct him to "climb the wall and leap down within it"; but, had he been supposed to do this, some intimation would have been given that he was to go out of eye-shot of Mer. and Benv.; as, for instance, in Love's Lab. L. . . . Again Benvolio's remark that Romeo "*hath hid* himself among *these trees*" must surely be made within the enclosure where Romeo is, unless we suppose Benv. able to see farther into a stone wall than most folk can.

Here we have the complete scene beginning with Romeo's entrance ("Can I go forward when my heart is here?") with Romeo already *within* the orchard along with Mercutio and Benvolio. If we accept this situation we cannot honor the stage directions that have come to be accepted in the later texts.

In any case, however, while it is difficult to have complete faith in Chamber's speculation, White's explanation also lacks absolute credibility. So, what should we do? Perhaps the best plan would be to reconstruct, using as much information as we can get from all commentaries and our own thoughts, the scene just before the entrance of Romeo. (And we must, as best we can, approach this scene from the actor's viewpoint.)

After the end of the Capulet ball scene, the garden scene begins (discounting the spurious chorus that separates the two). Our question is, just where is Romeo entering from, where is he and what is the motivation for his entrance? Let us accept the proposition that he is in the street when he first comes into view. His remark, "Can I go forward (i.e., on down the street and away from where Juliet lives) while my heart is here?" does not have to mean that he is actually inside the garden wall; the proximity of the actor to the house is certainly enough to give sense and meaning to the remark. He is probably trying to give his friends the slip even though he may not be completely aware of what he intends to do. Their calls are motive enough for him to hide and the hiding places are fairly limited. Going over the wall and into the garden seems a logical solution to his problem. Once Romeo is in the garden our attention must go with him; that is, we as designers must put ourselves in his place to see—our first time and probably Romeo's too— just how this garden appears.

But what do we see? And just how did we really find our way here?

The answer, quite obviously, is by following the progress of Romeo in our imaginations as he acts out the scene. With the aid of the action-drawing process we can begin to comprehend the action requirements of the scene as well as its visual needs. First, however, let us think back over what we already know about these two places—the garden and the street outside it. We know much more of the second than we do of the first; we know, for instance, a number of facts concerning the streets of Verona in general: narrow, dirty, the scene of brutal and cruel brawls, probably not well lit at night and subject to a number of roving bands of Renaissance "juvenile delinquents" who would, simply for the thrill of it, attack the single traveler unlucky enough to be walking these streets alone after dark. We can also surmise a number of things about the garden (although we know, at this point, considerably less about it than we do the streets). Being private property, it is probably not only secluded and protected but more peaceful, more carefully attended and, in short, all the things that the streets outside are not. These are literally, two different worlds separate and kept apart by a wall. Diagrammatically these places could be presented as shown in figure 82.

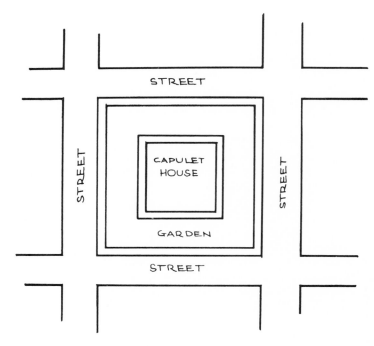

82. *Capulet house and surrounding area*

We are now ready to trace the action of this scene through the use of action drawings. Often young designers ask if this process is more or less practiced by all designers when they are trying to evolve a design for the stage out of printed text. The answer is quite obviously no. At least few do it to the extent and in the detail as presented here. Many of them can and do accomplish everything that is shown here without setting a pencil to paper; that is, they can *see* these actions in their imaginations. And some who have worked in this manner at one point in their artistic careers no longer do it as much at a later phase. The real value in this activity is, though, that the more you do this sort of analyzation in your formative stage of development, the stronger your spatial imagination becomes and the less you need detailed analysis as you become a more experienced designer. In other words, it is a technique of working that frankly is geared to the learning process but one that greatly aids the building of the imaginative skills peculiar to stage design. And while some designers continue to use these action sketches throughout their careers, the student learning his art should not underestimate the value of this activity even if, at a later time, he no longer feels it necessary to work in this manner. A simple sketch of the foregoing diagram might look something like figure 83. Remember, though, at this point we are not trying so much to work out a stage setting as we are trying to get a clear view of what elements must go into it.

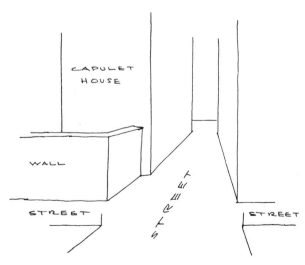

83. *Street outside Capulet house*

A. Romeo enters street. He is running away, we will discover, from his friends (fig. 84).

B. "Can I go forward when my heart is here?" (In the Capulet house with Juliet.)

C. He hears Benvolio and Mercutio calling for him and not too far

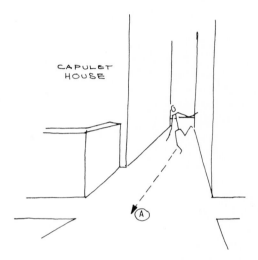

84. Street scene before garden scene

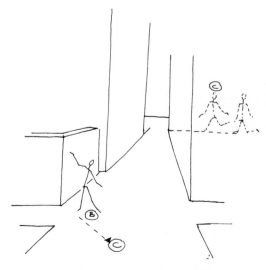

85. Street scene before garden scene

behind. He doesn't want to leave nor does he want to be discovered. He must hide somewhere (fig. 85).

   D. He climbs over the wall (How high is it?). But Benvolio must *see* him just as he goes over. (Benvolio remarks directly as to this action shortly after this [fig. 86].)

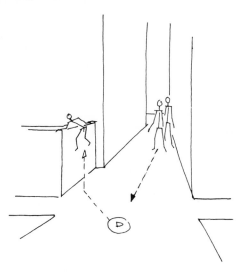

86. *Street scene before garden scene*

87. *Street scene before garden scene*

E. Benvolio and Mercutio come near the wall (fig. 87). Romeo is now hidden on the other side but can hear what is being said about him. Benvolio also remarks a little later that "he hath hid himself among these trees" (which are probably in the garden). *Problem:* We need to see both Romeo and the other two men. How?

F. Mercutio calls to Romeo (knowing where he is but pretending that he does not [fig. 88]).

G. Benvolio starts to go down the street. He tells Mercutio it is a vain quest to seek Romeo out any longer, he doesn't mean to be found.

H. Benvolio and Mercutio leave (fig. 89). *Problem:* Our angle of vision must now shift to the inside of the garden where the rest of the scene is to take place. (Perhaps this should happen as Romeo goes over the wall so that he is seen during the short scene with Benvolio and Mercutio.) How can this be done?

I. Now the second part of the scene begins. ("He jests at scars . . ." [fig. 90].) *Problem:* Romeo mentions a window. Where is it? Although we cannot help knowing it is a second-storey one (even though the stage direction "Juliet appears above at a window," does not appear in the 1597 quarto. No entrance is provided at all in that version. But, even if the play were completely unfamiliar to the designer (an unlikely possibility), he would shortly learn, from internal evidence, that it was a room not at ground level. We can also suppose from further study of the scene that she stands on a balcony structure. (What size?)

J. At this point, we still have a lot to determine before a design can

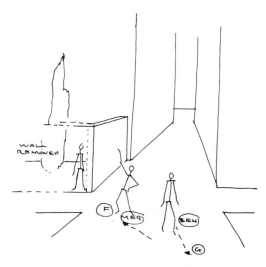

88. *Street scene before garden scene*

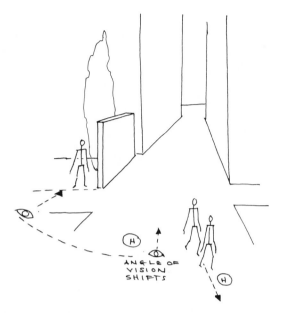

89. *Street scene before garden scene*

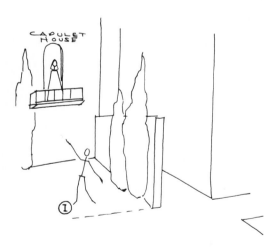

90. *Street scene before garden scene*

be made. (How big is the area we need in the garden? What kind of trees? How big is the balcony, what architectural style is it and the window, and how far from the ground are they? These are but a few of the questions that must be eventually answered [fig. 91].

91. *Street scene before garden scene*

Even though this discussion of *Romeo and Juliet* has consumed a great deal of time, the designer would soon discover, were he given the task of working out all the problems for an actual production, that only the surface has been scratched; a complete investigation, along the lines pursued here, would be worth a deliberation at least a dozen times as long as it has been given. But, for our purposes, there is a point of diminishing returns and we are very near it if, indeed, we have not passed over it already. For this reason we will stop now even though nothing very conclusive has been decided or shown concerning the production as a whole. Perhaps this will be incentive to the student designer to carry on from here to complete his own design or, maybe preferable, return again to the beginning in order that he may work out his own ideas of what the script "tells" him is important, what is trivial.

Let it be repeated once more that the conclusions to these investigations are not half so important as is the fact they were reached by a process that includes both rational and intuitional aspects of the designer's mind. Most important of all, it should be clearly understood that there is a process of scene design in the first place that does not depend merely on an emotional (or unthinking) response to a play by an artist peculiarly talented in stage design. This process, however, has been sufficiently exposed so that further explanation could serve no purpose. Furthermore, the actual problems of putting these findings into designs and onto the stage cannot be solved once and for all; although many of these findings may remain conceptually valid for the play in general, every different production will demand that the problems be confronted and resolved anew.

Nothing much more can be added at this point other than to demonstrate how one particular problem—the shift in scene from the street into the garden—was accomplished in an actual production. While it is certainly not the definitive solution to this scene, its evolution was based directly on the research materials and techniques of employing those materials into a design that we have just been studying. The setting for this particular production was, for the most part, nothing more than a series of walls some of which were stationary and some moveable. This plan allowed different areas on the stage to be given variable size and form for different scenes with a minimum of physical change. In the scene sketches that follow, both wall A and wall B were designed to open in toward the center of the stage. In the first sketch (fig. 92) we

92. *Setting for street scene*

93. *Wall mechanism*

94. *Setting for the garden scene*

see these walls in position for a street scene. In the second sketch (see fig. 94), however, wall A is opened in toward the center to allow the garden of the Capulet house to be better exposed. Wall A is constructed so that it can open, thus revealing more of the Capulet garden (fig. 93). Wall A is opened at the time Romeo climbs onto the wall—thus it is possible to see him climb over it and down into the garden without losing sight of his action. The garden is exposed by the time Mercutio and Benvolio have entered (fig. 94).

§23
Detailed Analysis of the Script:
The Church Scene in *Faust*

The first steps in designing for the opera is not unlike the approach to any other design project. Study and analyzation of the text usually takes precedence over any other activity. There is a basic difference, however, between the text of an opera and most other scripts. Reading the libretto alone can be an uninspiring experience since much of this text only becomes meaningful when it is amplified and underscored by the musical accompaniment. In opera, words and ideas, because they are not easily heard or understood when sung, are generally much more simple, repetitive, and straightforward in utterance with greater part of the emotional or poetic feeling left to the music. Still, this text must be as carefully studied as any playscript. It is gratifying to note, however, that modern operas have placed a greater emphasis on the libretto with the result that many of these newer works have more literary merit than has been the case in the past.

Faust, by Charles Gounod based on Goethe's drama of the same name, is an opera which belongs to the late-middle period of the romantic era, a movement that held the artistic world in its sway from approximately 1830 until well into the present century. Opera has yet to completely escape its influence (although as an art form it is not entirely alone in this respect), and probably will not as long as works written during the romantic period are still performed. At the present time, it is not possible to say just how long that will be, but it would seem that these works will be with us for some time to come.

In the Gounod *Faust,* much of the original legend, so powerful dramatically in the Goethe version, has, unfortunately, been weakened and obscured by the excessively sentimental attitudes of the period. (In Germany, this particular opera is generally advertised not as *Faust,* but *Marguerite.*) In the production we will examine here, it was decided early in the various conferences that precede such an undertaking to consciously counteract some of this gross (or that which seems gross to us now) sentimentality, which, while attractive and perhaps persuasive to audiences a hundred years ago (the first performance was in 1859), might prevent a present day audience from easily accepting it. This, by the way, is not meant as apology for the composer and the librettist; it is rather, an attempt to recover some of the original force and meaning they intended and did, apparently, achieve in the earlier presentations for audiences whose tastes were more in sympathy with the style and the period. This, perhaps, is the most defensible reason for updating the period of a work; to expose the form and meaning that lies beneath the often antiquated surface of its original mode of presentation.

The decision concerning period, therefore, became the first and most important consideration for all those responsible for the look and "spirit" of the opera. The time period was not, however, to be exactly pinpointed but, rather, to be treated with a certain amount of conscious anachronism. (German designers, especially those who have worked for Brecht or influenced by his philosophies—Teo Otto and Caspar Neher for example—have adopted this particular attitude toward design in general for a number of years.) This time period was to be placed roughly during the first years after World War I; a period, it was felt, which would contain some elements that might reflect attitudes found in the original legend and buried below the surface of the opera. *Faust* contains a number of situations and acts of violence that are all but completely hidden under the patina and guise of conventional romanticism. Carnal love, disillusionment, betrayal, revenge, murder, and insanity are all part of the story's web; the church scene itself is a short but intense study in the horror possible in a mind cruelly tortured to the point of madness. It was with this attitude in mind the production was approached; it was to be an exploration of the dark world that lay beneath the surface beauty of the music.

This was the period, then—the aftermath of a great war with its disillusionments, its sense of dislocation and destroyed values—in which the opera was to be set. It was also decided to use a trio of German expressionist painters—Nolde, Kirchner, Kokoschka—as a visual focal point, a point of reference and departure, and to consciously make certain scenes (the church scene for one, the Walpurgis Night scene for another) Expressionistic in nature. Some of the specific reasons why and how this was done will be discussed later in relation to the church scene.

For the moment, let us examine this question of consciously using a certain style, in this case expressionism, as part of a design concept.

To use expressionism at all in the theater can be a dangerous course for the designer to pursue, although it is a style popular and widespread, especially in university theaters. The term actually implies the way one (and only one) person sees the world, with whatever distortion that personal view entails. When we look at an artwork done in this style, we are seeing precisely what the artist wants us to see. This is his view, his outlook; it is subjective and personal. As perceived by the artist it may appear distorted since it is, by definition, a highly singular way of seeing. But while this singular vision is the prerogative of an individual artist creating an individual work, it is, with few exceptions, not a workable style for the theater designer since an audience is rarely required to experience a scene through the eyes of one artist only (or one character as in Elmer Rice's *The Adding Machine*). It is not entirely fair for a designer to impose an intensely personal subjective view on a play, and, consequently, on an audience.

In the church scene, however, it was felt that an expressionistic approach was not only possible but desirable, that we are asked to see through the eyes of one person—Marguerite—and that what we see is a distortion of reality. In other words, although the general principle that expressionism may be in most instances a dangerous course of action for the designer, in some cases it might be the right and proper one.

Let us take a closer look at the composition of this scene. Here is a synopsis. (In actual production, this scene is almost always played "in one"; this means that there is a larger scene set up immediately behind it hidden by a backdrop or curtain. In *Faust,* the scene that follows this one [the square scene in which Valentin, Marguerite's brother, has returned from the wars] was originally intended to precede the church scene, but it has become traditional to perform it afterward in order to give more emphasis to the famous "Soldier's Chorus" and the death scene of Valentin.)

> The interior of the cathedral. Organ music vibrates softly as Marguerite enters, kneels, and begins to pray. Suddenly the voice of Mephistopheles calls harshly that she must not pray ("Non! tu ne prieras pas!"). As Marguerite cowers in terror, a tomb opens and Mephistopheles stands before her, thundering that the devils in hell are clamoring for her soul. Marguerite cries out in horror and bewilderment. The choir behind the scenes chants of the awful Day of Judgment ("Quand du Seigneur le jour luira"). As Marguerite prays, Mephistopheles again proclaims her doom, then vanishes. She

faints with a piercing cry as the curtain falls. [Milton Cross, *Milton Cross' Complete Stories of the Great Operas*]

In most productions of *Faust,* the appearance of Mephistopheles is unquestioned; he simply appears, says what he has to say and then disappears. In the present production, where and how he appears was the cause of much discussion and debate. Finally, it was decided that he didn't just come to the church, *he was brought there.* By whom? There is only one other person in the scene—Marguerite. How does she bring him into the church? In her imagination. While the world where she is, the church, is real, what she is experiencing in it—the confrontation with Mephistopheles—is not necessarily real. What we, the audience see, therefore, is what she is imagining. The scene is actually an hallucination, a product of a mind that is slowly losing its grip on reality, not an actual supernatural occurrence as it has usually been played heretofore. We, the producers, felt this would be more acceptable to a modern-day audience. But what does this mean to the designer? How can he and the director use this concept? Most important, how can this idea be made clear to an audience?

Usually this scene is not presented very elaborately; often it rates nothing more than a narrow horizontal passage of space in front of a painted drop which masks a larger scene behind it. But actually, it is a key scene in the drama of the opera and deserves more attention than it too often receives. Yet, since it is a short scene and occupies an unfavorable position in the flow of scenes, great care must be taken in order that it does not become too cumbersome and difficult to set or strike. This was the main problem in the actual realization of the set on the stage and the solution to the problem demanded great care in planning, precisely because it had to be done quickly.

If there has been one major development or trend in opera production during the past seventy years, it has been the attempt to make the staging more acceptable on the realistic level. Even in the often grotesque and fantasy world of opera, audiences seem to be demanding greater skill both in presentation of character and in the design and execution of the scenery used in opera production. And yet, much of present-day opera design still is inspired by middle and late nineteenth-century settings. But, what was almost exclusively created in flat two-dimensional terms then, that is in painting, is now being built in three-dimensional form. What was then represented in a series of flat wings, backdrops, and groundrows—all artfully painted—have now become complex and practical structures.

Before we go further, let us examine the text more closely in order to get some idea of the form the church scene takes in relation to the physical actions it requires. Questions and notes accompany this text and were made by the designer as he studied the scene for possible clues to its design. (It would also be helpful to anyone studying this particular problem to listen to the passage on the recorded version of the opera. The Angel recording 3622 D/L is the only complete one to date and is an exceptionally fine performance.)

FAUST: Charles Gounod (Translated by Peter Paul Fuchs)
Act IV. Part 1—Scene 1, The Church
(Time: Approximately, 10 Minutes)

Actual Libretto	Designer's Notes
	1. Curtain rises on first bars of organ solo. (13 bars after music begins.) Stage very dark and shadowy.
	2. Marg. enters immediately after curtain starts to open.
	3. Marg. kneels at holy fount, dips fingers in water, crosses herself, rises, goes to another place, and kneels. (All this agreed upon with director.)
MARG: Dear Lord, to this poor sinner wilt Thou be Forgiving who would in Thy mercy confide.	
MEPH: (4) No—you are not to pray, No—you are not to pray! Strike her heart with misgiving, Spirits of dark, rush to her side.	4. Voice only—where it comes from unknown to Marg. or audience.
CHOR: (5) Marguerite! MARG: Oh, what voices!	5. Voices only—unseen. From behind or below? (*Problem:* Where is chorus to be put so they can see conductor or so that the chorus master can see the conductor?)
CHOR: Marguerite! (6)	6. Figure of Meph. appears at this point. It should slowly emerge.

Actual Libretto

Designer's Notes

Quality of light around him should be different than that surrounding Marg. or in church proper. He should be, literally, "king of shadows." Not fully revealed, his appearance should have the effect of a snake peering out of a pit. (How?)

MARG: Who is calling? I'll die! Oh Heaven!   (7)

7.
Perhaps she has risen when first hearing the voice and sinks down at this point. She needs something to hold, some support.

MEPH: (8)
Think again of the past,
When, protected by angels,
Your pure heart knew no wrong,
When in church you would kneel,
Singing praise to the Heavens
In heavenly song.
Here your lips would pronounce childish
Prayers
In a voice filled with innocence and love.
You would feel in your soul your dear
Mother's caress.
And blessing from above.
But now these sounds that you hear
Are the demons of hell, claiming loudly

8.
Meph. reveals himself more. His movements should not be too hampered or confined. His position should not be level with Marg. but higher so that he can dominate most of the scene (fig. 95).

95. *Action by Marguerite*

Actual Libretto

Designer's Notes

Their right.
This is the voice of your conscience,
The voice of damnation,
Freed by the dark of the night.

MARG: Lord! Who frightens me so,
Whisp'ring words in the dark
ness? (9)
Heavenly hosts! What voice of terror
Grips at my heart?

9.
She can't see him. (Why?)

CHOR: (10)
Once the clouds are torn asunder
There will be eternal thunder,
And the world will be blown to dust.

MARG: No more, no more!
This holy song sounds even more
appalling!

MEPH: No! The Lord has no mercy for you.
For you the stars will soon be falling.
Go—go!

10.
Another chorus, different in
quality from first. Orchestral accompaniment sounds like winds
high in air. (Possible change of
light to help localize this chorus
in different place—higher than
first?)

CHOR: How shall I face my creator,
Where procure an arbitrater,
When the guiltless tremble with fear?

MARG: Ah—this song is harsh and depres-
sing!
I'm caught in a prison of gloom. (11)

MEPH: Goodbye to feasts of love,
Past are joys of caressing.
You'll go below! Your fate is doom!

11.
"Prison of gloom." Can the walls
of the church have a closed-in
aspect or seem slightly prison-
like. Narrow, confining—no exit
(fig 96).

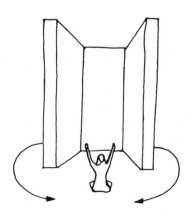

96. *Diagram of walls*

Actual Libretto	Designer's Notes
MARG: My Lord. (12) O Lord, do not spurn the contrition Of souls gone astray. Show their sins forbearing remission With one gleaming ray. O Lord, do not spurn the contrition, The contrition of souls gone astray. Show their sins forbearing remission, Show their sins forbearing remission, With one gleaming ray!	12. This is the main part of the scene, the highest point it reaches. She is borne up by this prayer and must be in a strong position for this section.
CHOR: O Lord, O Lord, do not spurn the contrition Of souls gone astray, of souls gone astray. Show their sins forbearing remission With one gleaming ray, With one gleaming ray, one ray! (13)	13. This section for chorus is simultaneous with Marg. last passage.
MEPH: Marguerite! Be accursed! (14)	14. He pronounces a judgment on her as if in a court. (Is this scene a trial?)
MARG: Ah! (15)	15. She collapses under the weight of the sentence. Curtain starts immediately after her collapse.
CURTAIN	

The scene, then, is fairly simple in structure; Marguerite comes in, kneels, prays, is tormented by the voice of Mephistopheles, prays again but is apparently not heard, collapses, curtain.

However, there is something that informs the scene and gives it its particular horror; wherever she turns, she cannot escape. She even calls the situation a "prison of gloom." She has come to the church for comfort—she gets, instead, torment. This is, perhaps, the key to the design of the scene: whenever she seeks one thing, she receives just the opposite. This is a clue, but only a start. Now, her actions must be more carefully analyzed and noted.

Let us picture this church in its simplest form; a stone structure not well lighted. The time of day, according to Mephistopheles, is night and Marguerite remarks about the darkness of the church itself. Her first action, after entering the church, would be to receive holy water (the original text has her doing most of the scene from this place). If we could see this action, it might look like what is shown in figure 97. First Action: She goes to holy-water fount, kneels, and crosses herself (fig. 98). Second Action: She rises, goes some distance (?), kneels again,

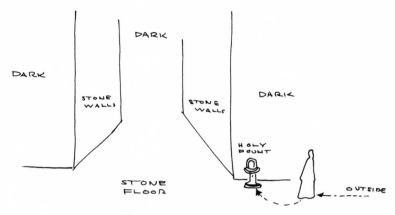

97. *Church essentials needed for actions*

98. *Action by Marguerite*

begins to pray (fig. 99)—probably in front of some object of devo-
tion(?). (In some productions, the curtain does not rise until after the
organ passage just before she begins to sing. It was felt, however, she
would have more opportunity, if the scene started immediately with the
organ music, to show her emotional state better by being seen coming
into the church instead of merely being discovered there.)

Now, let us sum up what we know to this point:

1. Situation as of this scene: Marguerite, abandoned by Faust,
alone since her brother is at war, has come to the church to ask forgiveness for succumbing to Faust's advances. (All this we know from study
of the complete opera.)

2. The church to where she has come: She probably has not gone
to a main part of the church. In disgrace, she wishes to hide so has
picked a time of day when not many people are likely to be there

99. *Action by Marguerite*

(night, according to internal evidence). The church is dark and full of shadows. By what illumination do we see her? What is the source of light—windows, votive candles? In any case, the walls and ceiling of the church are likely to be lost in darkness.

3. After the preliminary ritual (the holy water), she goes to some other place and kneels. It is in front, no doubt, of some religious object. The Christ figure is usually given the most prominent place, over the altar. She wishes not to be conspicuous, so perhaps goes someplace other than that most important area. Let us assume she goes to a Madonna figure in order to pray *through* her to God even though in the text she addresses Him directly.

She is now ready for the main part of the scene, the prayer, the confrontation, and the collapse. In the synopsis, Mephistopheles appears out of a tomb. And, even though this is a direction in the original work, this is only one of the many ways his appearance has been staged. Sometimes he appears in a column, sometimes behind a scrim wall, sometimes as in a revival at the Metropolitan Opera, not at all—just his voice is heard. Our problem at this moment is, therefore, where will he appear?

Earlier, it was said that this scene would be done expressionistically, through the eyes of one character, that character being Marguerite. And the decision was made that it was she who would

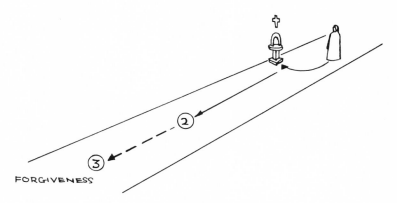

100. *Action by Marguerite*

bring Mephistopheles into the church in her imagination. We also have
assumed that wherever she turns, she is confronted with him.

A basic relationship suggests itself at this point. It might be diagramed in this way (fig. 100): (1) She enters church; (2) she kneels in
prayer for forgiveness; (3) if successful, she is free to go forward from
this point. This diagram is a combination of concrete actions and a conceptual goal (a desire to be forgiven). But she is intercepted by Mephistopheles and her path blocked. At this point her progress is checked
and she can go no further (fig. 101). A more detailed plan of this
confrontation might look like figure 102. (This also shows a level difference which increases the "power" of Mephistopheles.)

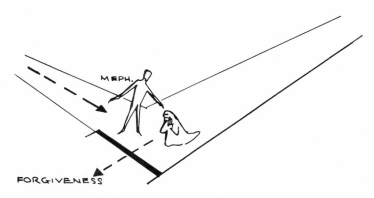

101. *Action by Marguerite and Mephistopheles*

DARK

DARK

DARK

DARK

AREA OF CONFRONTATION

102. *Action by Marguerite and Mephistopheles*

But, as of now, nothing stands between Mephistopheles and Marguerite: the scene demands concealment for him—at least at first—and some object for her to direct her prayer to, to focus on. The figure of the Madonna, suggested earlier, would serve both these needs. But just how would this serve both? In her torment, Marguerite has turned to prayer for relief. It is to this Madonna she has come to seek remission of her transgressions. Yet, instead of forgiveness, she is reminded by the voice of Mephistopheles of her sins and is taunted with the promise of damnation. She has turned to the Madonna figure for help but apparently receives just the reverse of what she seeks. This is another key to the design: a perverse response to her prayer—a metamorphosis of good into evil.

It was decided, therefore, to make whatever seemed like one thing at first to become just the opposite of what it had appeared to be. If she prayed to the Madonna, then, this figure must in someway become what it was not. Finally, it was decided that the Madonna figure would not actually change into Mephistopheles, but rather, would provide a place for him to hide behind and from which he could emerge when it became necessary for him to be seen. (In the actual presentation of the scene, he was made to appear, at first, as part of the robe of the figure and, after his first words during which he is not seen at all, to slowly detach himself from the main body of the statue. Marguerite, on the other hand, was instructed never to look directly at the figure or at Mephistopheles, but as if she were seeing [or hearing] the scene only in her mind. By directing her attention not to an actual object, she could better show that she was, in fact, going mad from the accumulative effect of guilt and grief.)

It is now time to begin to explore the other visual elements of the scene in more detail. The actual place where she spends the most time in this scene and the light sources were the next two questions to be studied. First, let us examine her playing area more closely. After she kneels and begins her prayer, Marguerite is fairly well limited in possibility of movement; actually, she is stuck in one place for the greater part of this short scene. This position must also be favorable in terms of sound, not only visually effective. Possibilities for use of this confined area, therefore, became important to the performer. The idea suggested earlier that this scene has similarities to a criminal trial, plus the fact that the church would almost certainly have altar railings around the various religious stations, made some structure desirable both to aid the singer and as a scenic unit. For these reasons, then, a railing was devised that would help define the space while at the same time providing something for Marguerite to use directly in the action of the scene. (There are moments when she very much needs something to hold on to, to provide support.) Since this rail served in a symbolic function as well as a practical one, it was designed to enclose Marguerite in the manner of the European prisoner's dock, but shorter since most of her scene is played from a kneeling position (fig. 103).

The statue, since one of its functions was to provide a hiding place for Mephistopheles, had to be fairly large. It was decided to overscale it, that is, make it much larger than any such statue one might find in an actual church. (Again, the expressionist viewpoint was adopted: dur-

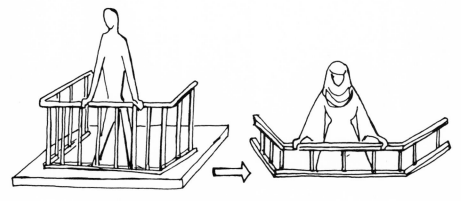

103. *Prisoner's railing and altar railing*

ing this scene, the things to which Marguerite directs her attention
loom larger to her than they might under different circumstances. The
figure of the Madonna, therefore, becomes an overpowering symbol of
refuge at first and later, in her distorted vision, an equally powerful
reminder to Marguerite that Heaven may be denied her.) It was also
designed so that the Madonna looks above and beyond the place where
Marguerite kneels; she is, in fact, overlooked. Actually, Marguerite is
more in the shadow of the statue than addressing it directly. This
brings in the question of light source in the church. Where does it
come from, what are its qualities?

Several possibilities exist for light motivation. The windows are
stained glass and would give patterns of light that could emphasize or
suggest the fractured planes of color which one finds in expressionist
paintings. But it is night and little light would be coming through the
windows from outside. What light does exist, then, in the church and
around the various statues? The most prevalent source would be, at
night especially, from votive candles lit by supplicants. They do not,
moreover, give out much light; the church could still remain mostly in
shadow. The light from the votive candles also suggest another means
by which the design concept may be reinforced, especially if they are in
the small red glass receptacles as is often the case. Let us suppose,

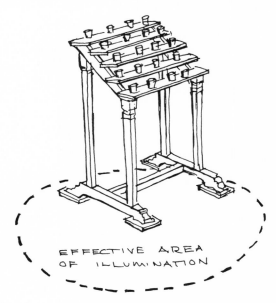

104. *Votive candle rack*

therefore, that these candles will be our motivating source of light; they would probably be placed on a stand in tiered rows. Our research reveals something like fig. 104.

There isn't time for Marguerite to light a candle (or really a need) so perhaps it should be placed somewhere out of her direct path. Since she is in the shadow, the light in her area quite possibly should be kept on the cool side; on the other hand, the votive candles in their red holders would give off a reddish glow (which would have to have auxiliary light from lighting instruments—with red mediums—so that this area will be bright enough; the candles alone would not provide nearly enough light or exactly the desired color). The stand was placed on the opposite side of the Madonna from the area where Marguerite spends most of the scene (fig. 105).

We now have two general areas of light: a red one near the place where Mephistopheles appears and a cool one where Marguerite kneels. The votive candle stand in this position also helps in another way; it further supports the plan to make the ordinarily religious objects of the church take on perverse uses. Although these candles are lit to honor the sanctified dead, when Mephistopheles appears, the flickering quality of the light and its red color becomes reminiscent of hell-

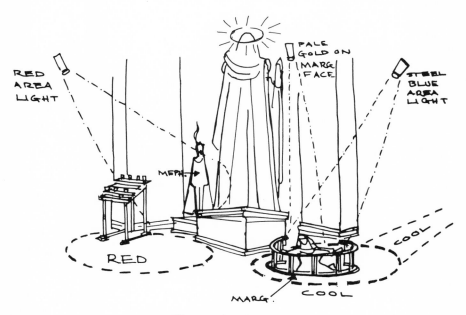

105. *Warm and cool areas of light*

fire (especially if the light in this area is intensified after he emerges from the shadows of the statue).

It is about this time in the design process that all the design elements and action plans must be brought together. At this stage the designer should be able to make drawings that will not only show pictorial and decorative possibilities, but will take into consideration the needs of the performers as well. Many designers also make a practice of including in these drawings (usually small and quickly made) pertinent notes. Figure 106 is such a drawing. Approximately two by three inches, it is only meant to be a crude indication, not a complete or final drawing; it is not uncommon for a designer to make several dozen of these small sketches, most of which he throws away.

From this point on (and the point at which we will leave this example) the designer's work becomes increasingly more technical and specific. He must now find ways of putting this product of the imagination in physical form; working drawings must be made, the builders and craftsmen in the shops supplied with detailed information, and

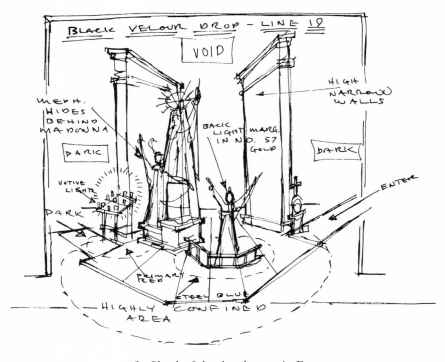

106. *Sketch of the church scene in* Faust

their work carefully overseen. A thousand decisions must be made, scrutinized, and, if necessary, changed or discarded. It is all the more important, then, that a firm design concept be evolved *before* the technical phase is reached so that the designer is provided with a firm base from which to work and a security of purpose so that his imaginative vision is not lost in the hectic world of production (fig. 107).

There are seven scenes in *Faust*; our concern has been with only one of that seven. In a multiscene work, however, the designer must think of the production as a visually integrated total, not as a series of independent nonrelated designs. He may, for instance choose common visual elements or a range of colors which are repeated in a number of all of the scenes. He is almost certain to find that a playwright or composer has consciously—although sometimes intuitively—constructed every scene so as to contain not only clues that aid in the realization of that particular one but also others as well. How does this affect the designer's overall scenic scheme?

In analyzing the text of the church scene it was necessary to follow

107. *Model of the church scene in* Faust

closely the train of Marguerite's thought; it was through her remarks
that we obtained valuable clues to the scenic environment. She believed, at the beginning of the scene, that she had come to a place
where solace and peace of mind could be found. By degrees she finds it
is something entirely different from what she expected. In fact the
church has become a "prison of gloom." In order to produce the desired mood, the qualities of a prison were emphasized—heavy stone
walls, unrelieved with any softening detail or ornament—instead of
those of a church. At the end of the scene she has been tried and found
guilty of a moral crime and she believes damnation to be her fate. In
the final scene of the opera, however, she has committed an actual
crime—the killing of her child by Faust—and has been put in a real
prison. The question the designer must answer is, then, how do these
two different places—the church and the prison—visually relate to each
other? Or should he draw some sort of visual comparison? Quite probably he should and in so doing strengthen the unity of the production.
(Actually Gounod's dramatic scheme contains a fairly obvious equation
concerning these two scenes: Marguerite finds in the church, condem-
nation; and in the prison, salvation.)

Here is the very last part of the libretto. It describes what is supposed to happen to the prison at the very end of the opera.

FAUST:	O Marguerite!
MARG:	What blood is that which stains thy hand!
	[pushing him away]
	Away! Thy sight doth cause me horror!
MEPH:	Condemned!
CHORUS OF ANGELS:	Saved! Christ has arisen!
	Christ is born again!
	Peace and felicity
	To all disciples of the Master!

[The prison walls open. The soul of Marguerite rises toward
heaven. Faust gazes dispairingly after her, then falls on his
knees and prays. Mephistopheles turns away, barred by the
shining sword of an archangel.]

End of the Opera.

Whereas the church was a prison, the prison now becomes the portal to
heaven. In the production under discussion it was decided to make
these two scenes strongly linked; the walls of the church would also be
the walls of the prison, only certain details would be changed (fig. 108).

At the appropriate moment this is what took place (fig. 109): first,

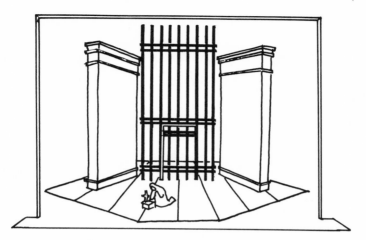

108. *Design for the prison scene in* Faust

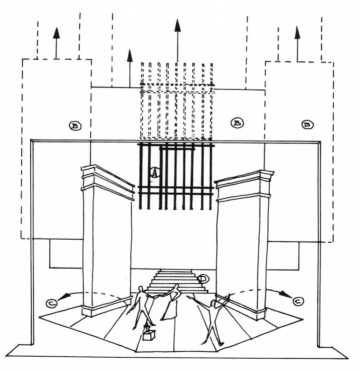

109. *Diagram for the scene transformation in* Faust

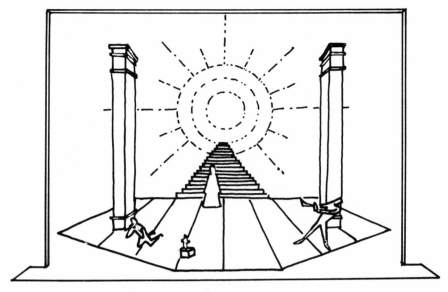

110. *Design for the finale in* Faust

the prison grillwork was flown out (A); second, the black velour drop and masking legs were also flown out (B); and third, the walls pivoted outward (C), revealing a golden stairway leading into a sunburst projection on a sky cyclorama (fig. 110).

§24
The Design Concept on the Stage: *The Glass Menagerie*

It has been many years since the first performance of *The Glass Menagerie,* Tennessee Williams's initial success in the theater. It would be almost impossible to recount just how many times it has been put on the stage since then and how many ways it has been done. Jo Mielziner first designed it and there probably have been many more individual and original interpretations by actors and directors than there have been by designers, not that his design has been merely duplicated down through the years. Still, the basic concepts behind this particular design have all but gone unquestioned in a great many of those productions seen on the stage. And the fact that Williams himself agreed with the design offered by Mielziner, at least tacitly, has further reinforced the feeling that this is the "right" way, the correct solution. But before we go further, let us look at a simplified version of the plan of the setting used in the original production. Basically it consisted of certain specific areas arranged as shown in figure 111. In this design, the setting is oriented to a proscenium theater arrangement and in no way violates the limitations of such a theater which, usually, keeps audience (A, fig. 112) and actors (B, fig. 112) in separate and isolated units. Movement in depth and at oblique angles is limited; action of the play is essentially horizontal rather than multidimensional. In short, the design approach is basically pictorial.

Let us, for a moment, examine this question of approach and, at the same time, examine the question of originality. Every designer should always ask himself for what reasons would he want to redesign a basic plan thought out by a talented and successful professional designer. Is it merely to be different? Is it just to "show you can do it

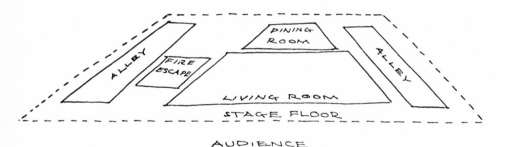

111. *Mielziner's setting with acting areas*

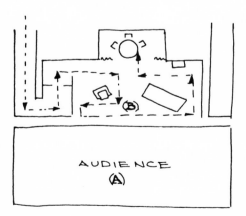

112. *Plan of Mielziner set*

too"? This is, in many instances, part of the motive, but it's not the whole truth, the complete rationale. No, the creative urge in most designers lies in a somewhat different direction or at least has a deeper impetus and motivation.

Quite often a student designer will say that what he wants to do with a project, a design, is to "think it out for myself and do something different." And while it is difficult to disagree with this desire totally, some objection could be made to the last words of that statement, to the implication of the "do something different" part. Originality is certainly not a bad thing to strive for, but one should always carefully examine the motives inherent in the desire for it. Perhaps this statement should be amended to read, "When I approach a play with the intent of designing it, I would like to think it out." Period. Dylan Thomas once said that the business of posterity was to look after itself; maybe it is the business of originality to do likewise and not be pursued as the most important element of the design. This is especially true in an age which has put such an emphasis and premium (too much possibly) on originality for its own sake. To be new and different just to be new and different is a reason, it must be admitted; it is not necessarily a good reason however, at least not good enough for the serious mature designer to make it his complete *raison d'être*.

This, then, often becomes the truly creative designer's problem when faced with designing the "war horses" of theater; not trying to be just original or new, but to be able to see the play in a new light and with fresh eyes, to be able to create a right environment (very few will deny there is more than one acceptable variation) and not just an impressively new or cleverly different setting. All too often, when we attempt to evolve a style for a production, we add on a veneer when our real problem should be to clear away and start from scratch. A designer must not be afraid to begin at the beginning; he should not be afraid of being simple. The process would be as if a man gave a piece of furniture another coat of paint when what he really wanted to do was strip all the old paint away and reveal the original beauty of the wood.

The designing of *The Glass Menagerie* was begun with the basic assumption that the world of the play is a macrocosm, a complete and specific world, even though it is merely conceptual and one that is unlimited by artificial restrictions (such as the proscenium arch). Someday, all too soon as it usually happens, this larger world must be presented as a microcosm and will be bound by the limitations of the stage, that is, accomplished with its devices and subject to its principles. But, it is valuable, as long as possible, to keep the freedom of the first from being unduly hampered by the shortcomings of the second. This is the best reason one can find for not blindly accepting the design solution of another artist, no matter how successful that design might have been.

The design of the production of *The Glass Menagerie* began, then, by attempting to clear away what was already known and going back to the script itself. Along with this, however, certain considerations could not be avoided entirely. First, the various ways it had been done before either in the theater or seen in photographs could not be obliterated from the mind entirely; there is really no good reason for doing this anyway. This backlog of observation included such diverse items as a cinema version, a telecast, and a recording, as well as a number of stage presentations (at least a dozen or so) ranging from proscenium arch productions to thrust stage to full arena. All helped in some way; there are always those little revelations—sometimes planned, most often accidental—even in the worst productions that make it worth seeing or hearing. But, still, this accumulated information is of little use to the designer confronted with the job of realizing Williams's particular world of memory on an actual stage.

A second consideration, and a more useful one, was Williams's own words in a short essay accompanying the recorded version of the play. While this material is primarily "literary"—not directly related to stage production of the play—certain thoughts in it are valuable.

When my family first moved to St. Louis from the South, we were forced to live in a congested apartment neighborhood. . . . The apartment we lived in was about as cheerful as an Arctic winter. There were outside windows only in the front room and kitchen. The rooms between had windows that opened upon a narrow areaway that was virtually sunless and which we named "Death Valley" for a reason which is amusing only in retrospect.

There were a great many alley cats in the neighborhood which were constantly fighting the dogs. Every now and then some unwary young cat would allow itself to be pursued into this areaway which had only one opening. The end of the cul-de-sac was directly beneath my sister's bedroom window and it was here that the cats would have to turn around to face their pursuers in mortal combat. . . . For this reason . . . she kept the shade constantly drawn so that the interior of her bedroom had a perpetual twilight atmosphere. . . . My sister and I painted all her furniture white; she put white curtains at the window and on the shelves around the room she collected a large assortment of little glass articles. . . .

When I left home a number of years later, it was this room that I recalled most vividly and poignantly when looking back on our home life in St. Louis. . . . The areaway where the cats were torn to pieces was one thing—my sister's white curtains and tiny menagerie of glass were another. Somewhere between them was the world that we lived in.

In the actual play, this bedroom is not required, but what is revealed here is a basic relationship clearly set forth and which must, in some way, be put on the stage. The grim, cruel aspect of the outside "real" world and the twilight, quietly luminous quality of the inside of the apartment is constructive information, pertinent to the play and useful to a designer. In any case, this double world, simultaneously represented, seems to be the most important element in the play's environment. In the successful productions of this play (and this was true of the Mielziner design), this fundamental relationship was observed, regardless of the differences in the way it was accomplished; in the unsuccessful ones, it has been lacking or was mishandled and the play suffered accordingly.

Yet, the most valuable clue to a workable solution to the design was obtained, as it often is, by accident. It was revealed by a young student actor quite unaware that he summed up in one short phrase the whole key to the riddle.

The play was being discussed in a context totally unrelated to any design problem. Questioning him about how he would feel and react were he Tom and faced with the economic and family ties Tom had, he said, "I would do what was necessary as quick as possible. I guess that you have to do that. But then I'd split." Almost immediately his word, "split," seemed to have meaning, although it was not until sometime later that the full realization of just how valuable this word was became apparent. He had simply referred, of course, to the present-day vernacular for the act of leaving; the train of thought he provoked, however, had more to do with the situation of the three people who composed the family than it did with his meaning or use of the term.

About this time there was another disturbing and intriguing question that was occasioned by a statement of Tom's made during the final moments of the play: "time is the longest distance between two places . . . [and so I] followed, from then on, in my father's footsteps, attempting to find in motion what was lost in space." With these thoughts in mind, an image began to evolve of this family as they existed in time rather than in their allotted space, their apartment. The problem, then, was to construct a diagram that would resolve these two insistent thoughts, time and a split, into a meaningful visual image, an image that would clarify and describe the basic action of the play. After many tries, this diagram was evolved (fig. 113). This image immediately gave several ideas in which there were possibilities. Some of those were:

1. They were a single unit at one time. In the past, when they first moved to St. Louis, Tom was younger and, although not happy with his lot, was not in the stagnant position, both in his work and family life, he occupies during the course of the play.

2. At the time of the play's action, they have reached the point when the splits are, although ignored actively by the mother and Laura, just beginning to become serious.

3. Tom does eventually go his own way, but Laura is left, as is Amanda. For both Laura and Amanda, this is the end of the road, as it were. However, one other split is suggested here, (although not actively examined in the course of the play) and that is the split between Laura and Amanda after the last attempt (the plot of the play) to get a husband for Laura. Amanda, when this attempt fails, does move away from Laura and allows her to be alone, which, of course, is what she has come to accept already.

4. While we cannot be absolutely certain of the future of these three, we can be relatively sure that the end of the play should somehow imply they will never be "together" as a unit again. Each is left, at last, in his own separate world.

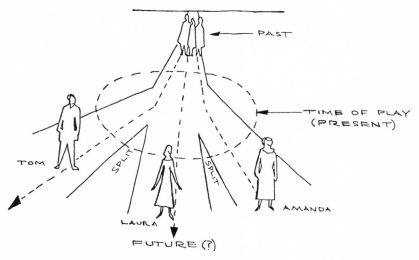

113. *Scenic image*

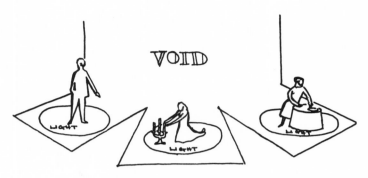

114. *Last scene of* The Glass Menagerie

From here, there was a direct jump to those final moments of the play, the time when the three are at last alone and separate (fig. 114). This brought to mind, incidently, that the first scene of the play, directly following the prologuelike speech of Tom, was one which showed them together at the table, and, although there is an uneasy peace among them, all three are as close as they ever are in the play.

This image also suggested several practical ideas; for one thing, it clarified a desire to violate the proscenium arch (which was the type of theater where the design would be done) so that the separateness of the individual characters could be intensified. Secondly, if Tom chooses the outside, i.e., the world, and Laura is left in the room where she was happiest, with her menagerie, then Amanda also needed a place of her own, a practical world where she can keep busy and useful. In the Mielziner design, this world of Amanda had been stuck off in the back and was subordinate to the other two worlds. Quite possibly it needed to be out where it could be visually and practically more important. A kitchen also seemed a natural and necessary adjunct to Amanda's particular place and so that too should somehow be included in the total design. By now the areas needed had increased from the two basic ones described in the play to three. This meant, in all probability, that space on the stage would be more limited than if the script's plan was followed.

Environment is not always or entirely a matter of *how* a place looks. It takes into consideration its spatial qualities as well. In *The Glass Menagerie,* environment is concerned primarily with the juxtaposition of spaces along with their individual and opposing qualities, not alone with a historically accurate pictorial representation, i.e., showing how a St. Louis alley looked in 1939. There is no doubt this period of time and its peculiar look and feel should be evoked; but this is not simply a matter of copying factual visual details.

In other words, the space through which the characters of this play move, the shape of it and the objects and barriers it contains, is more important than the background against which they are seen, no matter how visually right it is. We cannot avoid the diagrammatic implication of Williams's last sentence: "The areaway . . . was one thing—my sister's white curtains and tiny menagerie of glass were another. Somewhere between them was the world that we lived in."

Whenever more than one place is put on the single stage space, the designer is faced with a basic problem; he must compress the individual spaces to fit the total space, and at the same time, expand the possibility for movement of the actors in those spaces. Practically no major play Williams has ever written deals with a single limited area. In almost all his plays, he writes into the fabric of the play, situations that cannot be acted in a single unit of space, such as a room. The designer cannot avoid these demands for settings more fluid than single locales, nor is he given time to substitute one place for another in a sequence (changing one set for another by mechanical means). But the sense of space can be created without an actual large amount of space if certain things are done with it; for instance, substituting time and distance for space. This simply means that the designer causes a character to walk a much longer distance to get to a place that is actually and physically quite close if approached the nearest possible way. The actor's path and progress (fig. 115) is carefully controlled by various means so that he cannot go from A to B in a direct manner but must make his approach in this longer way.

In the Mielziner design, the main part of the action was confined to the boxlike structure set in the middle of the stage (fig. 116). The proscenium arch theater, with its relatively poor sight lines, undoubtedly dictated the placement of crucial areas in his design. (The second alley, quite possibly, was created because of the sight-line problem, even though in the directions of the playwright—and in the description

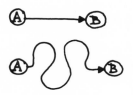

115. *Actor movement*

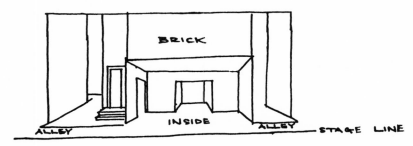

116. *Diagram of Mielziner setting*

of his original model, the actual locale itself—there was no second possibility of access or escape.)

Now, since there was a desire to show more of the dining room and also add a kitchen area (not used in the original design), this added space must be paid for at the expense of the other two areas (the alley and the living room). It also became clear that an expanded hall area was necessary in order to go from room to room and a bedroom door was needed primarily for escape purposes during the short blackouts. The need for a *sense* of space becomes, therefore, even more critical than before. In the Mielziner solution, the space is resolved basically as shown in figure 117. By using this dining-room-kitchen area in a more prominent way, it would be necessary to make the paths of movement more circuitous than he did, and, at the same time, work in depth rather than horizontally as he had done. The traffic followed roughly the pattern in figure 118.

In the present design, the proscenium arch line was violated and no curtain used in order to bring the action of the play, which is ex-

117. *Movement possibilities of Mielziner setting*

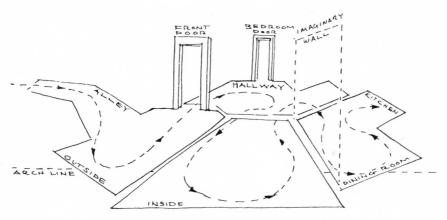

118. *Alternate movement possibilities*

tremely intimate in scope and nature, in closer proximity to the audience. This made it necessary for most of the actual physical boundaries of the rooms, the walls, to be removed. The feeling of being "boxed in" which Tom constantly alludes to and reacts against, so well conceived in the Mielziner design had, therefore, to be resolved in a different manner altogether. This was accomplished primarily through the use of a brick wall placed at the rear of the apartment which rose up behind and over the rather low ceiling line of the exterior. The wall, blank and unpenetrated by any opening, was carried out of sight and lost in the darkness of the upper portion of the stage house. There was, literally, no way out of Williams's "cul-de-sac" except the narrow passage of the alley into the street.

This wall (along with all the other details of the setting), while as literal environment was token in nature, was realistic in execution and did, although not entirely surrounding the apartment and alley, give the desired feeling of claustrophobic enclosure. It should also be noted here, perhaps, that even though the details of the setting examined separately, were almost naturalistic, the composition of these elements was not, at least not to the extent of the Mielziner design. If any prevalent influence is discernible, it would be, probably, Brechtian in nature.

The greatest advantage of the open stage form featured in this design (fig. 119), however, was that in extending the acting areas out and beyond the walls and into the auditorium, the actors could, by light, be more effectively isolated and separated from the setting. This ability to isolate a character from his environment is essential to the structure and nature of this particular play since it purports to be

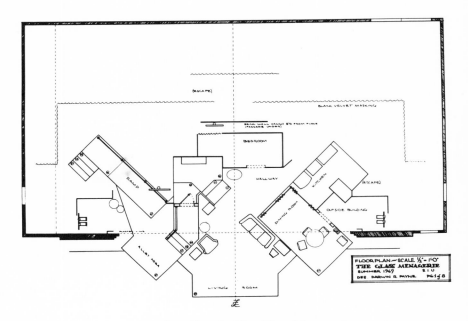

119. *Floor Plan for* The Glass Menagerie

memory, and memory tends to disassociate and separate the significant act and detail from its original all-inclusive, comprehensive background. This need to define and isolate characters, and at the same time obliterate all else, is especially necessary in the Laura-Jim section during the final scene of the play. Williams, himself, motivates this need by causing the action to be confined to a small circle of light from a few candles.

In the final stages of the design, what had evolved was this: a mood, a feeling of period and place was accomplished (this is something that the Mielziner design did superbly). At the same time, it was necessary to depart from his basic plan in order to (1) open up the apartment and expose more effectively some areas that he and his director decided not to show or use, and (2) make use of the image of the three major characters split one from the other and each alone on his own solitary path. What has been done in this design (fig. 120) is certainly not newer (except chronologically), or more original (that was never an intent or even a serious question), or better; that is a matter of how well the design served the actors and director; in fact, that is the only criterion really acceptable in judging the merit of any stage design.

120. *Set sketch for* The Glass Menagerie

What was attempted, and to some extent accomplished, was a resolution of the original thesis, which was to think the problem through from the ground up, finding in that process, a workable and satisfying solution rather than relying on or reacting against an earlier one by another designer. Finally, let it be said, if there is a sense of competition in the designer's makeup, and it is hard to believe that any creative artist is totally without it in some respect, it should be directed more inwardly, striving with one's own limitations, and not outward, that is, attempting to "do it better" than someone else.

§25
A Note on the Progress of Scene Design during
the Past Decade

Until now most of our attention has been directed toward scene designs created from a traditional and fairly literal point of view; in these designs an audience would have little difficulty relating what they saw on the stage with their own conceptions of what reality was or should be. Hopefully this procedure has had some value, partly for its own sake but also as a preparation for studying design concepts that are not as literally based.

It is time, then, to take a step beyond this approach (or at least to affirm there are others) and to make a brief examination of how the designer creates a scene design which has as its premise that the stage setting need not always be a representational image of reality as perceived somewhere outside the theater. While discussion of this view has been purposely avoided until now, even the most cursory glance at the output of today's designers will quickly reveal to the student designer a wide spectrum of possibilities of which he should be aware. At the same time, it must be remembered that the most advanced design theory owes much more to past concepts than might appear at first glance.

Theater, until quite recently, has been a closed system; "show business" was an escape from the "real" world not only for audiences but for those who made it their profession; few theater artists today, however, are as insulated from that outside world as they formerly were. As a result, the scene designer working now finds that he must look at the world outside the theater with different eyes than his predecessors did. The odd thing about this situation is that it is leading away from naturalism and the reproduction of literal images on the stage instead of toward it; the more outside events intrude on and affect the designer, the more seems to be his desire to uncover and to display that which lies beneath the surface of physical things and events. There seems to be an intense desire, in fact, to fracture, reorganize, and synthesize raw visual impressions into hybrid forms and structures that do not mirror life so much as present its dominate feature more directly: change as it occurs in time and motion.

It is easier to note, however, that profound alterations are being made in the way the designer thinks and performs than to chart the directions and import of those alterations. Moreover, by the time new concepts and practices filter into the classroom, often they have lost their initial vitality and usually much of their original "meaning"; for this reason, the young designer sometimes adopts only the outer forms of these newer approaches (and all too often only the most obvious and spectacular elements of them) without really understanding the underlying reasons for their initial creation. (There is probably more truth than we care to admit in William Faulkner's observation that, "immature artists copy, great artists steal." Knowing what and when to steal is very much a part of the designer's self-education.) It must be admitted, too, that the most that can be accomplished in any text on scene design is to draw attention to some of the salient features of recent and current trends in the whole field; in this case, approximately the last ten years.

Although the theater of the last decade has been the target of numerous forces, undoubtedly the most significant change has been the emergence of a more ritualistic form of theater which has put an emphasis on the emotional, nonverbal (sensory) engagement of an audience. Along with this trend there has been a marked de-emphasis on elaborate production as well as an intense effort to break down the traditional barriers between performer and audience which have grown up during the past three hundred years. A corresponding trend has been the virtual dethronement of the playwright as the single most important person in the theater. As a direct result of this development, the play, once considered as the sacrosanct corner block of the production, has become less important. The hierarchy of the theater (playwright down to director down to actor, designer, and technician) in a great many instances has all but given way to a loosely bonded confederation of artists who, by mutual agreement, each "does his own thing." Many of the playwrights of the new theater are more "idea" men who supply scenarios and situations to actors who then improvise from those germinal ideas. This does not imply, however, that everyone in theater has suddenly jettisoned the old methods and standards of theater production; tradition in theater is much too strong and production is still being handled in most companies much as it has been for centuries. Nevertheless, there are few professional artists, especially directors and designers, who have not been influenced by the experiments of the more avant-garde theater groups which have gained attention during the last ten years. For the designer, in particular, self-expression, so long antithetical to the concept of the production as a unified whole, has become more acceptable as a legitimate stance than it was heretofore. Directors are giving the designer more liberties; in some cases, the designer simply seems to be taking them. This does not necessarily imply that he is becoming a self-serving, ego-oriented exhibitionist; most designers still are designing settings (now more generally referred to as scenic environments) which they sincerely believe are in the best interests of the total production. But they are accepting less outside advice as to what those best interests are; this, in part, accounts for the great number of designers who have turned to directing in addition to designing. At the very least, there is a distinct understanding among most designers that the situation in which they work has become a more coequal one than it was in the past. In some ways, this thinking is less an innovation of today than it is a return to theater practices prior to the middle of the nineteenth century when Wagner and the Duke of Saxe-Meinigen began their crusade to make all aspects of a production merge into a unified whole (and if this production was to be reflective of any single personality, it was to be theirs). The difference between then and now, however, is that the designer, then often only an artisan who supplied scenic backgrounds according to strict specifications, is now very much an individual with strong artistic views and a philosophy to support those opinions.

What is essentially new to the present-day theater (and something for which the modern designer is greatly responsible) is the conception of the stage setting not as a static or fixed unit—a "set"—confined to a limited, predetermined area of space, but, rather, as an image or series of images which, like the human universe it reflects, is in a constant state of flux. This concept gives rise to a number of principles, some of which have been conventions of past ages of theater, although others are strictly twentieth century in origin. A few of these conventions—although not all—are:

1. That the action of the production can take place anywhere within viewing range of the spectator (and may even require the spectator to move from place to place to view the action—rather than having the performer come to him) and that the spectator's vision may be amplified, channeled, or distorted by mechanical means (closed-circuit television—cinema—projections or light effects).

2. That the setting need not be a single unified image but can be a number of unrelated ones shown in series or simultaneously.

3. That the duration of any single image or group of images is not directly related to the duration of the script's stated or intended divisions (acts, scenes, episodes, etc.). That, in fact, the images may move and change in arbitrary rhythms contrary to the progression of the script's intentions or to the actions of the performers. The scenic environment, in short, may be every bit as kinetic as any of the other elements in the production.

4. That the scenic environment may visually (as well as physically) support the nature of the production without literal or historical references. That this scenic environment may consist solely of forms and images the designer feels best displays the abstract qualities of the production.

In the next example, we will concentrate only on one area of these various possibilities: making the setting an embodiment of abstract qualities instead of a literal representation of a historical or geographical locale. Multimedia productions certainly figure importantly in current production practices. To discuss them adequately is, however, far beyond the scope of this text and presupposes a level of investigation which we have not intended. Little has been written on this subject to date; the material which has found its way into print usually deals with past productions (accounts of how a certain production was accomplished) or observations in the most general terms. The young designer should expect these newer trends in scene design to accelerate in the future; but much of what he learns about how to produce such a design must be empirically gained. A distinct shortcoming of studying multimedia designs in books is the fact that, unlike the static stage setting which lends itself to pictures, one of the prime features of a multimedia production—the mobility of images—is incapable of being shown.

§26
The Scene Design as a Physical Embodiment of Abstract Qualities: *The Caretaker*

Although the designer may use actual realistic source materials in the preparation of a design, he may sometimes be more interested in refining from those materials what he considers to be the visual and tactile essences. His purpose is to create a design that, while not recognizable "real," will in some way increase the involvement, understanding, and pleasure of the spectator viewing it and the actor performing within it. In creating such a design, the designer is still doing research much in the manner which we have already observed, but he allows his imagination to take greater liberties with his findings than has been the case in previous examples. He may, for instance, strip away surfaces from their substructures, juxtapose incongruent images and objects in various scales, fracture natural elements or architectural forms, and then recombine them into new structures and arrangements. Let us take a closer look at how and why a designer might choose to work in this manner.

Harold Pinter's play *The Caretaker* takes place in a single location, a room in a derelict building in an old section of London; the time of the action originally was 1959 (the date of the play's composition), but it could very well be the present time with little harm done to the text or intention of the play. While there is no reason to believe that the actual room in which Pinter sets the action of the play exists, it is quite probable that hundreds of such rooms not only do exist in London but could be found and duplicated on the stage (or, as Belasco once did, bought outright, taken apart, and then reassembled in a theater). But would this really satisfy the underlying requirements of the script? Would a naturalistic setting necessarily make the play more correctly produced—or better in the eyes of the spectator? Would it possibly hinder the production in any way? While these questions could never be completely answered without thinking in terms of an actual proposed production, any close inspection of the play will quickly reveal that Pinter relies heavily on physical things to create an atmosphere that, while it is never less than real, is always something more than factual reportage; nor does the dialogue, no matter how disjointed or abstract it becomes, ever proceed very far without direct reference to or use of something physical and close at hand. (In many ways, the locales of his plays are almost always totally closed systems; that is, the rooms in which the actions of his plays take place are not only complete worlds in themselves, they are isolated from any others.)

Any designer would agree that it is impossible to design this particular play without a very careful analyzation of the physical features of the room where the action transpires—the exact placement of doors, windows—with an equally intense study of the objects in it (and since it is a kind of storehouse, the problems of placement and relationships of objects become critical). But what about the intent of the play itself; what about its verbal structure? Who could deny that the dialogue is naturalistic to the point of being pointless? Or is it? Is it possible that Pinter is operating on more than one level and with more than one purpose? Quite obviously he is. It is equally obvious that his locale is closely tied to what he is trying to show. But should the designer create a room—or a scenic environment—that mirrors exactly only one level, the naturalistic one? Can you, in fact, have naturalistic acting (and that is obviously the technique demanded of the performers if not the underlying intent) in a "theatrical" setting, that is, a setting that is not "real"? Of course, only an accepted philosophy of presentation can give the answer to such a general question, but the answer it gives us in this case (and in today's practice in general) is yes.

This is not so contradictory as it might seem to be at first glance. Perhaps one of the solutions to understanding this situation lies in the fact that an actor's performance can and should lie on several levels simultaneously; whereas the designer's work, while also striving to possess levels of meaning other than the purely literal one, is more restricted to harder-lined images and symbols which are not as illusion-creating (and therefore not as mysterious) as those created by the actor.

But what if the designer decides to create a design that exhibits a level of meaning other than the naturalistic one; a level in which he presents to an audience the qualities he perceives in this room in abstract form, not hidden behind the details of naturalistic reproduction? In essence, this is what has happened in much of today's production;

the designer has been given just such a liberty. And whether or not one agrees with this philosophy (there are, in fact, many who do not), it should be recognized that it does exist; the designer training today would be well advised not only to expect this freedom of expression, but, more and more, to expect that many directors will not only allow but will also thrust it upon him.

Let us take a closer look at how the design for this play, *The Caretaker,* was approached in an actual production, a production where the questions we have just raised were part of the designer's problem. But these were not the only problems; there were others:

1. The production was an open stage one. How, then, to obtain the atmosphere of a closed-up, cut-off place; how to get this effect on a stage with only one wall possible on one side and none on the other three?

2. How to make the characters seem to be held down and contained; or, as the director desired, "wedged into a situation." While the actors were to perform their roles as naturalistically as possible, the place where they were to perform should be "less an actual room than a structure which is open and closed at the same time; a particular room and a timeless place; a construction that catches smells, is permanent but capable of disintegrating momentarily—a world solid and full of holes."

3. A floor pattern which allows for the maximum mobility of action (there is much more of this inherent in the script than seems at first reading) while seeming to prevent it.

Preliminary research turned up enough materials to allow a drawing to be made that would satisfy many of the integral necessities of the play's action: a room on the second floor of a fairly large house with a number of rooms, hallways, etc., all in a state of disrepair (fig. 121). Literal features of the room thus reconstructed: walls—wallpaper dirty with age, peeling, stained; plaster beneath cracked, patches falling off to reveal substructure (lath and rough plaster); moldings and trims scarred, dirty, rough from repeated coats of paint and varnish; floors—worn, warped, scarred, edges of planks chipped and splintered. The whole building shows the effect of heat, cold, moisture, and hard use with little upkeep. But while these are all facts (strong possibilities at least), research cannot end here; a greater refinement of these findings is necessary before they can be directly incorporated into a final design. But where to from here; what direction will turn up anything more useful than this information or determine its possible use?

Research, as it has been pointed out before, is not always just a matter of finding appropriate visual details. Literary sources can be

121. *London House*

tremendously helpful to the designer when he is seeking to pinpoint illusive qualities of a playscript; they might very well assist the designer in knowing what out of his raw research materials to keep and use and what to discard. Granted, these sources are much harder to find than visual materials; you almost have to know where this written material is before searching for it. But this is all the more reason for the designer to maintain a wide undirected reading program. Paradoxically, being able to verbalize images is more important to the designer of abstract settings than it might be for the designer creating more literal ones; words become clues to visual ideas. For instance, when I first read *The Caretaker,* and began to consider what the room where it takes place should look and (more important) *feel* like, at the back of my mind was the dim recollection of something once read. It was some time before that passage could be recalled (although I am sure the contents of it were already at work in the unconscious levels of my mind). Finally, however, it did rise to the surface and I remembered that it occurred in a book by Rainer Maria Rilke called *The Notebooks of Malte Laurids Brigge.* The recalled passage was a description of an old tenement building that was being torn down. This is what the protagonist, Brigge, saw and recorded in his notebook:

> Will anyone believe that there are such houses? . . . But, to be precise, they were houses that were no longer there. Houses that had been pulled down from top to bottom. What *was* there was the other houses, those that had stood alongside of them, tall neighboring houses. Apparently these were in danger of falling down, since everything alongside had been taken away; for a whole scaffolding of long, tarred timbers had been rammed slantwise between the rubbish-strewn ground and the bared wall. I don't know whether I have already said that it is this wall I mean. But it was, so to speak, not the first wall of the existing houses (as one would have supposed), but the last of those that had been there. One saw its inner side. One saw at the different storeys the walls of rooms to which the paper still clung, and here and there the join of floor or ceiling. Beside these room-walls there still remained, along the whole length of the wall, a dirty-white area, and through this crept in unspeakably disgusting motions, worm-soft as if digesting, the open, rust-spotted channel of the water-closet pipe. Grey, dusty traces of the paths the lighting-gas had taken remained at the ceiling edges, and here and there, quite unexpectedly, they bent sharp around and came running into the colored wall and into a hole that had been torn out black and ruthless. But most unforgettable of all were the walls themselves. The stubborn life of these rooms had not let itself be trampled out. It was still there; it clung to the nails that had been left, it stood on the remaining handsbreadth of flooring, it crouched under the corner joints where there was still a little bit of interior. One could see that it was in the paint, which, year by year, it had slowly altered: blue into moldy green, green into grey, and yellow into an old, stale rotting white. But it was also in the spots that had kept fresher, behind mirrors, pictures, and wardrobes; for it had drawn and redrawn their contours, and had been with spiders and dust even in these hidden places that now lay bared. It was in every flayed strip, it was in the damp blisters at the lower edges of the wallpapers; it wavered in the torn-off shreds, and sweated out of the foul patches that had come into being long ago. And from these walls once blue and green and yellow, which were framed by the fracture-tracts of the demol-

ished partitions, the breath of these lives stood out—the clammy, sluggish, musty breath, which no wind had yet scattered. There stood the middays and the sicknesses and the exhaled breath and the smoke of years, and the sweat that breaks out under armpits and makes clothes heavy, and the stale breath of mouths, and the fusel odor of sweltering feet. There stood the tang of urine and the burn of soot and the grey reek of potatoes, and the heavy, smooth stench of ageing grease. The sweet, lingering smell of neglected infants was there, and the fear-smell of children who go to school, and the sultriness out of the beds of nubile youths. To these was added much that had come from below, from the abyss of the street, which reeked, and more that had oozed down from above with the rain, which over cities is not clean.

The observations that Rilke has Brigge make are essentially those I found in my own research; but there is a vast difference, it can be easily seen, between my casual catalogue of isolated "facts" and this intensely depicted total vision. Of the two, Rilke's words are more helpful to me than my own visual findings; his description is not a substitute, it merely clarifies my own thinking by helping me to recognize the "right" solution when I hit upon it. Moreover, there is a direct relationship between the subterranean levels on which Pinter's play moves and the thoughts and feelings experienced by Brigge when he viewed those walls to rooms no longer in existence. It is precisely this mode of thought that the designer must apply to his work, especially when creating settings that present directly to an audience essences and abstract qualities instead of recognizable details in a literal context. It is also significant that Brigge is most affected by what is *not* there rather than what is; one could say exactly the same thing about Pinter's plays.

Both the director and designer agreed that the setting for *The Caretaker* should have a similar feeling, should evoke something of the same response from an audience that Brigge felt when he viewed the remaining walls of the torn-down building. But now it was time to begin the task of applying these thoughts to the particular production at hand; to begin solving the unique problems it presented. Since the nature of the open stage made it impossible to close in the sides of the room with solid walls, it was decided to make the best use of the remaining elements; that is, the ceiling and the floor as well as the back wall (fig. 122). It was also decided to intensify, in some way, the overhanging force of the ceiling (and, incidentally, facilitate the hanging of lighting instruments); this was accomplished in two major ways:

(1) by slanting it (this idea presented itself in several photographs showing rooms with outer walls merging into roof lines; the earlier drawing
[fig. 122] includes this feature in it); and (2) forcing the perspective in
an obvious manner (fig. 123). As a result of these two decisions, a
strong downward thrust was given to the whole ceiling (fig. 124). This
helped obtain the director's desire for a space into which the action
could be "wedged." (In the final design, as it was realized on the stage,
there was an ominous quality imparted by this ceiling that would be difficult to explain in terms of design principles; i.e., strong downward
force equals dynamic instability when coupled with diagonals.)

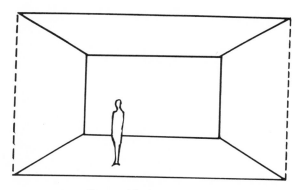

122. *Room with three walls removed*

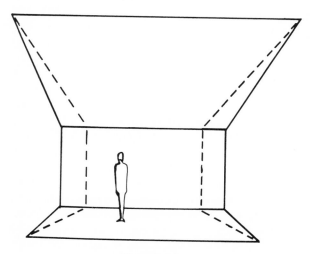

123. *Slanted ceiling*

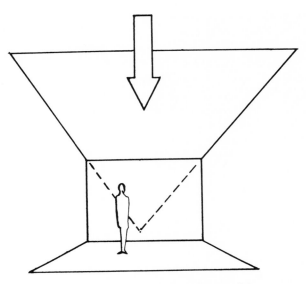

124. *Slanted ceiling showing downward force*

There was only one access to the room (and there should be only one); this was placed in the back wall. This door led to a hallway which led to downstairs and other parts of the house. Architecturally, a ceiling such as we had now didn't make much sense; esthetically, we felt, it did: feasibility lost out to artistic license. Figure 125 is a photographic image that seemed to sum up a number of desirable features (a stark simplicity, but, at the same time, a certain mysterious quality: perhaps the resulting combination of the aged wooden structures with the extreme angle of perspective?).

Thus far, a basic form had been evolved, although at this stage of development it is certainly not a complete or usable one. Various possibilities for treating this shell now came under consideration; one possibility was to make the ceiling and wall a simulation of what might be found in the actual building. (And this was considered at one point in the planning stages of this production.) This did not, however, seem to take full advantage of the images summoned up by Rilke: a room whose physical existence was all but destroyed but whose "stubborn life . . . had not let itself be trampled out." Perhaps there was something in the actual construction of the building that would provide the feeling of enclosure and at the same time seem to be in the process of disappearing. ("A world solid and full of holes.") And so the walls and ceiling had its various layers of building materials—wallpapers, coats of

125. *Wooden house by Charles Lichtenstein, from* Art Has Many Faces *by Katharine Kuh. Courtesy of Katharine Kuh*

paint, plaster—removed until only the bare lath and framework remained (fig. 126).

But unlike the framework of a house being constructed which plainly exhibits its new wood, this structure must show the effects of its age and disintegration; moreover, these effects should be presented on their own terms, not merely as naturalistic details. They are, in fact, the physical correlatives of Rilke's verbal images, "the tang of urine . . . the burn of soot . . . the grey reek of potatoes . . . the heavy, smooth

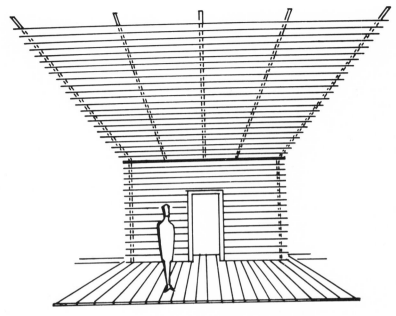

126. *Slanted ceiling with lath construction*

stench of ageing grease." Verbal images suggest physical ones; but how they are put into physical form is not always an easy or predictable task. The designer must assure the required result not only through the creation of appropriate forms and structures; he must also provide instruction to the shops for the application of textural surfaces to these forms (special sand mixed into the paints, crumbled cork, appliqués of metal foils, fiber-glass forms and finishes, vacuum-formed plastic, etc.). The day when scenery was only wood, canvas, and scene paint is probably gone forever. A designer must also insure that these forms and textures are finished with a careful selection of color (and, again, Rilke provides valuable clues to a proper palette for *The Caretaker*: "blue into moldy green, green into grey, and yellow into an old stale rotting white"). Even though the designer may have made many careful color sketches and paint specifications, they are rarely sufficient. It is not uncommon in actual production for him to go to the shops and seek the proper effect by working directly on the actual scenery, handling three-dimensional materials much as a sculptor would and painting and repainting the scenery a number of times. Only the amateur gets what he wants on the first try.

As it has been noted before, this room is filled with a great number of items; ostensibly, there is no apparent order to their placement. In reality, a random order to these things would immobilize the actor (and the relationship of each item to the others is implicitly—and carefully—worked out in the text of the play) (fig. 127). What must be done, therefore, is determine (with the director) just what these space relationships are and then mass all the items that are necessary to the progress of the play (along with those that are simply needed for visual effect) into islands around and through which the action patterns of the performers can move (fig. 128). Sight lines, naturally, limit the height of the objects that could be placed around the outer edge of the stage; this made it necessary to "store" furniture and objects above the heads of the performers. It also intensifies the feeling that they are hemmed in by these things without really being so.

While a structure was designed specifically for this purpose, it also functioned in other ways as well; the pipe frame with its outrigger

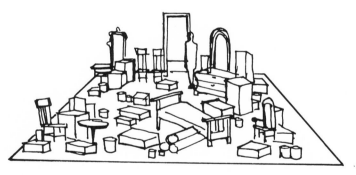

127. *Floor with random objects*

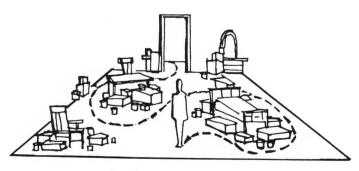

128. *Floor with objects in islands*

beams not only provided hanging room for overhead storage, it also helped to cut off and define the total area of the room into smaller more individual areas. This frame not only seemed a logical supporting device for the ceiling—as well as a structure around which the actors can gravitate, lean against, and otherwise use in numerous ways—it also helped to integrate the physical setting into the total stage space without hindering the spectator's vision (fig. 129). Once the basic form of the setting was settled, a floor plan had to be determined that would incorporate all the needs of the play (and the actors) and then resolved in terms of actual space available, which, on the open stage is always at a premium. The basic form of the stage could not be extended in any of these directions (fig. 130). This made it necessary to expand the playing area in the only directions possible while still preserving the basic thrust of the stage (fig. 131).

While the preceding pages should give a fairly clear picture of how a design for *The Caretaker* evolved, it would be impossible to draw attention to all the many steps and decisions that are made for any one project; some of these will be reasoned out along the lines presented here, not a few will be compromises. Finally, what resulted in this case was, more than anything else, a large sculpture in which the action of the play, it was felt, transpired appropriately.

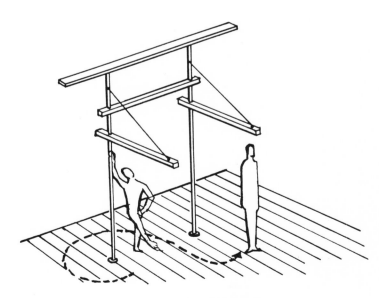

129. *Supporting pipe structure*

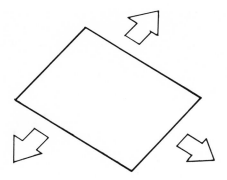

130. *Floor extension possibilities*

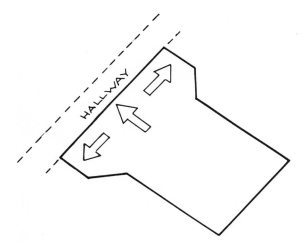

131. *Floor extension possibilities*

There is no doubt that the designer of the future must be much more knowledgeable in the fields of sculpture, painting, and architecture than his immediate predecessors have been; not necessarily each for its own sake but for what it can contribute to the scene designer's individual art-form. While none know what the future of scene design will be—or for that matter theater in general—it is safe to assume that the old world of only canvas flats and backdrops is gone, and with it the box-set mentality that has plagued the theater for so long (figs. 132, 133).

132. Set sketch for The Caretaker

§27
"On Being Upstaged by Scenery"

By John Hatch

The theatre in the 1960's is the heir to so many inventions and traditions of stage design—expressionism, constructivism, the box set, the unit set, the apron stage, theatre-in-the-round, Reinhardt's fly-specks, Gordon Craig's screens, Adolphe Appia's expectant emp-

133. *Photograph of set for* The Caretaker

tiness—that any orderly review of their evolution and intertwined influence is a task for the historian, not the essayist. But it has been,
speaking very broadly, a two-edged inheritance. We are the benefi-
ciaries of the Greek amphitheatre and Shakespeare's "Wooden O"; we
have also incurred a guilty knowledge of those architectural splendors
and natural stupefactions (Vesuvius in spate, the great seas in uproar)
that in centuries past threatened to efface the drama in the cause of
spectacle. True, it has been a generation or more since Eliza skipped
across the tumbling ice; large and exotic animals are at present out of
stage-fashion; and I cannot remember the last time a performer made
his entrance upon a cloud. Still, the temptation to confuse the magic of
the theatre with the trickery of the stage is in our blood, and sets today
fall roughly into two categories: they offer a picture or they offer a
playing space.

Obviously, these alternatives are almost never presented in pure
form—the most picture-oriented set must still provide the actors with
the physical essentials of their trade, and only the most dedicated

theorist will sweep his stage as naked as a laboratory table. Neverthe-less, you can usually tell whether the stage was set primarily to flatter the eye or to facilitate the actor's assignment. I can illustrate the dif-ference by describing an experiment that was unaccountably aban-doned in 1957 at the Shakespeare Festival in Stratford, Connecticut.

The Stratford theatre, a remote descendent of Shakespeare's Globe, is a house of inviting proportions, admirable acoustics, and a great technical versatility. But its stage is vast in all its dimensions, and sets scaled to fill it place the action in jeopardy. I well remember the dress rehearsal of *Julius Caesar* in 1955, the company's first season, when shortly after midnight it was decided to scrap Horace Armistead's breathtaking panorama of Rome because it was diminishing the affairs of Cassius and Brutus to triviality.

For the second season, Rouben Ter-Arutunian designed a stage that seemed to me an ideal frame for Shakespeare. It consisted of tremendous panels of lattice, walling the entire playing area; neutral in tone, these took light and shadow beautifully. Moreover, they were infi-nitely flexible: openings could be made almost at will; sections could be thrust forward to provide balconies, rostrums, battlements; inner stages, dungeons, grottoes, private doors, or ceremonial gateways could be conjured out of the pliant slatwork. Since the lattice was am-biguous—interior or exterior, nature or fabrication—any object added to it was vividly suggestive, and a very few props—a tapestry, a throne chair, stacked arms, a glowing brazier—would sharply focus the scene. The space was as great as ever, but it was space undefined by perspec-tive or scale, and in that limpid element the actors took on the height-ened presence that is part of what makes theatre magic. I don't know why the Shakespeare Festival shelved this exemplary scene for the pas-tel and papier-mâché agitation that became its style in later seasons. This theatre does business primarily with the summer colonies along the shore; perhaps such an audience does not appreciate self-effacement raised to an art.

The question of whether the stage is to be a vision or an in-strument is linked to equivalent theories as to the relationship between the audience and the occasion; it has been given particular relevance in our time by the proliferation of theatres in accommodations never meant for the drama. If the playwright is the manufacturer of more or less intelligent pastimes for a market that can pay well to be amused, then everything possible should be done to present a beguiling pack-age. I have considerable admiration for the professional efficiency of *A Man for All Seasons,* but it falls, I think, into the category of entertain-ment. And its eye-catching unit set, dominated by a magnificently pro-portioned spiral ramp, its scene changes wittily engineered into the action, suit the intentions of the work and contribute to its popular success.

Such decorative virtuosity, however, makes an almost tangible barrier of the proscenium frame; the audience feels itself in exile from fairyland. I recall still the elegant sensuality of Christian Berard's set for the production of *L'École des Femmes,* which Louis Jouvet brought to America a good many years ago. The insolently aristocratic chandeliers, the exquisitely scaled street arches, the garden walls that parted on silken hinges to disclose the most perfect of formal gardens—these blandishments of texture and proportion made the audience purr. But I also remember that I watched Molière through flawless plate glass: one looked in rapture, but one was not touched.

The playgoer who forsakes such luxury of the senses for the opportunism of off-Broadway may feel himself curtly received, unless at the same time he shifts his view of himself from pampered guest to committed participant. No one perched on the bleachers of the 4th Street Theatre—that railroad flat bisected by a card-table stage—deluded himself that the theatre is a spectator sport. If a play took life in those surroundings, it was because the challenge was so obvious, the miracle occurred there with dependable regularity. I don't pretend that this former American home of Chekhov and Ibsen was ideal for its purposes: I was disconcerted by spying a second audience, a kind of mirror image, dimly across the lighted playing area; the little stage was so crabbed that one ground plan had to be used, play after play.

The off-Broadway definition of a theatre is any room that can seat one hundred or more persons without incurring the instant hostility of the fire department. Sometimes these unlikely warrens are brilliantly suited to the material at hand. José Quintero's production of *The Iceman Cometh* at the original Circle in the Square (it has since been torn down to make way for an apartment house) fitted with almost no artifice at all into the long, bleak room, broken by pillars supporting the low ceiling. And the Provincetown Playhouse, mean in dimensions, grimy, threadbare, neglected, was a den ready-made for Krapp's prowlings. I recall, finally, the throat-constricting expectancy of that operating table of a stage deep below the tiered seats where *The Blacks* was played. It was made a place or ritual merely by the vertiginous pitch of its sight lines.

There are evident limitations to the lucky compatibility between house and play. These absurd theatres of Greenwich Village and the East Side have proved excellent frames for the Theatre of the Absurd that now dominates our avant-garde; but their idiosyncracies and raffish squalor do not always suit: Congreve's *The Way of the World* stepped its minuet bravely at The Cherry Lane, but it seemed to be slumming.

Despite an almost continual ululation in the profession, poverty can be a tonic in the theatre, but I would not therefore prescribe it as a principal diet.

What is so inspiriting about these makeshift stages, however, is that the room for a play often seems to have been created by main force. The audience feels itself a crowd of witnesses on the verge of trespassing upon the minimal arena where the performers are getting on with their imperative task. At The Living Theatre it has become almost a matter of style that the actors exhort to join the act. The revivalist appeal is hardly necessary, for the house itself throws everyone into the melee.

Uptown in the more decorous houses, formalized by their curtains and proscenium stages, it is not as easy to mount a performance that takes on the quality of a communal ceremony. Nevertheless, the distinction between picture-scape and playing space still operates. A set, when it is first revealed, should make you inch forward in your seat; too often, it urges you to lean back after perfunctory applause. The designers, members of one of the few real guilds left in the world, work with such authority, so fill the stage with their strong personalities, that there often seems no opening for author or actors. Tennessee Williams's *The Night of the Iguana* is a case in point. The play impressed me as the most relevant, most humane, dramatically most engrossing work that Williams has done in some time. But I was aware that the playwright was fighting the set for my attention. This fully conceived hotel of dubious propriety, deep in the Mexican jungle, projected so much personality of its own, its cunning angles and subtle imbalances were so diverting, its vegetation so feverishly rich, that the cross purposes, precarious sanity, and rampant vitality of the play's personnel were gentled by the visual boisterousness. The performances, though good, were perhaps a little too consistently strident. That could be accounted for by the presence of Bette Davis, whose professional aura does not encourage reticence in her colleagues, but the steaming jungle must take a share of the blame.

I dislike a set that stands on its own feet: it should be like a bicycle—functional only in motion. Thus the sets for *Ross,* a play I did not much admire, seemed to me excellent. They were so shallow, sometimes so perfunctory, as to be disagreeably saltless in repose. But they keyed the action and stood well aside to let the actors get everything humanly possible out of the script. Of course *Ross* is a play in innumerable scenes, and the budget for individual tableaux must have been spartan. A writer these days who constructs a one-set play invites the designer to paint him off the stage.

Box sets are out of favor just now, but they have a great virtue: they allow the performance to build emotion under the pressure of confinement. Still, the emphasis of these boxes should be on the space they enclose and not on the furnishings the designer can plausibly pack them with to "heighten" the illusion. Nothing so deflates illusion as bric-a-brac that upstages the actor. Such sets invariably draw applause as the curtain rises on a parlormaid dusting the armor; in my view, any set that draws applause should instantly be scrapped for a plain back-drop. Stage design is like editing or undertaking—no trade for prima donnas.

I say that, realizing that the two greatest figures of modern stage design—Adolphe Appia and Gordon Craig—were prima donnas of the first rank. But they were also seers, men transfixed by all-embracing visions. Appia decreed a stage of neutral emptiness to be transformed by light; Craig appealed to the theatre world to be saved by his "thousand scenes in one scene"—a distillation of the total human environment which, translated, became: "flat floor—flat walls—flat roof." The stage structures, imagined by these men were noble, expectant, almost religious, and fairly crying out for great deeds and inexorable decisions. But in both cases they also bore a strong resemblance to Stonehenge or the Giant's Causeway; had they prevailed, they could have restricted repertory to Wagner, *King Lear,* and Ibsen's *When We Dead Awaken.*

However, the theatre has never been in danger of succumbing to the high-minded rigors of Craig and Appia. The kind of threat it does have to be on guard against is the staircase that is more beautiful than the heroine, the living room that is busier than the villain, and the forest of Arden in which you cannot see Touchstone for the trees.

Suggested Reading:

Burris-Meyer, Harold, and Cole, Edward C. *Theatres and Auditoriums.* 2d ed. New York: Reinhold Publishing Corp., 1964.

Cogswell, Margaret, ed. *The Ideal Theatre: Eight Concepts.* New York: The American Federation of Arts, 1962.

Gorelik, Mordecai. *New Theatres for Old.* New York: Samuel French, 1955.

Hodges, C. Walter. *The Globe Restored.* New York: Coward-McCann, Inc., 1954.

Nicoll, Allardyce. *The Development of the Theatre.* 5th ed. London: Harrap & Co., Ltd., 1966.

Southern, Richard. *The Open Stage.* New York: Theatre Arts Books, 1959.

———. *The Seven Ages of the Theatre.* New York: Hill & Wang, 1961.

Theatre Check List: A Guide to the Planning and Construction of Proscenium and Open Stage Theatres. Edited by the American Theatre Planning Board. Middletown, Conn.: Wesleyan University Press, 1969.

Index